Y0-CAR-896

Common Core Meets Education Reform

What It All Means for Politics, Policy, and the Future of Schooling

Common Core
Meets
Education Reform

What It All Means for Politics, Policy, and the Future of Schooling

Edited by

Frederick M. Hess

Michael Q. McShane

Teachers College, Columbia University
New York and London

Published by Teachers College Press, 1234 Amsterdam Avenue, New York, NY 10027

Copyright © 2014 by Teachers College, Columbia University

All rights reserved. No part of this publication may be reproduced or transmitted in any form or by any means, electronic or mechanical, including photocopy, or any information storage and retrieval system, without permission from the publisher.

Library of Congress Cataloging-in-Publication Data can be obtained at www.loc.gov

ISBN 978-0-8077-5478-8 (paper)
ISBN 978-0-8077-5479-5 (hardcover)

Printed on acid-free paper
Manufactured in the United States of America

20   19   18   17   16   15   14   13   8   7   6   5   4   3   2   1

Contents

Acknowledgments   vii

Introduction   1
Frederick M. Hess and Michael Q. McShane

1. **The Lay of the Land**   14
   Michael Q. McShane

2. **The Role of Governors**   35
   Dane Linn

3. **Teacher Quality Reforms**   54
   Morgan Polikoff

4. **Will Charter Schools Lead or Lag?**   76
   Robin Lake and Tricia Maas

5. **Accountability: A Story of Opportunities and Challenges**   96
   Deven Carlson

6. **The History of History Standards:
   The Prospects for Standards for Social Studies**   118
   Peter Meyer

7. **Technology**   140
   Taryn Hochleitner and Allison Kimmel

8. **Visions and Challenges for Multistate Governance
   and Sustainability**   162
   Patrick McGuinn

9. **A Reform at Risk? The Political Realities**   185
    Ashley Jochim

Conclusion: The Common Core and the "Reform" Agenda   206
    Frederick M. Hess and Michael Q. McShane

About the Editors and Contributors   219

Index   222

Acknowledgments

On March 25, 2013 we convened a daylong public research conference at the American Enterprise Institute (AEI) to discuss a complex and multifaceted question: What do the Common Core State Standards mean for education reform in America? This gathering included representatives from a variety of stakeholder groups including researchers, advocates, teachers, principals, state education leaders, and union representatives.

What resulted was a spirited dialogue that raised as many important questions as it did answers. Some left the day as confident as ever that the Common Core would be the glue to bind together the next generation of school reforms. Others left with the feeling that many issues that could derail the standards lurked in the shadows, waiting to thwart the efforts of the standards writers.

The chapters that follow provided the framework for that discussion and surfaced many important issues. What does the Common Core mean for accountability, a reform lever that policy makers have been pulling in an attempt to corral schools for over a decade? How will the Common Core affect teacher preparation, professional development, and the variety of burgeoning methods to measure teacher performance? Will the Common Core accelerate a transition to schools and classrooms that rely more on technology or will it hinder these efforts? Who will govern the standards moving forward?

We purposely picked scholars who could not be easily categorized into the "pro-" or "anti-" Common Core camps. They took to their particular piece of the puzzle with a fair-minded skepticism that recognized that even if the standards are of high quality, they might do more harm than good over the long run if they are not implemented with care.

We would like to thank the following discussants for providing outstanding feedback throughout that day: Mark Bauerlein of Emory University, Kimberly Worthy of the Howard University Public Charter School, Ann Bonitatibus of the Frederick County (Maryland) Public Schools, Mitchell Chester of the Massachusetts Department of Education, Lily Eskelsen of the National Education Association, Jeanne Allen of the Center for Education Reform, Russell Armstrong of the office of Louisiana governor Bobby Jindal, Richard Laine of the National Governors Association, Linda Darling-Hammond of Stanford University, Chester E. Finn Jr. of the Thomas B. Fordham Institute, Neal McCluskey of the Cato Institute, Mark Murphy of the Delaware Department of Education, and Joshua Parker of the Baltimore County (Maryland) Public Schools.

We are also indebted to the steadfast support provided by AEI and its president, Arthur Brooks. The Gates Foundation generously provided financial support for this project, and we are deeply grateful for their involvement and encouragement throughout the process. We'd also like to thank the terrific staff at AEI, especially Allison Kimmel and Max Eden for their work managing and overseeing this project, Lauren Aronson for her work coordinating the conference, and Daniel Lautzenheiser, Taryn Hochleitner, and K.C. Deane for their vital assistance. Finally, we express our gratitude to the Teachers College Press team, particularly our editor Brian Ellerbeck, who offered skillful and timely guidance throughout the course of this project.

Introduction

Frederick M. Hess

Michael Q. McShane

IN A REMARKABLY short period of time, the Common Core State Standards (also called simply, the Common Core) have moved to the forefront of discussions about K–12 schooling. Little more than a vague notion in 2008, they were introduced in 2009, unveiled and adopted by thirty-nine states and the District of Columbia in 2010 (to be joined by 6 more states in subsequent years), and celebrated with near-universal acclaim in 2011, before becoming an increasingly contentious issue in 2012 and 2013. As smooth sailing has yielded to choppier waters, many Common Core enthusiasts and observers have had to remark on the challenges of "implementation." As Chester E. Finn Jr., president of the Thomas B. Fordham Institute, said, "the biggest potential pot hole, by far, is failed implementation."[1] William McCallum, the University of Arizona professor who cowrote the math standards, similarly said "implementation is everything."[2]

They are undoubtedly right, but *implementation* is a painfully broad word that obscures all manner of sins. Its very ambiguity allows any number of policy missteps, dumb decisions, or miscalculations to be dismissed as nothing more than "implementation challenges." Yet the last half century of school reform includes a remarkably long list of once-celebrated, now-discarded ideas, accompanied by the common lament that they were undone by implementation.

What's more, this familiar phrase tends to hide more than it reveals. It bundles together those missteps produced by a lack of forethought, by political and institutional resistance, by the innate difficulty in scaling new programs, by insufficient attention to the nuts and bolts of change, or by unforeseen and unforeseeable surprises, and treats these missteps as if they were the same.

This all matters immensely when it comes to the Common Core. First, the Common Core is simply standards—a listing of what students should know, aspirational words on a page. For the Common Core to deliver on its promise requires states, districts, and schools to make a slew of complementary changes to curriculum, tests, teacher training, and the like. Adopting the Common Core (as impressive a political feat as it was), in and of itself, is just not that significant. Almost everything that matters about it depends on what happens next—in other words, on implementation.

Second, unlike any number of once-promising reforms that were undone by implementation—from block scheduling to site-based management to small high schools to comprehensive school reform—the Common Core has far more capability to do harm if it doesn't work out. While those initiatives could create headaches, disruption, and frustration at individual campuses or in certain districts, their reach was limited and their impact muted. The Common Core, on the other hand, is intended to displace old state standards, alter state assessments and accountability, revamp K–12 instruction, force changes in teacher preparation and professional development, and more. If it blows up, or is undone by implementation, the costs in terms of time, dollars, and disruption will be enormous. The stakes are high.

IMPLEMENTATION AND THE COMMON CORE

When we think about the Common Core, there are at least three kinds of implementation challenges worth keeping in mind.

One is instruction. Teachers, principals, teacher educators, and policy makers have been told that it's essential to align preparation, instructional materials, and classroom practice to the Common Core. This kind of *instructional implementation* will prove a pressing concern for teachers, principals, and system leaders. They may well need to alter what content is taught, how it is organized, and what pedagogical strategies are used. Common Core proponents note that the standards focus more deeply on fewer items, that the new assessments being produced for the Common Core will focus on different knowledge and skills, and that classroom instruction will have to change in turn.

Teachers and principals are concerned with this form of implementation. The 2013 *Metlife Survey of the American Teacher*—an annual polling of 1,000 teachers and 500 principals—found 59% of teachers and 67% of principals believing that implementing the Common Core Standards would be either "very challenging" or "challenging."[3]

A number of organizations have rushed to address these needs. Just type "Common Core" into the Amazon search bar and you'll get over 30,000 results—the lion's share for textbooks and tools for classrooms. *Education Week* regularly sends links for professional development webinars with titles like "A Full Day of Common Core Strategies Live on Your Computer" and "Attend Virtually! Road Maps to Common Core Success." Student Achievement Partners, a nonprofit organization that provides free Common Core–aligned resources to states, districts, and schools, has received $18 million from the GE Foundation to engage in this work.[4] We have no idea whether these efforts will suffice, but this piece of the implementation challenge has drawn substantial attention.

The second challenge to Common Core implementation involves the political dimension. The success of the standards will turn heavily on decisions around policy, procurement, spending, and the rest. Over the next half decade this will require sustained support from governors, legislators, state superintendents, and state school board members, many of whom were not in office in 2010 and 2011 when their states signed on to the Common Core. This broaches the *politics of implementation.* Successful implementation across more than a handful of states will require broad-based, bipartisan support. Otherwise, the new costs, potential disruptions, and various frustrations will give policy makers plentiful opportunities to let the effort become one more in the litany of implementation failures. The early political success of the Common Core was impressive. The National Governors Association (NGA) and Council of Chief State School Officers (CCSSO) could draw on the support of prominent Democrats like President Obama and U.S. education secretary Arne Duncan as well as notable Republicans like former Florida governor Jeb Bush and New Jersey governor Chris Christie. This coalition was also backed by enthusiastic advocacy groups like Democrats for Education Reform and philanthropies like the deep-pocketed Bill & Melinda Gates Foundation.

Over time, however, the politics have morphed. The Obama administration's decision to champion the Common Core—in Race to the Top, NCLB waivers, Obama's 2013 State of the Union, and much else—fueled suspicion in the conservative grassroots. By 2013, a number of states that had previously adopted the Common Core were debating whether to abandon it, with Alabama and Oklahoma backing out of their testing consortia and state legislatures in Michigan, Indiana, and Pennsylvania pausing funding for the implementation of the standards. Meanwhile, progressive critics feared that the Common Core reflects the post-NCLB testing culture. In 2013 both of the major teachers unions, the American Federation of Teachers (AFT) and the National Education Association (NEA), called for a moratorium on any stakes attached to new Common Core–aligned exams. In response to this the Department of Education granted states flexibility in their NCLB waiver applications to allow more time to implement their new tests before attaching stakes to them. In short, the politics of implementation have grown heated, with big practical implications. This is an issue that will draw some attention in the chapters ahead, but most of what follows is focused on the third kind of implementation challenge.

This third challenge deals with what happens when Common Core implementation intersects with various ongoing school improvement strategies. As convenient shorthand, we can think of this as "Common Core meets the reform agenda." More prosaically, this is about *policy implementation*. How does Common Core implementation complement or clash with such ongoing efforts as those addressing teacher quality, school accountability, educational technology, and charter schooling? How will the Common Core further or hinder those efforts, and how will any tensions impact the Common Core push? These are the questions that will primarily motivate this volume.

WHAT IS THE REFORM AGENDA?

When we talk of the Common Core encountering the reform agenda, just what do we have in mind? What do we think of as the "reform agenda"? Do we presume that this agenda is an obviously terrific thing? And whatever one thinks of the reform agenda, isn't the Common Core already part of it?

First, by "reform agenda" we intend to refer to the range of efforts in the past decade that have focused upon teacher quality, school and system accountability, charter schooling, and the role of education technology. Second, we're not seeking to judge this broad swath of activity in any blanket fashion. Indeed, in each of these areas, we can point to proposals that we've staunchly supported and others that have given us pause. Common Core proponents have given the impression that their efforts will readily complement and further each of these. We're not so sure. That is why we've asked the contributors to this volume to look more fully at what the Common Core means for these efforts. Third, in a broad sense, the Common Core is surely supported by many who have helped champion this agenda, and is widely seen by many as part of it. But many reform efforts date back a decade or more, while the Common Core is a relatively new addition. In light of that, we're curious whether peering around the bend suggests that the Common Core could undermine, impede, or otherwise hinder these other efforts in various ways (and, if so, what might be done about it).

Such a possibility has scarcely been acknowledged by proponents of the Common Core, who have enthusiastically promised that the effort will simplify accountability, support professional development and teacher evaluation, do only good things for charter schools, and stimulate the development of better digital learning tools. In fact, Secretary Duncan himself went so far as to describe opposition to the standards as "misguided" "misinformed" and "based on false information" in a speech to the American Society of News Editors in June of 2013.[5] Meanwhile, skeptics have tended to focus more on concerns about federal overreach or the quality of the standards than on the more practical questions posed by implementation. Largely lost has been the simple but vital point that the interaction of the Common Core with other improvement efforts may have complex or unforeseen consequences—which could well compromise either the Common Core or these other strategies.

In other words, even if one is willing to stipulate that the Common Core Standards are good, and even if the Common Core can overcome instructional implementation hurdles, the whole effort could still ultimately do more to retard than to accelerate school improvement. That's why addressing policy implementation and political implementation, and doing so now and not as part of a postmortem, is such an important exercise.

That tension motivated this book. We're not concerned with whether or not the Common Core is "good" or "bad" per se, or whether it can survive the oft-discussed instructional challenges. We leave those worthwhile debates to others. Rather, the contributors here offer insights into two critical, linked questions. First, how likely is it that the Common Core might have negative, unanticipated consequences, and where are they most likely to emerge? Second, what might policy makers, practitioners, and advocates do to anticipate and address these kinds of tensions?

We think you will see that the contributors here are not motivated by a desire to advocate for or oppose the Common Core. Rather, our interest is in helping to ensure that the Common Core, however beneficial it proves to be on its own terms and however smooth or choppy its implementation, does not casually or unintentionally fail due to predictable implementation challenges, or unnecessarily undercut or compromise other promising school improvement efforts.

WHAT IS THE COMMON CORE?

Before we get too far along, it's probably worth offering a quick refresher on the Common Core for those who are less versed in some of the particulars. The standards initiative was announced by the NGA and Student Achievement Partners on June 1, 2009. Almost one year to the day later, the English and language arts standards were released, and states scrambled to adopt the standards by the early August 2010 deadline for their Race to the Top applications. By November of 2011, 45 states and the District of Columbia had adopted the standards.

It's worth noting that national standards are not a new idea. Leaders have sought to establish common goals for education at least since the National Education Association convened the Committee of Ten in 1892. While that effort endeavored to create broad requirements including the number of courses students should take in given subjects, as Peter Meyer details in Chapter 6 of this volume, efforts to create a set of uniform national standards came to a head in 1989 when president George H. W. Bush sent out a clarion call for "national performance goals . . . that will make us internationally competitive, second to none in the 21st century."[6]

Bush's effort, however, fell flat. The committee that he appointed to draft such standards, the National Council on Education Standards and Testing, was not able to put together a set of standards that could win political support. More conservative members of Congress, who were tasked with funding the development of these standards, feared a federal takeover of education. More liberal members did not agree with the plan's proposed tests to measure how well students were reaching these goals. While this led to the ultimate sinking of the math and English language arts standards initiatives, the social studies standards had a particularly nasty, and public, downfall. After working for years to lead the development of the standards, then chairwoman for the National Endowment for the Humanities Lynne Cheney withdrew her support in a *Wall Street Journal* op-ed titled "The End of History."[7] She cited the "political correctness" of the standards, stating that they had been "hijacked" by "those who were pursuing the revision agenda" and who had "great hatred for traditional history." As Peter Meyer recounts, the history standards—which had cost $1.6 million and took 32 months to develop—were voted down 99–1 in the U.S. Senate. It would be years before the effort recovered.

In 2001 the passage of the No Child Left Behind Act (NCLB) side-stepped the notion of national standards. In lieu of trying to specify norms for reading and math, President George W. Bush, Senator Edward Kennedy, and other key figures settled on a compromise that required states to test all students annually in reading and math in Grades 3–8 and once in high school, but allowed them to select the standards, tests, and bar for determining student "proficiency." At the time, the effort was marked with great enthusiasm. Senator Kennedy hailed NCLB as "a defining issue about the future of our nation and about the future of democracy, the future of liberty, and the future of the United States in leading the free world," going so far as to say, "no piece of legislation will have a greater impact or influence on that."[8] The law passed the House 381–41 and the Senate 87–10.

But, as Deven Carlson details in Chapter 5, states responded to the law by setting vastly different proficiency levels. This "gaming" tended to reward states that set low bars by allowing them to claim lots of high-performing schools and students. Meanwhile, states that set a high bar for themselves, like Massachusetts, got only a black eye for their pains. Using National Assessment of Educational Progress (NAEP) scores to standardize performance, Paul Peterson and Frederick Hess examined this phenomenon in a 2006 article in *Education Next*.[9] They found that many states, including Mississippi, Georgia, West Virginia, North Carolina, Oklahoma, and

Tennessee, set vastly lower proficiency thresholds on their state tests, and that, over time, states from Arizona to Kansas decreased the threshold of proficiency on their state exams. As Ashley Jochim describes in Chapter 9, because Adequate Yearly Progress (AYP) was measured by the proportion of students that cleared the proficiency bar, political leaders had one of two options if they wanted to get more students over it: One, they could invest the time and resources in making schools better, or two, they could simply lower the bar. As Peterson and Hess—as well as an analysis by the Institute for Education Sciences show—many chose the latter.[10]

Out of these concerns rose a concerted effort between state leaders, national education organizations, and private philanthropy to reverse this trend and create a common set of academic standards. In order to sidestep the perils of history, the designers opted to just draft standards for math and English language arts, deciding that these are the backbone of most K–12 instruction, that the content is less politically charged, and that there's less obvious justification for variation from place to place in math instruction than, say, in history instruction.

Coupled with the development of standards, Race to the Top provided $330 million to two consortia of states to develop assessments aligned to the Common Core. The Smarter Balanced Assessment Consortium (SBAC), a collection of 24 states and the District of Columbia, received $160 million of those dollars. The Partnership for Assessment of Readiness for College and Careers (PARCC) received $170 million of those dollars to develop the tests for 22 participating states.

By signing on to the standards, states agreed to have them fully integrated into their accountability systems by 2014–15. As of this writing the tests have not come online, but the consortia have explained several key features that will make them different from the proficiency tests of the No Child Left Behind era. First, the tests are designed to explicitly measure higher order thinking skills. Test items will require students to make more sophisticated demonstrations of reading comprehension, including using evidence from a piece of writing to support an argument. The tests are also designed to be taken online and to be computer adaptive. Computer adaptivity allows the test to alter the sequence and difficulty of items presented to a student so as to hone in on the exact level of knowledge that the student possesses.

But will it work? The confidence of various experts and practitioners appears to stem, in large part, from how the speaker feels about No Child Left Behind.

Those enthusiastic about the Common Core tend to argue that one reason that No Child Left Behind failed to live up to expectations was because it was agnostic about the standards to which students were taught and the performance that states expected. As Chester E. Finn Jr. and Mike Petrilli of the Thomas B. Fordham Institute argued in *National Review*, "The vast majority of states have failed to adopt rigorous standards[;] . . . in some places, students could score below the tenth percentile and still be considered 'proficient.'"[11] In 2009 President Obama told the Hispanic Chamber of Commerce that "today's system of 50 different sets of benchmarks for academic success means 4th grade readers in Mississippi are scoring nearly 70 points lower than students in Wyoming—and they're getting the same grade."[12]

A very different view is proffered by skeptics of the Common Core who think that the problem with No Child Left Behind was its overly ambitious effort to federalize and nationalize schooling. The Cato Institute's Neal McCluskey holds such a view, arguing that NCLB failed because "federal politicians don't have to worry if the spending does any good."[13] Specifically referencing Common Core in a 2012 *Education Week* commentary, McClusky argued that "some people think that the solution is to double down on government power by imposing a federal curriculum" but that ultimately "we don't need more federal intervention, but to sidestep imbalanced incentives by letting parents control education funds and educators teach as they see fit."[14] Similarly, in 2011 over 100 conservative education thinkers signed a document declaring that a "one-size-fits-all, centrally controlled curriculum for every K–12 subject . . . threatens to close the door on educational innovation . . . and transfer control to an elephantine, inside-the-beltway bureaucracy."[15]

Outside of these two groups is a school of thought that sees the Common Core as a Rorschach test. As is the case across the political landscape, policies that have not been fully implemented can mean a lot of things to a lot of different people. Rather than seeing the Common Core integrated with the tests and accountability systems that are designed to be connected to it, this group sees the Common Core in isolation.

A great example of the Common Core as Rorschach test was New York principal Carol Burris's 2012 book *Opening the Common Core*. In that volume, she argued that the Common Core was an opportunity to improve the quality and equity of instruction. She argued that the standards move away from the curriculum-narrowing rote memorization of the previous generation. When it became clear that the standards were part of an overall push that included assessments, she then had to pen a *mea culpa* in the *Washington Post* to say that she had been "naïve" about the Common Core, and that she "should have known in an age in which standardized tests direct teaching and learning, that the standards themselves would quickly become operationalized by tests."[16] This group, while optimistic about the Common Core as they see it, will most likely become far more skeptical once they realize just how far reaching its implications are with respect to accountability and teacher policy.

MISSING PIECE OF THE PUZZLE

This volume grew out of an ongoing conversation on the practical issues state and district leaders will face when trying to make the Common Core a coherent facet of their education system. Our thinking crystallized at a research conference held at the American Enterprise Institute in March, 2013. For that meeting we recruited an outstanding set of researchers and thinkers, both up-and-coming and established, and asked them to investigate the aspect of Common Core implementation in which they have expertise. They presented their initial findings at the conference and their work was discussed by Common Core proponents and skeptics alike.

What struck us then was how such important concerns for educators and policy makers had been by and large ignored in the scholarly study of the topic. And yet perhaps this is not necessarily surprising. For one, those in schools and classrooms are generally more interested in what teachers need to teach and what students need to know, not the broader policy implications of the effort. For another, nationally, it makes more sense that the larger debate is on the *quality* of the standards, as it is more interesting than nitty-gritty issues of implementation and alignment.

For the first part of that discussion, numerous popular works have been developed for teachers to understand the Common Core and how it relates to their classroom. Books like *Pathways to the Common Core: Accelerating Achievement* (a book consistently ranked in the Amazon top 1,000 books for the year after it was published by Heinemann in 2012) by Teachers College professors Lucy Calkins, Mary Ehrenworth, and Christopher Lehman, offer plainly worded explanations of the standards and instructional techniques for teachers to align their practice with what the standards expect.

Other books offer quick primers on the standards. *Understanding Common Core State Standards* (ASCD, 2011) by John Kendell, senior director of research at McREL, an organization that advocates for higher standards, is illustrative of this type. Short (only 63 pages) and inexpensive (the initial price was $13.95), the book outlines the goals of the standards, how they were developed, what schools need to think about as they implement them, and how the assessment systems are being designed. Published by the Association for Supervision and Curriculum Development, it is paired with webinars and interactive web tools to make approaching the ideas and frameworks of the Common Core easy for teachers, principals, and parents.

Those seeking the political arguments for and against the standards need look no further than the editorial pages of most major news publications. From the pages of the *Washington Post,* to the *Wall Street Journal*[17] and the editorial board of the *New York Times*[18] offered a similar defense.

In looking for a book that offers analysis of the politics of the effort, readers can start with Robert Rothman's *Something in Common: The Common Core Standards and the Next Chapter in American Education* (Harvard Education Press, 2011). In that volume, Rothman, a former *Education Week* reporter who then went to work for the Alliance for Excellent Education, an organization that promoted the Common Core Standards, situates this most recent effort in the history of the standards movement. He recounts the story of the standards, from the push in the 1990s to the NGA's coalition with the CCSSO, Student Achievement Partners, and the Gates Foundation to develop the Common Core.

These are all valuable contributions for stakeholders and participants. But, as we look to the book before us, it is clear that they do not wrestle with the same issues as this volume. We will leave curriculum and pedagogy to those who know more about it. What we're concerned with is how the Common Core will interact with the policies in place to educate, train, develop, and hold teachers accountable. Similarly, we will leave the judgments of the wisdom of national standards to historians, but we will discuss what national standards mean for governance, governors, charter schools, and technology.

PLAN OF THE BOOK

We have encouraged authors to avoid making normative declarations regarding the quality of the Common Core Standards or the wisdom of their adoption. The following chapters have clear-minded examination of vexing problems that need to be understood and discussed in order for the Common Core to be successful. Fundamentally, we hope these chapters promote discussion that will prevent the "Gee, why didn't we think of that?" questions that often linger after a policy has failed to live up to its promise.

In Chapter 1 coeditor Michael McShane lays the groundwork for the politics and policies of Common Core implementation. He walks step-by-step through the decisions that state, district, and school leaders will need to make to ensure that the standards are integrated with the school improvement agenda. Borrowing an analytical tool from Pressman and Wildavsky's 1973 classic *Implementation: How Great Expectations in Washington Are Dashed in Oakland; or, Why It's Amazing That Federal Programs Work at All, This Being a Saga of the Economic Development Administration as Told by Two Sympathetic Observers who Seek to Build Morals on a Foundation of Ruined Hopes* (University of California Press, 1973, 1979, 1984), he calculates the probability of success for the endeavor and highlights just how difficult it is to coordinate such a diverse set of actors.

In Chapter 2, Dane Linn describes the role of governors in this process. As leader of the National Governors Association's education wing, he oversaw the standards' development process. He offers a firsthand account of how the standards were written, modified, and adopted, stressing the uniquely state-led process that governors undertook to develop the standards. He discusses the challenges that governors will face to maintain support for the standards, including the role of public opinion and the demands on state budgets, and uses his intimate knowledge of the NGA and its constituent members to offer advice to governors as they transition from adopters to implementers.

In Chapter 3 Morgan Polikoff discusses what this effort means for teacher quality initiatives around the country. Teachers will be the lynchpin for implementation of the standards, and if insufficient care is taken to understand how the standards interact with the policies we have in place to educate them, develop them, and hold them accountable, the standards could do more harm than good.

In Chapter 4 Robin Lake and Tricia Maas examine the relationship between charter schools and common standards. Through a series of interviews with charter school leaders, they uncover a lingering tension bubbling under the surface of the charter school community. Some of those leaders see the Common Core as a great opportunity to access new materials and more fairly compare themselves to the traditional public schools with whom they compete for students. Others are extremely wary of the standards and fear that they will impinge on the instructional autonomy that charter schools so prize.

In Chapter 5 Deven Carlson describes the Common Core's connection to state accountability systems. He highlights the tension between common standards and assessments and the state prerogative to set standards for proficiency and uncovers numerous lingering issues of integrating scores from the new Common Core–aligned exams into existing No Child Left Behind remedies. More than anything, though, he remarks on just how much is riding on these new assessments, and how challenging it will be for them to live up to their hype.

In Chapter 6 Peter Meyer offers a history of social studies standards in the United States and considers if we will ever see Common Core social studies standards. After the disastrous attempt in the 1990s to approve a set of history standards, those interested in trying again have a new playing field. The math and English language arts standards have cleared a path and softened a great deal of opposition to the "national" nature of the standards that proved such a hurdle in the 1990s. However, the issue of social studies standards is still a controversial subject, and one that appears relatively unlikely moving forward.

In Chapter 7 Taryn Hochleitner and Allison Kimmel dive deep into the world of technology. With both assessments and instructional materials for the Common Core designed to be more technology-based than ever before, there are real concerns as issues with bandwidth, infrastructure, hardware, and software stand firmly in the way of the innovation that the standards make possible. Through a series of in-depth interviews with key staff members in states and districts, as well as leading thinkers in the field, they highlight several practical concerns and offer words of caution as technological advances develop.

In Chapter 8, Patrick McGuinn of Drew University addresses the question of governance. At this time, it is unclear who is going to control the standards, amend them when necessary, and track state cut scores and proficiency definitions. McGuinn talks through many of the possible governance models, which individuals and organizations should be represented in the governing entity, as well as the deeper concerns of how the entity should be funded and managed, and the optimal role of the federal government in this process.

In Chapter 9 Ashley Jochim explains the messy politics of implementation. The Common Core, and all of its associated expenses, will have to compete with other claims for tax dollars in already squeezed state budgets. State leaders will have to make difficult tradeoffs to ensure that assessments, professional development, instructional tools, and infrastructure are adequately funded. She also discusses how results from the new assessments may affect public opinion about the Common Core and concludes by walking through strategies for policy makers tasked with managing support for the standards.

In the conclusion we will try to distill some of the key insights and lessons from the nine chapters, exploring what those mean for smart implementation of the Common Core, and what they imply for school improvement more broadly.

At this time, it is unclear if the Common Core will complement or conflict with current efforts underway to reform the American education system. It is our hope that this volume may contribute, if only slightly, to promoting discussion as to how would-be reformers can maximize the opportunities presented by the Common Core, while mitigating the risks that the effort will upend (or be upended by) ongoing school improvement efforts.

NOTES

1.   Chester Finn, quoted in Gewertz, C. (2013, April 25). Success of standards depends on translation for classroom. *Education Week*.

2.   William McCallum, quoted in Weingarten, R. (2013, April 30). Making Common Core Standards work before making them count: Remarks for [sic] AFT president Randi Weingarten, Association for a Better New York [Speech transcript].Retrieved from the AFT website: http://www.aft.org/newspubs/press/weingarten043013.cfm

3.   Markow, D., Macia, L., & Lee, H. (2013, February). *The Metlife survey of the American teacher*. New York: Metlife.

4.   Richards, E. (2012, February 1). $18 million GE grant helps train Milwaukee teachers. *Milwaukee Journal Sentinel*.

5.   Duncan, A. (2013, June 25). *Remarks at the American Society of News Editors Annual Convention*. Capital Hilton, Washington, DC. Retrieved from http://www.ed.gov/news/speeches/duncan-pushes-back-attacks-common-core-standards

6.   Bush, G. (1990). *Address before a joint session of the Congress on the state of the Union*. Retrieved from http://www.presidency.ucsb.edu/ws/index.php?pid=18095

7.   Cheney, L. (1994, October 20). The end of history. *Wall Street Journal*.

8.   Edward Kennedy, quoted in Rudalevige, A. (2003, Fall). The politics of No Child Left Behind. *Education Next, 3*(4).

9.   Peterson, P. E., & Hess, F. (2006, Summer). Keeping an eye on state standards. *Education Next, 6*(3).

10.   Bandeira de Mello, V. (2011). Mapping state proficiency standards onto the NAEP scales: Variation and change in state standards for reading and mathematics, 2005–2009 (NCES 2011-458). National Center for Education Statistics, Institute of Education Sciences, U.S. Department of Education, Washington, DC: Government Printing Office.

11.   Finn, C. E., & Petrilli, M. J. (2010, July 22). The Common Core curriculum. *National Review Online*.

12.   Obama, B. (2009, March 10). *Remarks to the Hispanic Chamber of Commerce on a complete and competitive American education* [Speech transcript]. Washington, DC: White House Briefing Room.

13.   McCluskey, N. (2012, January 9). No Child—And the latest lost decade. *Cato Institute Commentary*.

14.   McCluskey, N. (2012, January 5). NCLB: Perspectives on the law. *Education Week*.

15.   Evers, W., Greene, J. P., Forster, G., Stotsky, S., Wurman, Z., et. al. (2011). Closing the door on innovation. Available from the Heartland Institute website: http://heartland.org/policy-documents/closing-door-innovation

16.   Carol Burris, quoted in Strauss, V. (2013, March 4). Principal: "I was naïve about Common Core." *Washington Post*.

17.   Bush, J., & Klein, J. (2011, June 23). The case for common educational standards. *Wall Street Journal*.

18.   The Editorial Board. (2013, April 20). Moving ahead with Common Core. *New York Times*.

CHAPTER 1

The Lay of the Land

Michael Q. McShane

DECADES OF STUDY of public policy have led to an almost immutable truth: Implementing large, national initiatives that require diverse actors to cooperate is really, really complicated. As a result, the landscape of American history is littered with policies that, while grandiose in vision and rhetoric, fell apart during implementation.

The Common Core State Standards (CCSS) initiative is an example of such an enormous undertaking. Not since states across the country implemented large-scale accountability systems to comply with the No Child Left Behind Act in the early 2000s has such a diverse set of national, state, and local actors been called upon to work together to align instruction, develop assessments, and reform teacher and school-level accountability systems.

Between the formal adoption of the Common Core Standards by most participating states in 2010 and their full implementation by the 2014–2015 school year, states, districts, and schools have quite a bit of work to do. All members of the education system—from classroom teachers to the secretary of education—will need to coordinate their efforts and work together toward a common goal.

On the national level, organizations like the Council of Chief State School Officers (CCSSO) and the National Governors Association (NGA) will need to continue to manage a political climate that has large swaths of legislators, politicians, writers, and practitioners uncomfortable with the Common Core. The more the standards become synonymous with the Obama administration, which repeatedly took credit for the initiative during the 2012 campaign and provided incentives for states to adopt the standards through the Race to the Top program and their Elementary and Secondary Education Act (ESEA) waivers, the more reticent many Republicans (who, at the time of writing, control the state houses and governorships in 24 states) will be to support them.

On the state level, leaders will need to coordinate funding and manage teacher preparation programs and professional development to equip teachers with the skills and content knowledge necessary to teach to the Common Core. They will also need to set guidelines for adopting (or in some states, choose directly) new textbooks and supplementary resources (both technology-based and traditional) aligned to the new standards. At a time of declining budgets, they must fund new tests and the necessary technology to administer them, as well as pay for the new resources for students and teachers that will become available. When new test scores are released, which are almost universally believed to be much lower based on the increasing difficulty of the tests, leaders will need to determine how to integrate them into existing accountability programs and manage public perception about the standards. They will need to coordinate with teacher education programs to ensure that preservice teachers are prepared to teach to the standards. And they will also need to determine how to best leverage newly comparable performance data across states.

At the local level, leaders will need to assess their capacity to fulfill the new responsibilities that the Common Core presents. They will bear the brunt of national calls for new professional development, new technology, and new teacher quality management systems. Do schools have the necessary number of computers to complete testing within the allocated assessment windows? Do they want to invest in one-to-one technology to leverage online resources for students and teachers? Schools and districts will need to contract with aligned professional development groups and, in many places, decide which new textbooks to use. In the short term, they will need to decide if they want to use so called "bridge" textbooks with Common Core–aligned resources as addenda, or purchase new books and resources across the board.

This chapter will map the decisions that leaders at all levels will need to make at various points in the implementation process. In doing so, it will highlight the enormous challenges and the very real likelihood that the initiative will be less than successful across all domains. In closing, it will offer recommendations for maximizing the probability that the Common Core initiative will be successful.

THE CIRCUITOUS PATH OF THE COMMON CORE, IN THREE PHASES

For ease of understanding, I've divided Common Core implementation into three phases (illustrated in the flow chart in Figure 1.1). *Phase One* consists of the time between state adoption and when standards-aligned tests come online. The Smarter Balanced Assessment Consortium (SBAC) and the Partnership for Assessment of Readiness for College and Careers (PARCC) are the two largest developers, though providers may get involved in developing

FIGURE 1.1. Flow Chart of Common Core Decisions

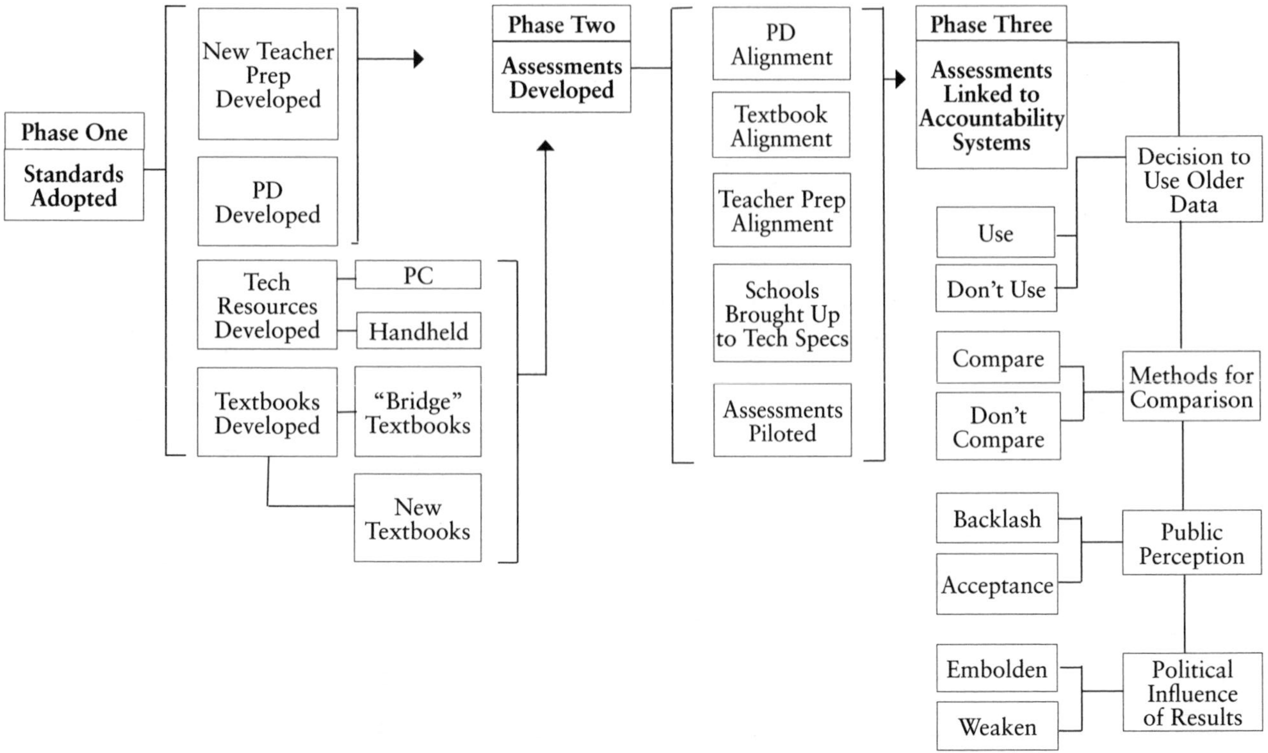

tests that measure the standards. This stage of Common Core implementation is marked predominately by practical concerns—namely, determining what resources will need to be brought to bear to make sure that the Common Core enhances current efforts to improve schooling, and how they will be paid for in austere times. *Phase Two* consists of the time after the tests are brought live, but before they are fully integrated into accountability and teacher quality management systems. It is marked most notably by concerns about alignment and whether all of the different facets of the education system will work in concert with the standards' end goals. *Phase Three* begins when the Common Core becomes the status quo and the standards are integrated into accountability systems. This phase is marked by the decisions that will need to be made to maintain public support for the standards and to ensure that the standards and their associated assessments continue to complement, rather than conflict with, concurrent efforts in states to improve schooling.

Phase One: Adoption and Development

The vast majority of participating states adopted the Common Core Standards in the summer of 2010 under the agreement that the standards would be fully implemented into accountability regimes by the 2014–15 school year. Adoption was driven, in large part, by the Obama administration's incentives for states to adopt the standards by virtue of its "standards and assessments" category in its Race to the Top competition. Seventy of the 500 total points awarded in the competition measured standards, including subcategories such as "developing and adopting common standards," "participating in consortium developing high-quality standards," "developing and implementing common, high-quality assessments," and others, which were clearly a nod to the Common Core.[1] Race to the Top also granted $330 million to fund the PARCC and SBAC consortia to develop tests to measure the standards. Regardless of the adoption process, states will need to integrate the Common Core Standards into the already crowded school reform space. Specifically, states will need to ensure that teachers are prepared, instructional materials are aligned, and schools and systems have the technological capacity to implement the standards.

Teacher Preparation. There is wide agreement that the Common Core Standards are going to ask teachers to instruct students in new ways.[2] With the standards' emphasis on critical thinking and problem solving, as well as on the importance of evidence-based inquiry and literary analysis, many teachers will be asked to teach students things that they were not taught during their own education, either as children or as preservice teachers.

Therefore, colleges of education and teacher preparation programs are going to be called upon to change the way that they train teachers in order to prepare them to teach to the Common Core. Courses in pedagogy will need to promote strategies for teaching critical problem solving, close reading, using textual evidence, and other skills that may be new and difficult for prospective teachers. Colleges of education may need to remediate these skills for their students.

Unfortunately, many observers believe that teacher preparation programs are not up to the task. In the summer of 2013, the National Council on Teacher Quality released a scathing indictment of teacher preparation, calling colleges of education "an industry of mediocrity."[3] The report found that less than one elementary teacher education program in nine instilled the content knowledge necessary to teach the Common Core. High school teacher preparation programs fared better, but only slightly, with just over one third of programs meeting NCTQ's standards.

Professional Development. Under a best-case scenario, colleges of education and other teacher preparation programs will infuse the system every year with a crop of new teachers ready and able to teach the Common Core. But even under those circumstances, there are still millions of teachers currently employed in schools who will need to be brought up to speed on the new content and skills. School leaders are going to rely on professional development to an almost unprecedented degree. Unfortunately, professional development has a dubious track record. When the Institute for Education Sciences attempted to review the academic literature on the topic, only 9 of the more than 1,300 studies reviewed met their evidence standards. Of those, the only programs that were found to be effective were those that offered intense, longer term professional development (averaging 49 hours of workshops).[4] If that is the standard necessary for adequate professional development, this will constitute an enormous undertaking.

The Common Core's national scale does have certain advantages. Today, each state is on its own to find, hire, and vet professional development providers. Because each state has its own standards, professional development options are more limited. With common standards across the vast majority of the country, the number of available programs should grow exponentially. Moreover, the booming "app" market for smart phones and tablets offers a great opportunity for a diverse group of increasingly technology-based providers to create tools for teachers across the country. However, with all of these new providers comes a greater need for quality control, as it takes little effort to brand a new product as "Common Core–aligned," even if it isn't.

Technology. Technology is an integral part of the Common Core initiative. Both of the new assessments being developed by SBAC and PARCC are designed to be administered on computers. Many of the resources for teachers will be digital. However, the level to which such tests and resources are designed (either to mesh with existing technology or the next generation of handhelds and tablets) will be important in determining the hardware and software that schools and districts will need to procure in the coming years.

Computer-based assessment offers a mix of opportunities and challenges. Computer-adaptive tests are far more accurate than traditional paper-and-pencil exams.[5] As SBAC and PARCC move away from mere measures of proficiency to a more complicated assessment of college and career readiness, tests will need to be able to better diagnose where students are and where gaps exist in their knowledge and skills. Adaptive tests offer a clear opportunity to accomplish this with greater precision. However, states will have to navigate new hardware and software considerations in order to bring these tests to scale across the country. Given that states only allow accountability testing during particular "windows" throughout the school year to ensure test security and comparability, schools will need a large number of computers to administer tests. While many schools, especially in more affluent areas, are pushing "one-to-one" programs that pair every child with his or her own computer, wide swaths of the country are still lagging behind in their hardware.[6] Similarly, for web-based testing, schools are going to need a large amount of Internet bandwidth in order to download testing materials and upload student responses. This will not be cheap. Furthermore, as tablets and handheld devices become more and more popular, user-friendly, and stocked with useful apps, schools are going to have to decide if they would like to purchase them all at once, phase them in, or stick with older technology.

Computer-based resources drive a similar set of questions for leaders. For years, many prominent thinkers have called for moving away from costly paper-based textbooks and resources to online student and teacher development tools.[7] New providers like LearnZillion, MasteryConnect, BetterLesson, and the Khan Academy are developing videos, quizzes, and activities for students aligned to the Common Core that are available for free or for a nominal fee, provided that schools have the necessary technology. Leaders may need to incur some upfront capital costs to purchase computers and upgrade inter- and intranet infrastructure, but very well could realize substantial cost savings over the long term, as less expensive resources supplant more expensive ones. Given the tight budgets with which many states are working, it is not clear that schools will be able or willing to meet these upfront costs.

Textbooks. While some districts have adopted digital resources, by and large, schools around the country still rely on paper-based textbooks that will need to be updated or replaced to align with the Common Core. In 2012 alone, schools spent $2.35 billion on textbooks, and that was simply to keep pace with current standards and assessments.[8] Given that most existing texts are not aligned to the Common Core, state and district leaders will have two choices moving forward. First, they can purchase (or in some cases textbook producers will provide free of charge) so-called bridge textbooks, which are addenda to existing textbooks and will offer Common Core–aligned supplements.[9] For schools that cannot afford wholesale textbook replacement, this looks like the most reasonable course of action. For those that have more money available, or happen to be at a time in their textbook purchasing cycle when it makes sense to buy new textbooks, they can replace wholesale with Common Core–aligned books.

There are three major challenges that state and district leaders will need to address in order to make sure new texts benefit their efforts to improve schools and not hinder them. First, states are going to need to develop ways to vet texts to make sure that they are actually aligned to the Common Core. Currently ten states (Arkansas, California, Florida, Kentucky, Mississippi, Oklahoma, Oregon, South Carolina, Tennessee, and Texas) select their textbooks at the state level. An additional seven states (Idaho, Indiana, Louisiana, North Carolina, Utah, Virginia, and West Virginia) create a "recommended list" from which states must choose their textbooks, and four more states (Alabama, Georgia, Nevada, and New Mexico) are required to do some combination of the two.[10] Thus state leaders will need to be involved in vetting and selecting textbooks, and school- and district-level personnel will need to examine them to ensure that they are aligned to the Common Core.

Second, states and districts are going to need to select and most likely pilot new texts. In a first foray into this process, the state of Louisiana tested several different textbooks for various subjects and found all of them inadequate. State superintendent John White, who was reported to have personally examined the proposed textbooks, was quoted as saying that all of the book series that he examined did not "consistently reflect the level of work we see in the PARCC prototypes."[11] If White is correct, many states may find themselves without adequate classroom resources.

Finally, states and districts are going to need to align supplementary materials with the new texts. Previously, publishers explicitly linked the majority of supplementary materials to particular textbook series. This will change when school leaders have the opportunity to mix and match from a surfeit of options at their disposal. Rather than simply having the Prentice Hall math series supplemented by Prentice Hall's workbooks, flash cards, and overhead transparencies, a school or even an individual teacher might have a Prentice Hall textbook, a slate of Khan Academy videos, and a set of quizzes from online assessment warehouse MasteryConnect. Wading through all of these resources will be a daunting task, as most teachers and leaders in the past have accepted all of the resources that simply came along with their textbook series. Common Core–generation school leaders and policy makers will need to develop processes to find, mix, and match the best resources.

Decisions made in Phase One will determine whether the Common Core initiative begins on the right footing to dance well with current reform efforts. As states learn more about the tests that will be used to assess the standards, we move into Phase Two, wherein preparation, instruction, and assessment are brought up to speed.

Phase Two: Alignment

Phase Two of Common Core implementation will begin once the assessments for the Common Core are developed and will conclude before the tests are integrated into state accountability systems. During this time period it will be crucial for leaders at all levels to develop the capability and infrastructure to administer tests and then collect and analyze the data they produce, to pilot tests as a check that textbooks, resources, and professional development are aligned with the standards, and to prepare the public to understand new test results.

Capability and Infrastructure. Phase One was marked by general conversation about the technical needs and capabilities of the Common Core assessments and resources. In Phase Two, leaders will have to get down to the intricate details of implementation. After making decisions about the level of technology they will procure when it comes to assessments and resources (this generation's PC-based operating systems or the next generation of handhelds and tablets) districts will need to budget, purchase, install, and troubleshoot this new hardware.

Professional development and educator training will play an equally important role in ensuring that teachers are prepared to teach to the Common Core. Districts will need to ensure that the professional development programs they selected in Phase One will not only help teachers master new content and skills required to teach the Common Core, but that teachers are also able to utilize new resources available to supplement instruction. This will be a long process. The content and skills alone will take multiple professional development workshops, and follow-up sessions and trainings to select and utilize new technology will be equally laborious. Hopefully, this work will be informed by what schools and districts across the country are learning through assessment pilots, but this hinges upon data being made available in a timely and accessible manner.

Pilot Testing and Alignment. Schools and districts are not going to get the alignment between the Common Core content and assessments right the first time. As Morgan Polikoff outlines in this volume (see Chapter 3), alignment is as important as it is difficult to properly execute. In Phase One, schools and districts picked resources essentially in the dark, as the consortia had not released the item specifications. The standards clearly serve as a guide, but until the assessments are released, school leaders will not know exactly *what* will be tested and *how* it will be tested. As the tests are released, states will need to pilot their administration and use results as a check on whether their resources are aligned to the standards. This is a difficult process because leaders could very reasonably come to different conclusions when given the same results on these new tests. If students perform poorly, is it because their resources are improperly aligned, because the teachers did a poor job conveying the new material, or because the students simply do not know the information? Depending on the answers to these questions, vastly different policy prescriptions emerge. Leaders are going to have to be extremely careful as they analyze results to ensure that they don't draw the wrong conclusions and prescribe cures to ills that the system does not actually have, while ignoring the real problems.

Similarly, competition between test providers could lead to opacity in interpreting proficiency measurements. If providers outside of the state assessment compacts get involved, individual states could contract for their own "Common Core–aligned" assessments that have their own cut scores. How this will translate into interstate comparisons or uniform standards of proficiency remains to be seen.

Piloting the new assessments—by whoever develops them—will be a difficult task. Teachers are old hands at administering paper-and-pencil-based tests. They have worked out testing schedules, practiced administering assessments, and developed integrity precautions around the paper model. Administering computer-based examinations will change all of this. Testing schedules will need to navigate limited lab space and time, and teachers will need to know how to troubleshoot not only student questions about test administration or content, but also technical problems with the testing hardware and software. Issues of test security in a web- and technology-based format will also become extremely important. There will need to be a clear set of protocols developed and explained to teachers.

Michigan can serve as a useful example of a successful pilot exam protocol. Even though SBAC tests are not available yet, state leaders decided to administer the social studies portion of the current state exam, the MEAP, to 35,000 students on computers to serve as a scaled test run of computer-based testing. From all accounts it appears to have been a rousing success. As Kate Cermak, an analyst at the Michigan Department of Education, told the *Detroit Free Press*, "It's gone incredibly smoothly . . . the schools are reporting that their students seem to be more engaged and interested in taking the online assessment."[12] This is not surprising, as state leaders decided to choose a manageable subset of students and only pilot one exam. Taking an entire new statewide exam at full scale is a huge undertaking, but the Michigan model of gradually scaled-up testing capacity can serve as a valuable example for other states as they move into Phase Two of implementation.

Preparing the Public. The widely predicted dip in proficiency rates on the new Common Core–aligned assessments risks endangering the razor-thin margin of public support the standards currently enjoy. According to the 2012 Gallup/*Phi Delta Kappan* poll on education, only 50% of Americans believe that the standards will "improve the quality of education in [their] community."[13] Leaders need to prepare teachers, parents, and community members for the very likely scenario that school proficiency levels will drop dramatically after the first administration of these new tests.[14]

Why will this dip happen? Currently, state tests are designed to measure proficiency, an admittedly low bar (when compared to the NAEP, international tests, or college requirements) that was designed simply to ensure that students were not being "left behind." With the Common Core's goal of "college and career readiness," the bar has been raised significantly. Thus the word *proficient* will change meaning from "clearing a basic threshold of achievement" to "ready to achieve at the high level necessary for postsecondary success."

The tests used to measure these goals are different as well. In the past, exams were designed with the lion's share of questions at the difficulty level of the proficiency cutoff to give the tests the most sensitivity and accuracy when determining whether a student is proficient. Because the new tests are designed to be computer-adaptive, they will be sensitive across a much wider swath of the performance spectrum. As a result, many extremely high-performing and extremely low-performing students that were swept out in the tails of the less sensitive older tests will receive a much more accurate measure of their performance. This could indicate that they are doing better than they previously thought, also that they are doing worse than they previously thought.

If leaders do not prepare the public then, rather than parents, teachers, and community members responding to dips in proficiency levels by saying "Maybe our schools are not doing as well as we thought; let's work to make them better," they will respond with "Wow, these tests are nonsense." If stakeholders think that levels have dropped for some reason other than the definition of success changing, the system risks serious backlash.

States that are not currently concerned about this problem should look to the case of Florida. For the 2012 administration of the FCAT, the state accountability test, state leaders decided to make the writing portion more rigorous by emphasizing spelling, grammar, and using evidence to support claims. Test scores plummeted. The community was not prepared and the public backlash drove the state board of education to lower the cut score for passing the test, something aptly described by a state representative as "a barnyard way of trying to fix something."[15]

On the opposite end of the spectrum, Kentucky can serve as an example of a state that prepared its community well to accept the new tests. Kentucky was both the first state to adopt the Common Core and the first state to align its current state tests to the Common Core. After the first test administration in 2013, the state saw test scores drop as much as 28 percentage points in some grade levels and subjects.[16] However, Kentucky did not experience the backlash that Florida saw. Why? Because there was a year-long concerted effort on the part of the Kentucky Chamber of Commerce, the Kentucky PTA, and by state and district leaders to prepare stakeholders for the test results. In fact, the state went so far as to make public its predictions for how large the drop was going to be, estimating a dip as large as 36 percentage points in some places. So, when students did not do as poorly as was previously projected, Kentucky was actually able to give itself a small pat on the back! As Gene Wilhoit of the Council of Chief State School Officers told *Education Week*, "What you're seeing in Kentucky is a predictor of what you're going to see in the other states, as the assessments roll out next year and the year after."[17]

In total, Phase Two marks when the rubber meets the road. States will take their first crucial on-the-ground steps to ensure that the Common Core Standards accelerate current efforts to improve schools, not inhibit them. If school leaders are not careful and thoughtful at this stage, the entire enterprise could derail, especially when it comes to public support for the standards. Phase Two ends when the pilots have been completed and the new assessments are implemented into states' accountability systems. Phase Three presents an entirely new and daunting set of issues for funding, implementing, and managing public opinion about the standards.

Phase 3: Integration

In Phase Three the Common Core becomes the status quo. When this happens, the Common Core assessments will become the determinants for state, district, and school accountability systems. They will be the backbone for any teacher evaluation initiatives that include value-added test scores as a component, and they will be the measure by which schools are judged for accountability purposes. As the Common Core assessments are brought to scale, questions of how to integrate the new metrics into existing systems, how to manage the newly possible cross-school, cross-district, and cross-state comparisons, and how to navigate public opinion around education reform will move to the forefront. If policy makers and system leaders are not careful, all of their hard work in Phases One and Two could be undone.

Integration Into Existing Accountability Systems. State and district accountability systems are in for a major change as they implement the new Common Core assessments. With shifting goals and increased accuracy, state and district leaders are going to have to wrestle with how to integrate new test results into existing accountability systems. Remember, many states had large-scale accountability systems in place even before the No Child Left Behind Act of 2001 (NCLB) made them a nationwide policy.[18] States all across the country have been administering tests, collecting data, and using the data to inform decisions for well over a decade; will they simply throw this information out? Will schools that have been enmeshed in the multiyear cascading punishments because they have failed to make Adequate Yearly Progress (AYP) be able to reset the clock because the new tests are providing new (and arguably more accurate) information? How will the patchwork of state waivers from NCLB accountability mandates interact with these plans? Policy makers will need to decide if they are going to integrate these new test scores, and if so, how.

Accountability programs come down to cut scores. As Deven Carlson will discuss in this volume (see Chapter 5), there is substantial evidence that states have systematically lowered their cut scores in response to political pressures due to low achievement.[19] It is unclear whether states will have the latitude to set their own cut scores and determine their own proficiency levels. If states are allowed to set their own levels, there will be a measure of incongruity across states; two different scores on the same tests will yield proficiency for one student and not for the other. It is unclear how states will manage this. But even if this process is centralized, or at least if there is some agreement across the various consortia of states on common cut scores, there is no guarantee that cut scores will be set high. The fundamental political calculus is the same, and the higher the cut scores are set, the less likely it will be that traditionally lower performing states will want to join. This could very easily drive states to use different tests, or to abandon the consortia for new providers that will give a more favorable assessment of their students' performance.

Managing Comparison. Administering the same tests aligned to the same standards across the entire country will offer an unparalleled level of comparability between schools, districts, and states. In the past, those wishing to make cross-state comparisons needed to cross-walk state tests scores to NAEP and then convert all of the scores, which is psychometrically dubious at best.[20] While cross-country comparability seems like an almost unmitigated good, leaders will have to navigate serious issues in making such comparisons.

The education landscape in the United States has a terrible history with drawing unwarranted conclusions from comparative data. One must not look past the response to books like *Surpassing Shanghai* and *Finnish Lessons* that take snapshot looks from the international Trends in International Mathematics and Science Study (TIMSS) or Programme for International Student Assessment (PISA) tests and then develop a series of policy prescriptions based on these countries' "best practices."[21] As it turns out, almost every high-performing country's "best practice" is also used somewhere in a low-performing country.[22] To borrow from the language of statistics, this approach continuously selects on the dependent variable; researchers find countries or school systems that perform well and then attempt to intuit backwards how they got there. It is rarely successful. If the cross-state comparability of student performance leads to this type of ineffective mimicry, it will not be productive. If, however, it drives policy makers to take serious and systematic looks at differences in performance and attempt to determine root causes based on data and statistical inference, this could be a very successful enterprise.

Public Perception and Political Influence. In Phase Two, leaders will need to prepare the public for a dip in school performance. In all likelihood, there will be some variation in how successful states accomplish this goal. In Phase Three, leaders will reap what they have sown. For those states that have prepared the public, managing opinion will still be important, as it will take a great deal of continuous hand-holding to keep communities engaged in and positive about the gradual alignment process. For those states that did not, there will likely be a serious backlash from parents, teachers, and the public writ large. There will be political pressure to lower cut scores or leave any sort of cross-state agreements regarding common proficiency levels. There could very well be backlash against the entire endeavor, with community members pushing to back out of the assessment consortia or out of the Common Core initiative entirely.

This new information will also play a central role in the political will to sustain the Common Core initiative. Maintaining this program over the coming years, especially with the public relations hit that a dip in scores or unfavorable comparisons might bring, will take political capital. At every turn, leaders will face incentives to leave the program for greener pastures and systems over which they exert more control. The organizations that support this endeavor including the National Governors Association, the Council of Chief State School Officers, the Gates Foundation, and any governing body developed to manage the standards will need to be cognizant of these incentives, and work to maintain the political coalition that supports the Common Core if they want the initiative to be successful.

If managed well, however, such new information could catalyze a new dimension of education reform. If, for instance, suburban schools are truly measured against a college- and career-ready standard and come up short, politically powerful suburban parents could call for reform to a new degree. Only 25% of students in the class of 2012 that took the ACT met the standard for college readiness in all four tested subjects. While these results are more acute when it comes to minority students, with only 5% of African American and 13% of Hispanic students meeting that standard in all four subjects, White students did not fare much better. Only 32% passed the college-ready threshold in all four subjects.[23] It is possible that scores from the new Common Core–aligned exams will bring that shortcoming to the fore and draw suburban parents into the school reform movement.

FUNDING

I have purposely avoided anything more than a very limited discussion of the elephant in the Common Core room—funding—up to this point, simply for the sake of repetitiveness. At every moment of Phase One, Two, and Three, I could have easily added a sentence or clause that said "and this is going to be expensive." From developing, piloting, and taking to scale new tests, to technological infrastructure upgrades, to new textbooks, professional development, and supplementary resources, adopting the Common Core is going to be an expensive enterprise. Compounding this problem are the difficult fiscal conditions that most states are currently experiencing. In the next several paragraphs I hope to unpack some of these funding issues in order to delineate the challenges state leaders across this country will face when it comes to funding this endeavor.

The first issue is simply the cost of procuring the tests, technology, professional development, and resources that are part and parcel of the Common Core. The Thomas B. Fordham Institute issued a report in May 2012 entitled *Putting a Price Tag on the Common Core: How Much Will Smart Implementation Cost?* in which they estimated the various situations that could influence this price tag.[24] The report includes three cost figures (*business as usual*, *bare bones*, and *balanced implementation*) based on different strategies that states might employ to fund the initiative. According to the report's authors, a "business as usual" approach would cost approximately $12.1 billion. On the opposite end of the spectrum, a "bare bones" approach to acquiring new textbooks and resources, assessments, and professional development would cost around $3 billion. The middle estimate, and the one for which the Thomas B. Fordham Institute advocates, would cost around $5.1 billion. Because the states that have adopted the Common Core Standards have already spent $3.9 billion collectively on these expenditures, the net cost for implementing the Common Core actually ranges from $8.2 billion for the "business as usual" model to a net savings of $900 million for the "bare bones" approach. The balanced approach would only represent a new expenditure of $1.2 billion nationwide.

While $1.2 billion in a $500 billion system may sound like a drop in the bucket, state leaders are scraping for every penny that they can gather. State budget dollars are being pulled in several different directions by everything from increased Medicaid costs to ballooning pension obligations. Taking a step-by-step look at the murderer's row of state budget issues paints a gloomy picture for any plans to increase expenditures.

State Pension Obligations

The Pew Center on the States estimates a $1.38 trillion gap between states' assets and obligations for public sector retirement benefits. Forty-two states are on the hook for $757 billion in pension liabilities and $627 billion in retiree health care costs that they do not have currently in state coffers. This does not bode well for other claims on state dollars, as most states have legal requirements that prevent this money from being repurposed.

States are in various shades of trouble when it comes to meeting these liabilities. The Pew report estimates that several Common Core adopting states are in dire straits, funding their retirement funds at far less than the liabilities outstanding. Louisiana, for example, has only funded 56% of its liabilities. Kentucky is faring even worse, at 54%, but every state pales in comparison to Illinois, which has only funded 45% of its obligations. In 2010, these states paid only 84%, 58%, and 87% respectively of the required contributions needed for pension funds to remain financially solvent. Stated plainly, mandatory contributions to these funds are going to squeeze out other claims on state dollars and put any requests, Common Core or otherwise, on the back burner.

Increased Medicaid Contributions

In 2012 the State Budget Crisis Task Force, an organization created by former New York lieutenant governor Richard Ravitch and former Federal Reserve chair Paul Volcker, painted a gloomy picture of increasing state Medicaid obligations.[25] According to their report, state-level Medicaid costs are likely to grow at a rate of 8.1% from 2012 to 2020. Unfortunately, the authors project an annual growth rate of only 3.9% for state tax revenue, creating an ever-increasing gap that could balloon as much as $22 billion *annually* for the next 5 years. This will be compounded by the growing elderly percentage of our population, which could increase by as much as

35% in the next 2 decades. As the authors point out, this will serve to crowd out other claims on state tax dollars.

Taken together, these yawning gaps in state funding and state obligations bode poorly for funding all aspects of the existing K–12 education system, let alone adding new expenditures. The Common Core will not only fight against Medicaid and pension obligations for funding, but against all of the other elements of the K–12 system, whether they are elements of the reform agenda or not. This is a disaster in the making. Imagine the district or state leader who has to decide between a round of teacher layoffs and a new suite of testing materials. If folks already do not like testing, there is little incentive to send that money to the element more essential for Common Core implementation.

PROBABILITY OF SUCCESS

Jeffery Pressman and Aaron Wildavsky's landmark 1973 work *Implementation* provides a framework for understanding how public policies are implemented on the ground level.[26] Its subtitle, *How Great Expectations in Washington Are Dashed in Oakland; or, Why It's Amazing That Federal Programs Work at All, This Being a Saga of the Economic Development Administration as Told by Two Sympathetic Observers Who Seek to Build Morals on a Foundation of Ruined Hopes*, tells you all you need to know about where their studies led them. To sum up their thesis, implementing large and complex programs involves marshaling large numbers of diverse actors whose incentives are not aligned to cooperate. As a result, making programs actually work is *an extremely difficult process.*

Below, I reproduce an exercise they undertake in their book, appropriately titled "The Complexity of Joint Action." In describing the implementation of a large public works program in Oakland, California, they counted the total number of decisions that needed to be made and the total number of agreements that needed to be forged between all of these diverse actors in order for the program to be successful. Through 30 different decision points, the authors accumulated 70 total agreements. By looking at a simple mathematical estimation, they argued that even if there is an extremely high probability that each agreement will be successful (say a 99% chance), after 70 iterations, there is less than a 50% chance of the endeavor working as a whole. Lowering the probability of success even to 95% drives down the cumulative probability of 70 successes to less than 0.4%.

Going back to the earlier discussion, there are 17 separate large-scale decisions that must be made correctly throughout the course of Phases One through Three in order to ensure that the Common Core initiative complements and does not conflict with current efforts to improve schooling. These decisions may be divided into 4 groups:

Professional Development

1. Teacher preparation institutions agree to teach prospective educators the Common Core.
2. Districts appropriate funding for new professional development resources.
3. State education agencies (SEAs) and local education agencies (LEAs) vet and select new professional development resources.
4. SEAs, LEAs, and individual schools pilot and check on the quality of new professional development resources.
5. SEAs, LEAs, and individual schools take new professional development resources to scale.

Technology

1. SEAs and LEAs select the level of technology to which professional development and student resources will be designed (current or next generation).
2. SEAs and LEAs accurately determine their existing technological capacity.
3. SEAs and LEAs accurately determine new technology needs.
4. State legislatures appropriate monies for hardware and Internet infrastructure upgrades.
5. SEAs, LEAs, and individual schools determine whether to purchase new textbooks or use bridge texts.

Assessments and Accountability

1. SEAs select new assessments.
2. SEAs and LEAs pilot new assessments.
3. SEAs align new data with existing accountability systems and determine whether or not to use pre–Common Core testing data.
4. SEAs and LEAs use new data in useful ways to make cross-school, cross-district, and cross-state comparisons.

Political Will

1. State leaders prepare the public for the dip in test scores.
2. State leaders manage public opinion once test scores are made available.

TABLE 1.1. Probability of Decisions

Number of Decisions	Probability of Each	Overall Probability of Success
17	.99	.843
17	.95	.418
17	.75	.008

3. State leaders use the new data constructively to inform political conversations.

Now, it is true that there are possible scenarios where not every one of these decisions is reached and yet the process is not derailed. For example, states with extra money in their budgets might buy new computers for their schools without assessing their current technological infrastructure. While wasteful, this would by no means prevent successful implementation. What this list does provide are questions that if not answered correctly, decrease the likelihood that the effort will complement and not conflict with existing efforts to improve schooling.

A look back to Figure 1.1 highlights the complex web and multiple phases in which these decisions will be made. Professional development, for example, stretches across all three phases, from initial development after the standards are released, to alignment with assessment once they are developed, to integration with student performance data once it is made available. The same is true with technology. From the initial decision between PC and handheld platforms to building large multistate data systems, school and systems leaders are going to have to coordinate at an impressive level in order for the project to succeed.

Using the Pressman and Wildavsky model and various levels of probability of success for each of these decisions (see Table 1.1) underscores just how difficult this process will be in the coming years. Even if every decision has a 99% chance of success, the overall probability of success is only 84%. If the probability of success of each decision drops to even 95%, the cumulative probability plummets to 42%. Decreasing the probability of success to 75% drops the overall probability of success to less than 1%. Such is the story of large, complex, and multipart policy implementation projects.

RECOMMENDATIONS

After the gloomy forecast above, it would be easy for a Common Core supporter to lose heart. In order for the initiative to be successful, there is a great deal of work that needs to be done and a large amount of coordination that must take place between a diverse set of actors. In order to make this process fruitful, there are three things that policy makers can do to increase the probability of success and help ensure that the Common Core complements and does not conflict with current efforts to improve schooling.

1. *Use this new opportunity to rethink pedagogical resources and professional development.* As the Thomas B. Fordham Institute report describes, the "business as usual" model is extremely costly and not always particularly effective. Today's market for resources, for students and teachers, is flush with new web-based tools that are drastically less expensive (even free) and have the potential to be every bit as high-quality as the textbooks and supplements of old. Finding them in the sea of apps and products is difficult, and leaders are going to need to develop winnowing skills that they have not always needed. However, savvy leaders and resource providers that take full advantage of this opportunity will be able to drastically decrease the cost while increasing, or at the very least not decreasing, the quality of their resources.

2. *Prepare all stakeholders for "the dip."* In taking the time to survey the landscape of Common Core implementation, teachers', parents', and the community's perception of the process will play a huge role. If people believe that these standards and their affiliated tests are inaccurate either because they lack validity or reliability, public perception will sink this project (and accountability efforts in general). In doing so, billions of dollars and years of hard work and political capital will be lost and the reform agenda will suffer a serious setback. However, if leaders anticipate what is coming and, like Kentucky, prepare their populace for decreasing scores, they can not only weather the storm, but use the dip in scores as a catalyst to promote reform. States should pay particular attention to Kentucky's strategy to project even lower scores than anticipated in order to soften the blow.

3. *Build a broad political coalition for the Common Core.* If the lesson of *Implementation* is that corralling diverse actors is a Sisyphusian task, one strategy is to align the incentives of all of the actors. The K–12 system can come together to protect itself by working together as a cudgel to decrease the cost of materials and development. However, if a particular party or particular interest group seizes the Common Core as "its" idea and makes it more partisan (as was the case when the Democratic Party made it part of their platform at the 2012 convention), this coalition will be threatened. As much as state and local leaders can retain the Common Core's nonpartisan nature, they should.

Surveying the landscape, the Common Core will face an uphill battle in the coming years. However, the hill is not insurmountable. Through careful planning and preparation, state and local leaders can use the Common Core as a lever for positive change and an accelerator for nascent reform efforts in their communities.

NOTES

1. U.S. Department of Education. (2012, February 15). Race to the Top Fund: States' applications, scores and comments for phase 1. Retrieved from http://www2.ed.gov/programs/racetothetop/phase1-applications/index.html

2. Powers, E. (2013, February 5). How will Common Core change what we do? *Edutopia* [Web log post]. Retrieved from http://www.edutopia.org/blog/common-core-change-teaching-erin-powers

3. Greenberg, J, McKee, A & Walsh, K. (2013, June). *Teacher prep review: A review of the nation's teacher preparation programs.* Washington, DC: National Council on Teacher Quality.

4. Yoon, K. S., Duncan, T., Lee, S., Scarloss, B., & Shapley, K. (2007). *Reviewing the evidence on how teacher professional development affects student achievement* (Issues & Answers Report, REL 2007–No. 033). Washington, DC: U.S. Department of Education, Institute of Educational Sciences, National Center for Education Evaluation and Regional Assistance, Regional Laboratory Southwest.

5. Weiss, D. J., & Von Minden, S. (2011). Measuring individual growth with conventional and adaptive tests. *Journal of Methods and Measurement in the Social Sciences, 2*(1), 80–101.

6. Pandolfo, N. (2012, January 25). As some schools plunge into technology, poor schools are left behind. *Chicago Tribune.*

7. See Christensen, C. N., & Horn, M. B. (2002). *Disrupting class: How disruptive innovation will change the way the world learns.* New York: McGraw-Hill; Moe, T. M., & Chubb, J. E. (2010). *Liberating learning: Technology, politics, and the future of American education.* Hoboken, NJ: Jossey-Bass; Peterson, P. (2011). *Saving schools: From Horace Mann to virtual learning.* Cambridge, MA: Harvard University Press.

8. Trachtenberg, J. A. (2012, July 1). Textbook case for expansion. *Wall Street Journal.*

9. Sawchuk, S. (2012, November 13). Retooled textbooks aim to capture Common Core. *Education Week.*

10. Thomas B. Fordham Institute. (2004). *The mad, mad world of textbook adoption.* Washington, DC: Thomas B. Fordham Institute. Retrieved from http://www.edexcellencemedia.net/publications/2004/200409_madworldoftextbookadoption/Mad%20World_Test2.pdf

11. John White, quoted in Sawchuck, S. (2012, November 29). Citing lack of Common-Core alignment, Louisiana poised to delay textbook adoption [Web log post]. *Education Week, Curriculum Matters Blog.* Retrieved from http://blogs.edweek.org/edweek/curriculum/2012/11/citing_lack_of_common-core_ali.html

12. Kate Cermak, quoted in Higgins, L. (2012, November 26). Michigan takes big step forward in online testing of students. *Detroit Free Press*.

13. Bushaw, W. J., & Lopez, S. J. (2012). Public education in the United States: A nation divided. *Phi Delta Kappan, 94*(1), 8–25.

14. Ujifusa, A. (2012, June 6). New test put states on hot seat as scores plunge. *Education Week*.

15. Postal, L. (2012, May 15). Schools won't be held accountable for this year's low FCAT scores. *Orlando Sentinel*.

16. Ujifusa, A. (2012, November 2). Scores drop on KY's Common Core–aligned tests. *Education Week*.

17. Gene Wilhoit, quoted in Ujifusa, Scores drop.

18. Hamilton, L. S., Stecher, B. M., Marsh, J. A., McCombs, J. S., Robyn, A., Russell, J. L., Naftel, S., & Barney, H. (2007). *Standards-based accountability under No Child Left Behind*. Arlington, VA: RAND Corporation Monograph.

19. Adkins, D. G., Kingsbury, G., Dahlin, M., & Cronin, J. (2007). *The proficiency illusion*. Washington, DC: Thomas B. Fordham Institute.

20. Ho, A. D., & Haertel, E. H. (2007). Apples to apples? The underlying assumptions of state-NAEP comparisons. Paper commissioned by the Council of Chief State School Officers. http://scholar.harvard.edu/files/andrewho/files/ho_haertel_apples_to_apples.pdf

21. Tucker, M. S. (2011). *Surpassing Shanghai: An agenda for American education built on the world's leading systems*. Cambridge, MA: Harvard Education Press; Sahlberg, P., & Hargreaves, A. (2011). *Finnish lessons: What can the world learn from educational change in Finland?* New York: Teachers College Press.

22. ACT. (2012). *The condition of college and career readiness*. Iowa City: ACT.

23. Murphy, P., & Regenstein, E. (2012). *Putting a price tag on the Common Core: How much will smart implementation cost?* Washington, DC: Thomas B. Fordham Institute.

24. Pew Center on the States. (2012). *The widening gap update*. Washington, DC: Pew Center on the States.

25. Ravitch, R., & Volcker, P. (2012). *Report of the state budget crisis task force*. New York: State Budget Task Force.

26. Pressman, J. L., & Wildvasky, A. (1973). *Implementation: How great expectations in Washington are dashed in Oakland; or, why it's amazing that federal programs work at all, this being a saga of the Economic Development Administration as told by two sympathetic observers who seek to build morals on a foundation of ruined hopes*. Berkeley: University of California Press.

CHAPTER 2

The Role of Governors

Dane Linn

RAISING STUDENT ACHIEVEMENT has never been so important to the United States. For the first time in this country's history, our children may face a lower standard of living than their parents. At the same time, many companies can't find enough qualified workers to fill current job openings. The Common Core State Standards (CCSS) are one of the most significant accomplishments in the education reform agenda, and have the potential to have more impact on improving student achievement than any other initiative over the past 20 years. If these standards are implemented with fidelity, American students will be prepared for whichever path—college and/or career—they choose, and the United States will return to being an internationally competitive nation.

Two national organizations played a key role in the development of the Common Core Standards: the National Governors Association (NGA), a membership organization representing governors in the 50 states, commonwealths, and U.S. territories; and the Council of Chief State School Officers (CCSSO), the national organization representing the state superintendents of schools. These groups decided to partner with Achieve Inc., a nonprofit supporting standards-based education reform, to create a task force that produced *Benchmarking for Success: Ensuring U.S. Students Receive a World-Class Education.*[1] This report laid out a set of recommendations articulating what it would take for the U.S. education system to be globally competitive.

The National Governors Association is an organization in which governors from both parties—Republican and Democrat—work together on a range of policy issues: education, health, homeland security, workforce development, energy, and more. Each party's caucus determines a leader to join a chairman, which rotates parties on an annual basis. In addition, there is also a committee structure (e.g., education, children, and workforce) that informs the organization's policy positions at the federal level. Unlike many organizations in Washington, D.C., governors make the decisions about where the organization will and will not focus its attention. The Common Core Standards were no exception.

In my 16 years as director of NGA's education division, I have spearheaded many national initiatives for the organization; few people have had the opportunity to influence state policy the way that I have over this time. Governors are uniquely political and practical animals, which makes them a delight to work with and for on education issues. In my work on the CCSS, I had an opportunity to level the playing field and ensure that *all* students have the opportunity to work toward meeting rigorous standards, regardless of their zip code.

In 2009, I was charged with figuring out how to address education as part of NGA's "Innovation America" initiative.[2] "Innovation America" largely focused on how governors could use innovation as a platform for rebuilding their state economies. There was one problem. The agenda did not pay any attention to the role of K–12 education. The governors decided to launch a national task force chaired by former governor Janet Napolitano and former Intel CEO Craig Barrett to determine what it would take for the U.S. education system to be internationally competitive. The NGA decided to partner with CCSSO and Achieve Inc. on the initiative, given the significant role these organizations play in the education reform movement.

THE GOVERNORS' ROLE IN CCSS

Who would have thought the United States would be in a position today where 45 states and the District of Columbia have agreed to implement a set of common standards in English language arts and mathematics? After all, we are a federalist-loving nation for the most part. The federal government drives a great deal of policy in areas from taxes to transportation. However, the U.S. Constitution is virtually silent on education. Instead, educating all students is defined as a state responsibility and delineated in each state's constitution.

It is important to understand that governors and chief state school offers started and determined the process for developing the Common Core State Standards. There's an ongoing myth that the federal government, and the White House in particular, asked the National Governors Association and the Council of Chief State School Officers to lead a process to create national standards. Others have suggested the federal stimulus package contained incentives for the two organizations to create the standards. As one of the leaders of the effort to develop common standards that were internationally benchmarked, I can attest that these statements are not and have never been true.

I believe the standards will prevail over time for several reasons. First, governors and state superintendents of schools drove the effort to create them. Keeping the federal government at bay was a key reason why so many states have not abandoned ship. Second, my experience with governors has taught me there is nothing that will drive action more than an economic decline. The current state of the economy—the high unemployment rate, especially among high school and college graduates—and our slipping international competitiveness are compelling state leaders to look for ways they can improve their education system. One key indicator is our performance on international assessments—students from former Eastern Bloc countries like Poland are now outpacing U.S. students. In order to ensure that the United States remains an economic superpower, we need to create an education system that prepares our students with the knowledge and skills required to compete for the jobs that will ensure they have as good or better quality of life than their parents. The Common Core State Standards are a first step toward achieving that goal.

THE HISTORY OF COMMON STANDARDS

Governors have been at the forefront of the standards debate ever since the first education summit in 1989. Since that time, the debate over whether to have federal or national education standards has continued. The most important argument against federal intrusion has been that state constitutions, not the U.S. Constitution, define education as a state responsibility. In addition, the federal government only contributes 8.3% of the cost of educating students.[3] This means, on average, that states and localities foot the bill for 92% of the cost of educating their students.

States have historically decided not to work together to develop standards for several reasons. Some state leaders believed that no state is the same and, as a result, all states should have the freedom to define the essential knowledge and skills their students should learn. On the other hand, some states feared that adopting a common set of academic standards would be the first step to federal overreach in other areas such as eligibility requirements for federal funds. Without federal standards, there is wide variation in the depth, breadth, and quality of state standards. Even states who have declared they have "internationally benchmarked" their standards have found it difficult to defend their performance on the National Assessment of Education Program (NAEP), a highly regarded assessment and the closest thing the United States has to a national test.

In 2009 then Arizona governor Janet Napolitano became chair of the NGA. She decided to focus on the role of innovation (e.g., commercialization of research in colleges and universities as a tool for increasing jobs) in order to strengthen the United States' competitive position in the global economy. The goal of the initiative was to give governors the tools they needed to improve math and science education and ensure that higher education was better aligned to state and regional economies. The initiative did not focus on what it would take for the country's education system to prepare students so they would be internationally competitive, even though the performance of U.S. 15-year-olds on the Programme for International Student Assessment (PISA), an assessment used by countries that represent two thirds of the world economy, indicates that our students perform near the bottom of the pile (25th) among participating countries.[4]

Early in the initiative, several governors asked Napolitano to create a national advisory group to focus its attention on what it would take to create a system that was internationally benchmarked to top-performing countries. The governors decided that NGA, CCSSO, and Achieve would join together in this effort. The advisory group was cochaired by Napolitano, then governor Sonny Perdue of Georgia, and Craig Barrett, former CEO of Intel. Other members of the group included former secretary of education Richard Riley, several state commissioners of education, and international representatives from the Organisation for Economic Co-operation and Development (OECD) and the International Association for the Evaluation of Educational Achievement.

As stated at the beginning of the chapter, the group came together to write *Benchmarking for Success*. The report laid out five key recommendations for governors on how to build an education system—K–12 and higher education—that could be internationally benchmarked.

Action 1: Upgrade state standards by adopting a common core of internationally benchmarked standards in math and language arts for grades K–12 to ensure that students are equipped with the necessary knowledge and skills to be globally competitive.

Action 2: Leverage states' collective influence to ensure that textbooks, digital media, curricula, and assessments are aligned to internationally benchmarked standards and draw on lessons from high-performing nations and states.

Action 3: Revise state policies for recruiting, preparing, developing, and supporting teachers and school leaders to reflect the human capital practices of top-performing nations and states around the world.

Action 4: Hold schools and systems accountable through monitoring, interventions, and support to ensure consistently high performance, drawing upon international best practices.

Action 5: Measure state-level education performance globally by examining student achievement and attainment in an international context to ensure that, over time, students are receiving the education they need to compete in the 21st-century economy.

Taking the Plunge: The Decision to Create the Common Core State Standards

The task force thought it was important to avoid issuing another national report that didn't lead to any action, and began the standards creation process. The group concluded the other recommendations (e.g., revising policies for recruiting, preparing, developing, and supporting teachers and school leaders) were dependent on the first recommendation—upgrading state standards by adopting a "common core" of internationally benchmarked standards in math and English language arts for K–12 education.

The advisory group decided to focus on the two subjects that they believed were critical to success in school—math and English language arts. This effort soon became known as the Common Core State Standards Initiative (CCSSI). An advisory group representing several national organizations—Achieve Inc., ACT, the College Board, the National Association of State Boards of Education, and the State Higher Education Executive Officers—helped shape the initiative and provided guidance throughout the process.

The governors were regularly informed during NGA meetings about the standards development process. But the most significant voice among the governors was Sonny Perdue, then governor of the state of Georgia and lead governor for NGA's involvement in the standards initiative. Perdue championed the standards effort for economic reasons. When he entered office, students in Georgia were performing near the bottom of the barrel among the southeastern states on the ACT. He repeatedly told me how tired he was that Georgia's students were being unfairly compared to students in other southeastern states and in the rest of the country. On more than one occasion, he told me that since each state has positioned the goal line at a different place, it is much easier to score a touchdown in some states than others. In other words, the rigor of each state's standards, the assessment, and the benchmark for demonstrating mastery were not only different, but also incredibly unfair to students. I was impressed with the significant amount of time Perdue spent learning about the standards and working to recruit his colleagues—other governors—to adopt the Common Core.

From his perspective, common standards were a way to both get more students ready for college and work and, as a result, improve the state's economy by being able to attract and retain businesses that needed highly skilled employees and also paid a salary on which an individual could support a family. Having more students leave high school better prepared for college meant that companies would not only locate in Georgia for the tax breaks, but they would also be attracted to the state because of the pool of potential employees who could meet the employers' needs.

As noted earlier, the initiative was completely state-led from beginning to end. While administration officials were regularly updated about the effort to develop common standards, they played no role in developing, reviewing, or approving the standards. Yet administration officials regularly voiced their support for the effort publicly. This led state leaders—governors and chief state school officers—and the public to conclude they were claiming the initiative as their own. It didn't help matters when the administration compelled states to adopt college and career readiness standards through the Race to the Top competition. Although the official language in the Race to the Top's request for proposals (RFP) was "college and career readiness standards," many thought federal officials really wanted states to adopt CCSS.

At times, the growing number of conditions put on the availability of stimulus dollars, Race to the Top, and other funds put the eventual adoption of the standards at risk. Clearly, it fed the argument being made by Governor Perry of Texas, whose state never considered adoption of the standards. The governor did not want to "Commit Texas taxpayers to unfunded federal obligations or to the adoption of unproven, cost-prohibitive national standards and tests."[5] To be honest, NGA and CCSSO made several requests to the U.S. Department of Education to (1) stop referring to CCSS and leaving many groups, especially opponents of the standards, with the impression the federal government was either creating the standards or asking NGA and CCSSO to lead the development of the standards on their behalf, and (2) not set preconditions for federal funds on whether or not states adopted CCSS. Even when the U.S. Department of Education made the adoption of "college- and career-ready standards" the requirement versus the adoption of CCSS, it was too late to change the minds of those individuals and groups who firmly believed the effort was a federal effort. Beyond Texas, some western states including Nebraska (once a leader of the Smarter Balanced Assessment Consortia, one of two assessment consortia being funded by the U.S. Department of Education) and Alaska, both of whom never adopted the standards, raised concerns about the federal government's involvement. These states believed if they adopted the standards, this would lead to other attempts by the federal government to preempt states' rights.

Once the standards were completed, no one was more surprised than Gene Wilhoit, former executive director of CCSSO, and I were by the number of states that adopted them. For example, we were surprised that some of the relatively conservative states saw the standards for what they are—much more rigorous than their own standards. State leaders acknowledged that student performance on their state assessments was not measuring whether their students were prepared to be college and career ready, let alone compete on an international stage. In my opinion, one reason for the swift standards adoption was that NGA and CCSSO worked tirelessly to engage governors and chiefs throughout the process so that they would champion the standards once they were released.

Getting It Done: Writing of the Standards

The English language arts (ELA) and math standards were written by a team of national experts. The ELA standards were led by Susan Pimental, founding principal of Student Achievement Partners (SAP). The math standards were led by William McCallum, University Distinguished Professor of Mathematics and head of the Department of Mathematics at the University of Arizona.

When critics argue that the standards were not based on empirical evidence, I respond by saying that our goal was to use the best available evidence. Governors did not want to waste another 20 years debating whether we have all the evidence to determine whether a particular standard should be included in the Common Core. Thus they marshaled the best available evidence from researchers, high-performing states, and international standards.

There was also a significant effort to ensure the process was transparent and inclusive. For example, the writing teams worked closely with six states—California, Colorado, Florida, Georgia, Massachusetts, and Minnesota —throughout the development of the standards. Several of these states spent significant time and resources to ensure their own standards were on par with those from high-performing countries. Researchers learned from Colorado, which was wrapping up a 2-year effort to develop new standards that were internationally benchmarked, as well as from Massachusetts and Minnesota, both of which perform very well on international assessments. Florida was interested in learning from the other states' work on standards, as well as in collaborating on assessments. Finally, NGA was interested in California because of its history in the development of the standards and also because it was a critical state that would determine whether the entire initiative was adopted.

NGA and CCSSO regularly held conference calls with each of the six states to collect feedback on the multiple drafts of the standards. Each state superintendent of schools put together a team of experts (e.g., English language arts and mathematics specialists; curriculum and instruction experts, and others) from their state education agency (SEA) to provide candid feedback and, most importantly, evidence to suggest why some standards should be included and others deleted. The teams also spent a considerable amount of time on the sequence of the math standards and deciding which skills should be taught in particular grades.

Engagement of National Organizations. The standards were developed with extraordinary input from education organizations. NGA and CCSSO, along with members of the writing teams, met with representatives from the Council of Great City Schools, American Federation of Teachers (AFT), National Education Association (NEA), National Council of Teachers of Mathematics, International Reading Association, from K–12; and the American Association of State Colleges and Universities and the American Council on Education, among others from higher education. More important, we spent a considerable amount of time enlisting feedback from content experts in the higher education field, who helped determine whether the standards, especially those in high school, would increase the number of students who would be successful in college coursework and would not need to enroll in remedial classes.

The feedback from national organizations resulted in important changes to the draft standards. The AFT's input probably had the most significant impact on both the math and English language arts standards. One Monday morning, representatives from NGA, CCSSO, and the lead writers met with math teachers who had spent an entire weekend reviewing the math standards, with a focus on which standards were missing and, equally important, where they thought the progressions—the timing of the skills taught (e.g., third grade vs. fourth grade)—did not match their classroom experience. When we entered the room, we noticed the entire walk was covered with strips of paper. The teachers had literally cut up all the standards and reordered them where they thought they made sense. They also included new standards they believed were missing, in addition to evidence to support their choices. The teachers also helped to achieve a better balance among the many issues in English language arts that continue to be debated today, including the types of texts that we "suggested" students read. The AFT teachers' input resulted in changes made to both the math and ELA standards.

Engagement of Concerned Individuals. The public also had an opportunity to submit comments on the draft standards on the Common Core's website. Over 10,000 comments were submitted by educators, parents, and other concerned citizens, and each was reviewed by the team. Many individuals agreed with the need to create a set of common standards across the states and, in general, liked what they saw in the draft documents. Some teachers, however, thought there were too many standards; others wanted to see standards in other subject areas such as history and science. Several teachers wanted to make sure students and teachers would have the supports they needed to ensure the standards were implemented well in classrooms.

Adopting the Common Core in the States

As the standards were being finalized, the NGA and CCSSO knew it was going to be critical to enlist vocal champions from the gubernatorial ranks. Fortunately, there were a couple of individuals who worked nonstop to convince their colleagues that governors played an instrumental role in this process. Then governor Don Carcieri of Rhode Island, a one-time high school math teacher, made several presentations around the country in support of the standards. He also made an effort to reach out to individual governors and encourage them to play an active role in supporting the standards. His knowledge about the standards development process and passion for education led him to spend a great deal of time on the issues at the state and national levels.

Some governors used the newly completed standards to push for other significant policy changes in their states. For example, then governor Jennifer Granholm made the case that the Common Core was an opportunity for the state of Michigan to legislate minimum high school graduation requirements. While several districts in the state had their own, there were no statewide requirements. It was clear that Michigan students would not be able to meet the new standards if they weren't required to take some of the rigorous courses aligned to the standards (e.g., Algebra 2). Under the governor's leadership, Michigan now has some of the highest graduation requirements in the country.

There are also signs that some states, such as Virginia, may adopt the standards in the future. Although the state recently completed aligning its English language arts and math standards, many superintendents and other key stakeholders see the Common Core as both a vehicle for leveling the playing field among disadvantaged populations and more affluent school districts, while others see the standards as key to improving the state's economy.

MEASURING PERFORMANCE AGAINST THE STANDARDS: COMMON ASSESSMENTS

The next step after states adopted the Common Core was to create common assessments to measure performance on the newly completed standards. Secretary Duncan set aside $350 million in federal stimulus funds to support the development of the assessments. While many governors, both Republicans and Democrats, were encouraged by this, there were several who raised concerns about "federal intrusion" in the state-led process.

Governors were very interested in the groups who responded to the secretary's request for proposals to create the assessments. When initially released in 2010, the RFP generated interest from several groups including Achieve, Inc., National Center on Education and the Economy, and a few groups formed by states coming together (e.g., one led by the state of Oregon that eventually became known as Smarter Balanced Assessment Consortium). NGA and CCSSO decided to convene the groups in order to reduce the number of interested organizations to no more than two (some had already discussed how they might work together.) At their 2010 winter meeting, the governors asked me join a governors-only session to discuss the status of the work on common assessments.

There I learned that the governors had two priorities when it came to common assessments. First, they wanted to make sure that the assessments allowed for fairer comparisons between states. Second, they wanted to create tests that moved beyond "color in the bubbles" and measured both students' knowledge of the content and their ability to apply information in different contexts. There were several points of view on the ideal number of consortia. For example, then governor of Colorado Bill Ritter thought it was important for the governors to encourage experimentation with tests that required students to apply their knowledge in a real-world setting; the number of assessment consortia didn't bother him at all. On the other hand, former governor of Georgia Roy Barnes thought six consortia would complicate any attempt to address his number one concern—comparability. At the end of the conversation, most governors including former governor Carcieri of Rhode Island, former governor Granholm of Michigan, and Governor Markell of Delaware supported former governor Barnes's proposal to support no more than two consortia.

NGA and CCSSO had to do very little work to encourage the groups to consolidate their efforts to develop common assessments. The groups' leadership worked independently to figure out how to build a proposal that addressed each group's interests (e.g., adaptive technology assessments), while remaining focused on developing tests that measure key skills (such as providing supporting evidence for the claims made in writing versus simply writing a well-constructed paragraph).

State superintendents and their assessment directors are leading the common assessment work. Higher education is also playing a role in both consortia as some of the decisions (e.g., whether the assessments would be used for college placement and cut scores) have a direct impact on them. Gubernatorial involvement in the technical work has decreased, as it should.

With the first administration of the assessments taking place in 2014, it is critical for governors to continue talking about the importance of the standards in their states and across the country. Parents and students need to both understand the standards and be prepared for the likely dip in proficiency levels. At the same time, governors need to help parents and others understand that the standards will help ensure their children are able to compete for the high-wage, high-skilled jobs that are currently going to students in other countries.

Simply talking about the importance of higher standards will not help students meet them. It's equally important for governors to focus on building supports for both students and teachers. For example, states will need to consider ways in which they can provide academic supports (e.g., before- and after-school programs; extended learning time) to students who will need more help in order to meet the standards.

CHALLENGES AHEAD

Common Core implementation presents several challenges for states. It is important that states begin to consider the ways in which they individually and/or collectively can begin to address them.

Tightening the Budget Belt

State budgets have not spared K–12 education over the last couple of years. This year is no exception. Some groups, including the Pioneer Institute, have indicated that Common Core implementation will cost states a significant amount of money.[6] As states begin to implement the common assessments, they will need to look beyond the stimulus funds that are currently supporting the assessment consortia's work. Many states, in partnership with the two assessment consortia, are developing a strategy for sustaining the assessment work. States are also examining how to use federal funds (e.g., Title VI) to sustain this effort. Beyond assessments, states will need to consider ways in which they will provide more support for disadvantaged students to meet the standards.

It may be true that states and districts need additional funding. But we should not make the case for new dollars until states and districts examine how they are using existing funds. For instance, states can reconsider how they are allocating Title I funds to support their lowest performing schools by ensuring that they are funding research-backed initiatives. The Alabama Reads Initiative is a good example where the state has invested in a research-based program over the past 10 years to improve reading proficiency. Additionally, federal funds such as the School Improvement Grants (SIG) and Race to the Top (for a limited number of states) can provide a significant infusion of resources to support implementation efforts. Governors can use these federal funds, in coordination with existing state dollars, to support implementation efforts, provided they are not using federal funds to replace supports traditionally provided with state funds.

States should also leverage technology to collaborate across state lines and create cost savings and improve their services. In 2009 Minnesota governor Tim Pawlenty and Wisconsin governor Jim Doyle engaged in a nation-leading effort to share services and become more efficient through cooperation. Minnesota and Wisconsin will work together on more than 80 projects to save money and improve government operations. At that time,

Governor Pawlenty indicated, "These challenging times provide us an opportunity to make state government more accountable and efficient. Working together with our neighbors in Wisconsin will advance these goals."[7]

The initiatives fell into one of five broad categories:

1. *Joint Procurement and Best Practices*—Collaboration to save on purchased goods or services, learning and improving from practices in other states
2. *Cross-border Collaboration*—Opportunities to improve by partnership along or across the border
3. *IT Systems*—Sharing, developing, or leveraging IT resources to improve government
4. *Reciprocity*—Making government work better by making borders permeable for customers
5. *Shared Resources*—Sharing resources to improve their utilization or unit cost

While this initiative was broader than education, it is instructive about the possibilities for states to leverage limited education funds to support this type of collective work. One area ripe for cross-state collaboration is in purchasing instructional materials (textbooks as well as digital materials). It's no secret that California, Florida, and Texas drive this market. Consortia of states could work together not only to create greater cost efficiencies, but also to drive publishers to respond to consumers' needs and, in this case, provide evidence their instructional materials are aligned to Common Core.

State Education Agencies' Limited Capacity

State education agencies have been directly impacted by the recent budget cuts. There are fewer staff in the agencies and, in many cases, the agency staff positions are supported with federal funds. Ultimately, this means that staff spends a great deal of time monitoring compliance against the federal regulations (e.g., Individuals with Disabilities Act).[8] State agencies have also lost talent to districts, where staff members can focus on supporting teachers and principals at the local level, in addition to enjoying higher salaries.

Several states are using Regional Service Agencies (RESA) or a similar structure in order to support Common Core implementation. Each RESA could develop expertise in a certain area (e.g., developing an online digital curriculum in partnership with teachers across the state) that teachers and principals could access. Higher education can also play a crucial role. For instance, there are some colleges and universities supported by state or federal funds that could play a direct role in helping educators and state agencies to implement the Common Core.

Resisting the Urge to Revise

Creating and implementing the initial set of standards will provide experts the opportunity to conduct research that will inform the next iteration of the standards. It will be important for NGA and CCSSO, in partnership with organizations such as Achieve Inc., the Hunt Institute, Alliance for Excellent Education, and others, to work with states to collect a range of data (not just test scores) to monitor implementation of the standards and assessments to inform future work. It will be equally important for these organizations to work with states to frame the research agenda that, in part, can help inform future iterations of the standards.

Based on other countries' experiences and the data needed to assess implementation, I do not think the standards should be revised until 2017, if not later. Some individuals even suggest that NGA and CCSSO should consider waiting 10 years to revise the standards. Let's not claim mission accomplished before providing adequate time for implementation.

Communicating the Importance of Standards and Assessments

No one should assume the general public knows much about the Common Core Standards. As a matter of fact, most individuals don't know anything about their current state standards. The reality is that most parents think their child is doing just fine in school, while they think everyone else's children won't be prepared for college or a career. If the draft test items from the work of the assessment consortia—PARCC or SBAC—are any indication, some may be surprised to find their children aren't as prepared as they thought. Governors should use this opportunity to educate the public about the standards—why and how they were developed—and why they are important to students' college and career readiness. New Jersey governor Chris Christie and former Florida governor Jeb Bush have used the bully pulpit to talk regularly about the importance of the Common Core and the opportunity it presents to help students demonstrate their abilities beyond repeating facts, especially when it comes to securing high-quality jobs.

Many national organizations have developed communications materials for state and district use largely aimed at helping individuals (e.g., educators, parents, and community leaders) understand the standards. Beyond educating people, there needs to be a more sophisticated campaign to help them understand what they can do to help make sure their child, grandchild, niece, or nephew is prepared to meet the standards and ultimately expectations in college or the workplace. The business community can help with this as well. For example, Intel is planning to train all their employees on the standards: why the standards were created; what is included in the standards; how students demonstrate performance on the common assessments; why the standards are important; and what they can do to make sure their state and school district is preparing students to meet the standards.

It's also important for governors to share important data points, such as how U.S. students perform on international assessments and how this competition may affect their ability to compete for well-paying jobs. Beyond the public, governors need to help state legislators understand why the standards and assessments are important to the state's education and economic agenda.

Building Political Will to Stay the Course

States need to have well-thought-out implementation plans that involve state leaders (e.g., governors, state superintendents, and state board of education members), business leaders, educators, parents, and community leaders. We've already seen some changes in the gubernatorial ranks (e.g., North Carolina) and legislative elections. There will be a significant number of new governors taking office in 2014, which will present an even greater challenge. None of them will have made the initial commitment to adopt the Common Core. It will be important to develop a strategy that doesn't make a state's ability to sustain the commitment dependent on which political leader currently holds office. Current and future governors have to remain steadfast in their commitment to implement the standards even when parents in more affluent communities begin to push back. Governors should also consider how to use state funds to leverage social services dollars to before-school and after-school programs to support student success in the classroom.

Teacher Preparation and Evaluation

First and foremost, teacher and leadership preparation programs are critical to ensuring that future teachers are prepared to teach the standards. This starts by setting higher admission standards for acceptance into teacher preparation programs. Governors may want to convene college and university presidents together with the goal of increasing entrance into preparation programs and, at the same time, work with agencies that control teacher and principal licensure and certification to increase the rigor of these programs. If this doesn't work, then I suggest the governor move toward changing licensure and certification requirements through the state board of education or legislature.

Teacher evaluation is getting a lot of attention in the states. Many governors used their 2013 State of the State Address to create or significantly revamp their teacher evaluation systems. That said, some states will be transitioning from a set of very low standards to the Common Core. It is important for states to think about how to make this transition successfully and, at the same time, set high expectations for teachers.

Professional Development

Professional development (PD) always gets the short shrift. In some cases, criticism against PD is well deserved. Some claim there's not enough time and resources devoted to PD. Others claim the PD rarely has any relationship to teacher effectiveness. No matter which side of the argument you buy, it's clear that we need more time and money to provide high-quality professional development that is grounded in student data. But we first have to identify existing funds targeting professional development, how they are being used, and whether these investments have any results on student achievement.

Technology can also play a role in creating rich professional development opportunities for teachers. For example, a consortium of states might collaborate to create online modules similar to the online lessons that are being collected on the Internet. In addition, states may want to consider developing an online community where teachers can learn from one another as they begin to implement the standards. Since teacher evaluation systems are moving toward making student performance on state assessments one component of a teacher's performance, it will be important to think about grounding all professional development in data, incentivizing excellent teachers to stay in the classroom, and, in some cases, deciding which teachers should no longer be educating students.

Transitioning from the Old to the New Assessment System

There's a lot of work that needs to be done to help students and educators transition to the new standards and assessments. States should not wait until 2014 to begin making policy changes. While many states have received waivers from the accountability provisions of No Child Left Behind, states will run into another bump in the road as they begin to implement the new assessments. Congress will either need to reauthorize the Elementary and Secondary Education Act (ESEA) or the U.S. Department of Education will have to provide another opportunity for states to modify their approved waivers. Either way, it is critical that states that have adopted the Common Core are not penalized for committing to help their students reach a higher standard.

There are several good examples of state implementation efforts. For example, North Carolina and Massachusetts have deleted questions on their current assessments that are not aligned to the Common Core. Kentucky has revised its current assessment to better align with the Common Core and has already administered the new Common Core assessment to students. As expected, student scores dropped in both subjects. However, Kentucky now has a head start on identifying potential student gaps, which will help state leaders start addressing them if or when Kentucky adopts one of the common assessments.

Creating a Governance Structure to Manage the Standards and Assessments Moving Forward

The beauty of the CCSS initiative was that it was state-led. Governors, in partnership with state superintendents of schools, should continue to consider options for a future governance model. However, there should be no rush to create such a structure. The focus should be on implementation of the standards. Key decisions states will have to confront include, but are not limited to, whether to create a 501(c)(3) to govern the standards work; how to create a nationwide communications strategy to educate and engage parents and educators; when to revise the standards; what will encompass the research agenda for informing the next iteration of standards; how to define the relationship between the ELA and math standards and the Next Generation Science Standards being led by Achieve Inc.; and how to define the relationship between the standards structure and assessment consortia. At a minimum, governors and state superintendents should play a lead role in creating the governance structure, since both organizations led the development of the Common Core.

PREDICTIONS FOR THE FUTURE

So, will the effort to adopt and implement CCSS succeed? I fully expect CCSS will be implemented and the goals that were laid out in the 2009 report *Benchmarking for Student Success* will be fully realized over the next several years. This will require everyone—governors, state superintendents, legislators, state boards of education, educators, and parents—to take advantage of the opportunities that the Common Core presents and overcome the challenges previously outlined. However, there are some key reasons that lead me to believe the effort will succeed.

Budgets Will Drive Collaboration

The short- and long-term state budget predictions make collaboration a necessity. The rising costs of Medicaid as a proportion of state budgets suggest that states cannot afford to continue increasing their education outlays. While the education community will always seek funding increases, I predict that states will look more actively for ways in which they can collaborate across state lines. Clearly, the implementation of the common assessments (beyond initial development costs) will provide an opportunity to minimize administration costs.

Further, CCSS provides a framework around which K–12 and higher education can collaborate. We've already seen significant progress around the creation of statewide data systems, building on the work of the Data Quality Campaign. I suggest that K–12 and higher education will work more closely to address several issues related to teacher preparation, particularly around teacher preparation and licensure standards and ensuring teachers have content-area expertise, as well as to increase postsecondary learning opportunities for students across the country. The Common Core sets the stage for ensuring students are mastering rigorous content and, as a result, are able to succeed when they enroll in college-level courses as high school students or upon entering college.

Productivity Will Matter More in the Future

For those individuals who are disappointed in the focus on accountability, I predict a greater attention to developing metrics to measure productivity in both K–12 and higher education. First, common assessments will provide student performance data that will help us figure out how to best spend limited state resources. This is already happening in some areas where, for example, remedial education has come under scrutiny. While K–12 has largely focused the productivity conversation around the accountability system defined by No Child Left Behind and, most recently, the waivers states have submitted to the U.S. Department of Education, there will be increased attention to the development of metrics created by NGA for higher education. State leaders will have no choice but to measure indicators such as degrees awarded, success in first-year college courses, time and credits toward degrees, and graduation rates.

The work of both assessment consortia—PARCC and SBAC—have significant potential to drive the system toward a greater focus on outcomes. Equally important, these assessments will drive a better understanding of students' ability to demonstrate what they know and their ability to apply knowledge in real-world settings. I also believe these assessments will require teachers to demand more from their students.

Business Leaders Will Demand More from the Education System

The business community has always played a significant role in the need to create a world-class education system, dating back to the 1989 Education Summit in Charlottesville. As the need for highly skilled employees, especially in the fields of science, technology, engineering, and math, continue to rise, the business community will continue to put pressure on both K–12 and higher education to produce more graduates who will fulfill labor market needs. Business leaders will become more directly engaged in creating new pathways such as career technical centers, in which industry-recognized credentials will be used to identify employees who fill market demand.

Technology Investments Will Start to Pay Dividends

For years states have been investing in data infrastructure. I'm the first to admit that we have a long way to go in this area (e.g., acquiring new hardware, training teachers to become more effective users of the technology, using technology to inform school, district, and state fiscal decisions). But the increased focus on creating greater system efficiencies, including giving teachers more time to focus on instruction, will lead to more effective uses of technology. One area that I predict will see increased attention is virtual schools. In many cases, states have not realized the opportunities (e.g., competency-based systems and sophisticated uses of multimedia as a component of demonstrating knowledge and skills) that virtual courses provide. State virtual schools will learn from examples such as the Florida Virtual School and APEX Learning about how to create rigorous coursework and ensure that all students have these opportunities, whether or not they are available at the local high school.

CONCLUSION

Despite the challenges, CCSS presents an opportunity to make fundamental changes to other parts of our education system, which are critical to successful implementation in states. Governors are in the position to accelerate reforms around issues including, but not limited to, professional development, technology use, and teacher evaluation. At the same time, Common Core implementation cannot be accomplished without meaningfully engaged educators. The business community can also play a role in helping ensure that governors, state superintendents, and legislators stay the course, especially when the first set of results from common assessments are released. The key will be to ensure that policies—state and local—are grounded in data, rather than tinkering around the edges and/or layering new policies on top of those that already exist. At the end of the day, successful implementation will depend on whether or not we have the political will and the capacity to stay the course. If not, we risk never realizing the potential of CCSS. And there's too much at risk for our children and the United States to fail to meet NGA and CCSSO's original vision.

NOTES

1.   National Governors Association, the Council of Chief State School Officers, & Achieve, Inc. (2008). *Benchmarking for success: Ensuring U.S. students receive a world-class education.* Washington, DC: Achieve, Inc. Retrieved from http://www.achieve.org/BenchmarkingforSuccess

2.   National Governors Association. (2007, April 14). *Innovation America: Building a science, technology, engineering and math agenda.* Washington, DC: National Governors Association Center for Best Practices.

3.   U.S. Department of Education. (2007). 10 facts about K–12 education funding. Retrieved from http://www2.ed.gov/about/overview/fed/10facts/index.html

4.   Organisation for Economic Co-operation and Development (OECD). (2010). *PISA 2009 at a glance.* Paris, France: OECD Publishing. Retrieved from http://www.oecd.org/pisa/46660259.pdf

5.   Perry, R. (2010, January 13). *Letter to Secretary Arne Duncan.* Austin, Texas: Office of the Governor.

6.   Pioneer Institute and American Principles Project. (2012, February). *National cost of aligning states and localities to the Common Core Standards.* Boston, MA: Pioneer Institute and American Principles Project.

7.   Pawlenty, T., & Doyle, J. (2009, March 31). Governor Pawlenty and Governor Doyle announce first joint Minnesota-Wisconsin efforts [Press release]. Retrieved from http://www.leg.state.mn.us/docs/2010/other/101583/www.governor.state.mn.us/mediacenter/pressreleases/2009/PROD009438.html

8.   Brown, C. G., Hess, F. M., Lautzenheiser, D. K., & Owen, I. (2011). *State education agencies as agents of change.* Washington, DC: Center for American Progress, American Enterprise Institute for Public Policy Research and The Broad Foundation.

CHAPTER 3

Teacher Quality Reforms

Morgan Polikoff

THE LAST HALF DECADE has seen a monumental shift in teacher policies in U.S. K–12 schools. Perhaps most notably, at least in part spurred by the Obama administration's Race to the Top (RTTT) program and Elementary and Secondary Education Act (ESEA) waivers, there is now unprecedented pressure to improve the quality and usefulness of teacher evaluations. Major elements of the teacher evaluation reforms being implemented include: (1) the inclusion of student achievement data in evaluations; (2) the use of research-based rubrics or observational protocols to rate pedagogical quality; (3) the placing of teachers into three or more categories of effectiveness (i.e., rather than *satisfactory* vs. *unsatisfactory*); and (4) the use of evaluations to inform teacher staffing decisions. High-profile backers, such as the Bill & Melinda Gates Foundation and Michelle Rhee's StudentsFirst, have supported these types of reforms. More than two thirds of the states have now revamped their teacher evaluation policies, requiring schools and districts to adopt these more comprehensive systems.[1]

Teacher and teaching policies are changing in other important ways as well. For instance, there have been widely publicized battles between public sector teachers unions and Republican governors in several midwestern states. There have been prominent pushes to change or end teacher tenure rights in other states, or to tie teachers' ongoing employment to performance as measured by the new evaluation systems. During the recent economic downturn, there has been a push to end so-called LIFO (last-in-first-out) policies that protect teachers with more seniority, regardless of quality, when layoffs are required. And finally, there has been a great deal of discussion and concern, perhaps spurred primarily by the recent report from the National Council on Teacher Quality (NCTQ), about the quality of preservice teacher education programs and their impact on teacher performance.

At the same time as these important changes to teacher policies have taken place, there have been tremendous changes in the nature of standards and accountability policy in U.S. schools. Arguably the most prominent reform in this area is the development and adoption of the Common Core State Standards (CCSS) in K–12 English language arts and mathematics. Originally a state-led effort, the Common Core was encouraged by the Obama administration's RTTT and ESEA waivers, and 45 states and the District of Columbia have now adopted the standards to replace their previous state standards in both subjects. The standards call for substantial modifications to the content and form of teacher instruction, and numerous organizations are developing aligned curriculum materials and assessments to the Common Core.[2]

Together, these two sets of reforms (the Common Core and teacher policies) are perhaps the most influential policy reforms happening now in U.S. K–12 education. In this chapter, I highlight some of the ways that these two reforms are likely to intersect and influence one another. There are two main goals of this analysis: (1) *to present both opportunities and challenges for the intersection of the Common Core Standards and the new teacher quality policies*; and (2) *to make policy recommendations that should maximize opportunities and minimize challenges when it comes to their intersection.*

My central premise is that, for the Common Core and teacher policies to be mutually beneficial, classroom teachers must faithfully implement the standards. Given this premise, I reach several conclusions about the necessary elements for effective standards implementation that will complement teacher policy reforms:

1. *The Common Core Standards are but one part of a larger standards-based policy system.* Thus policy makers must carefully align all components of these policy systems if we are to see the kinds of instructional effects we desire. This means getting serious about the alignment of assessments with standards in a way that we never have before.

2. *All beginning teachers need to be effectively prepared to implement curricula aligned with the standards.* Given the resistance in the teacher education community to preparing teachers to implement standards in the classroom, this will be a challenge that will require increasing attention and oversight.

3. *Teachers must be supported once they are in the classroom to teach aligned curricula.* They will need well-designed and effectively delivered professional development and high-quality, aligned curriculum materials. While the Common Core creates tremendous economies of scale, there is little trustworthy information to help judge the quality of both professional development and curriculum materials. Thus states and districts

will need a reliable way to vet instructional materials and ensure that they are aligned to the standards.

If each of these items is addressed, there will be an unprecedented opportunity to learn about effective instructional practices for teaching the content in the Common Core. While the Common Core movement may have a net positive influence on the effectiveness of teacher quality reforms, this positive impact may well be diluted or even reversed if policy makers do not carefully attend to the nuances of implementation.

The most difficult period for these two policy reforms will be in the 2013–2014 to 2014–2015 school years, when implementation challenges with the Common Core will clash with the rapid intensification of teacher evaluation policies. Because these changes are happening simultaneously, both reforms might be more faithfully applied if there were a moratorium on making high-stakes decisions about teachers (e.g., hiring, firing, tenure) until after the Common Core and its assessments are fully implemented. (This would also have the beneficial side effect of allowing us to learn more about these policies before using them to make important decisions about individual teachers.) Unfortunately, while both sets of reforms hold some promise for improving the quality of U.S. schools, political challenges arising from poor implementation may derail both policies in the long run.

TRENDS IN TEACHER QUALITY REFORM

Teacher Evaluation Policy

Teacher evaluation has long been a pro forma exercise; generally very few teachers have been rated unsatisfactory under traditional teacher evaluation systems.[3] Thus poor performance has gone unaddressed, and strong performance has gone unrewarded. The lack of meaningful evaluation has also meant that teachers have historically received little quality information about their effectiveness as educators, thus inhibiting their ability to improve their instruction. Recognizing these problems, policy makers have turned to teacher evaluation reform. Between 2009 and 2012, the number of states legislating that student performance must be an important criterion in teacher evaluations rose from 4 to 22; the number of states in which annual evaluations were required for all teachers rose from 15 to 24; and the number of states where evidence of teacher effectiveness was the preponderant criterion in teacher tenure decisions rose from 0 to 9.[4]

These trends will continue as the 40 states approved for ESEA waivers implement their reforms. A central condition for receiving flexibility from No Child Left Behind's (NCLB's) accountability mandates was that states create and adopt teacher and principal evaluation and support systems that take into account student achievement as a measure of teacher performance. States responded to the waiver requirements by proposing dozens of new teacher evaluation policies. For instance, states are implementing systems that rate teachers on 4-point scales (often *ineffective* to *highly effective*), require multiple classroom observations each year, and use student achievement as a substantial portion of a teacher's overall evaluation. While preliminary evidence suggests that inflated ratings continue to be a problem in new systems, there is hope that evaluation will become more meaningful and useful over time.[5]

Teacher Tenure

A second prominent teacher policy reform is the recent push to revamp tenure rules and curtail collective bargaining powers. These reforms are inextricably tied to evaluation reforms; with higher quality evaluations, it is only logical that we would begin to ask, "What should be done with unsatisfactory teachers?" Across a wide array of states, legislatures and governors have changed laws to make it increasingly challenging for teachers to obtain and keep tenure. A total of 34 states have made changes to tenure laws since 2008 (18 in 2011 alone).[6] While some states went so far as to end tenure, most states simply made tenure more difficult to obtain by strengthening requirements for evaluation and teacher performance. For instance, many of the states approved for NCLB waivers have proposed that teachers must be rated "*effective*" or higher on new evaluation systems in order to obtain tenure.

Teacher Education Evaluation and Reform

A third and final teacher policy trend is the increasing scrutiny being paid to the quality of traditional preservice teacher education programs, which collectively prepare roughly 90% of beginning teachers in U.S. schools.[7] There has historically been little to no rigorous evaluation of the impact of teacher preparation programs on teacher performance, let alone their impact on student outcomes. However, the recent growth in the use of achievement data to evaluate teachers' contributions to student learning has spurred a concomitant interest in evaluating teacher education programs using student performance to gauge teacher effectiveness. The most prominent example is the controversial "National Review of Teacher Preparation Programs" by the National Council on Teacher Quality.

There have also been federal- and state-level reforms targeted at improving teacher education. The 2008 rewrite of the federal Higher Education Act (HEA) contained significant reforms, including new reporting requirements for alternative certification programs and requiring programs to report mean scale scores of their graduates on licensure examinations. At the state level, Louisiana has been evaluating the performance of its teacher education programs using graduates' value-added scores for several years, with results showing large variance in preparation program quality.[8] These results are now being used to drive interventions for low-performing programs and learn from the best practices of high-performing ones.

INTERSECTIONS WITH THE COMMON CORE

In order for the Common Core to have a positive influence on student outcomes, it will need to be implemented faithfully. For that to happen, the initiative will need aligned assessments, adequate preservice education, and supportive professional development and curricular materials. If this happens, the Common Core offers opportunities to make serious strides in better understanding effective pedagogy, facilitating the comparison of teacher education programs, and decreasing the "standards churn" that has beset the reform movement for the past decade and a half. But there are serious challenges, such as the daunting timeline for implementation, a general lack of seriousness around alignment, and the tense politics around the initiative that need to be addressed for the Common Core initiative to be successful.

Common Core Implementation

It is almost tautological, but nonetheless true, to say that the Common Core can only influence achievement and the implementation of other policies if the standards affect teachers' instruction. The majority of evidence points to the conclusion that the Common Core Standards are superior to the majority of previous state standards in three ways.[9] First, the Common Core calls for instruction at more challenging levels of cognitive demand than is indicated by previous state standards or than is currently utilized by teachers. This means that faithful implementation of the Common Core will result in less teaching memorization and procedures and higher rates of analysis and demonstrating understanding. Second, the Common Core Standards are much more focused than the instruction typically practiced by U.S. teachers. This means that teachers will need to remove topics from their curricula, something that is often challenging for teachers to do.[10] Finally, the Common Core is somewhat more coherent from grade to grade than are state standards or teachers' instruction.[11] Thus there will be more pressure to effectively instruct students the first time they are taught new material, as there will be less emphasis on repetition.

While faithful implementation of the standards seems like a straightforward goal, research during the NCLB era clearly demonstrated that teachers' instruction was weakly aligned with the content of state standards.[12] Even within states, where teachers were supposed to be teaching roughly the same standards-aligned content, students' opportunity to learn advanced content differed substantially from classroom to classroom.[13] Instead of showing strong alignment, instruction in the NCLB era tended to follow old patterns—it was poorly structured from grade to grade, emphasized primarily lower level cognitive skills, and covered a broad array of topics very shallowly.[14] For instance, just one quarter to one half of the content taught by a typical teacher in a typical year between 2003 and 2011 was on content in the corresponding grade-level standards (though alignment did increase somewhat over time).[15] Moreover, research showed that mathematics teachers in elementary and middle schools during the NCLB era taught highly redundant curricula across grades, such that students were exposed to the same material over and over again (often for 3 or more years in a row).[16] These indicators are symptomatic of the abject failure of standards implementation under No Child Left Behind.

Supports Needed for Effective Common Core Implementation

Aligned Assessments. One of the major failings of standards-based reform under NCLB was the poor alignment of state student achievement tests with the standards they were intended to measure. For instance, an analysis of 138 standards-assessment pairs under NCLB found that 38–49% of the content on a typical state test was misaligned with the content specified in the corresponding state content standards.[17] There are at least two important types of misalignment that appeared on the NCLB tests. First, the assessments typically captured lower levels of cognitive demand than were called for in the standards. That is, the tests tended to be more procedural, and less likely to employ higher order thinking skills than the standards specified. Second, state tests under NCLB tended to be disproportionately focused on certain topics relative to their emphasis in the standards, therefore ignoring other essential subjects. The quintessential example of this is reading comprehension on state reading assessments—while reading comprehension is a key part of state English language arts standards, state tests disproportionately focused on those skills. These state reading comprehension tests often all but ignored essential standards content on grammar and spelling, writing, and speaking—indeed, roughly half the content in state English language arts standards was not tested at all.

The misalignment of tests with standards is a fundamental failure of NCLB. It sent teachers conflicting messages about what to teach—undermining, rather than supporting, state content standards.[18] And there is some empirical evidence that illustrates the negative effects of this incoherence—teachers in states where the standards and assessments were more aligned did indeed practice instruction more aligned to standards and assessments (i.e., coherence matters).[19] It is also undoubtedly the case that the low levels of cognitive demand emphasized on state tests contributed to the common claims that NCLB led to "dumbed down" instruction. That is, teachers acted perfectly rationally when they focused their instruction on memorization and procedures, because that is what appeared on standardized tests.

The Common Core Standards, in and of themselves, cannot solve this important problem. However, the two assessment consortia, together representing almost every Common Core adopting state, may. For one, the consortia are explicitly focusing on developing assessment tasks to capture higher order skills. Ideally, state tests would sample content from the standards such that, over time and across test forms, the alignment of the material tested with that in the standards would be perfect. That is to say, every piece of content in the standards would be tested, and every item on the test would represent the standards, in proportional agreement. New, promising techniques for test construction may help ensure alignment using test construction algorithms.[20]

At the very least, the computer-adaptive tests that the Smarter Balanced consortium plans to use should help ensure that a fuller range of standards content is assessed than is currently the case. This is because the computer adaptive assessments can draw upon a much larger item bank than the fixed-length test forms used under NCLB. Of course, only about half of adopting states are involved in Smarter Balanced (the other consortium is not planning computer adaptive tests), and there is the concern that computer adaptive tests may be less instructionally useful for teachers, since students complete different items. However, there is at least cautious optimism that test alignment to standards will improve in the Common Core era.

Preservice Teacher Education Focused on Standards. A second essential element for improved standards implementation is greater attention in preservice teacher education to standards implementation. There has been remarkably little focus on aligning instruction with standards in the teacher education community over the past decade. For instance, an ERIC search for the word *standards* in *Journal of Teacher Education* titles from 2000 to the present identifies just six articles. (In fact, just two of these six focus on content standards—the other four focus on professional standards for teachers or standards for program accreditation.) There are just five articles in *Teaching and Teacher Education*. In contrast, the word *pedagogy* appears in eight titles in the former journal and 19 in the latter, and the word *critical* (referring to the Marxian critique of society and culture) appears in 11 titles in the former journal and 17 in the latter. These admittedly crude figures highlight the fact that standards implementation is far from a focus in the teacher education community.

Some argue that this relative lack of attention to standards among teacher educators is because the United States lacks the "educational infrastructure" present in many other countries, including elements such as common curricula aligned to assessments.[21] Thus researchers argue that teachers cannot develop a common language around instruction, and teacher education must inevitably be generic and unrelated to the curriculum teachers will implement with students.[22] Therefore, teacher education cannot solve the problems of poor standards implementation unless teachers are going to be well supported once they reach the classroom.

Regardless of the decentralized nature of the U.S. education system, there are a whole host of impediments to teacher education training teachers to effectively implement the standards. One example is the rejection in the teacher education community of a "training" model for teacher education that provides novice teachers with demonstrable skills and knowledge.[23] According to leading scholars in the field, Marilyn Cochran-Smith and Kenneth Zeichner, training is viewed as "an oversimplification of teaching and learning, ignoring its dynamic, social and moral aspects."[24] Methods courses in teacher education programs are no longer intended to transmit knowledge about the most effective methods for teaching students. The refusal of traditional preservice teacher education to train teachers in how to effectively work with standards may leave novice teachers woefully underprepared when they arrive in the classroom.

Another teacher preparation–related impediment to standards implementation is the increased difficulty of the standards (particularly in mathematics) relative to existing state standards. The Common Core calls on teachers to deliver dramatically more coherent knowledge across grades than is true under existing state standards.[25] Furthermore, teachers must help students build both procedural and conceptual knowledge as foundations for future learning progressions. Given the generally poor mathematical abilities of elementary and middle school mathematics teachers, as well as the subpar academic performance of those drawn into the teaching profession, this new demand will be a tall order.[26] Again, this challenge calls for teacher education programs to take a more active role in helping prospective teachers develop the content knowledge to fully understand (as well as implement) the standards.

A final potential impediment to teacher education programs improving their preparation of teachers to teach the Common Core is an ideological one. While the public[27] and teachers[28] are largely supportive of the Common Core, there is some resistance to the initiative in the academy, particularly among teacher educators. It is easy to find examples of opposition to the

Common Core (or standards in general) among educational researchers, and particularly critical theorists who often populate the ranks of education school faculty.[29] For instance, Leslie Burns argues that the Common Core Standards "privilege a traditional and corporate-friendly lingua franca rather than preparing students for what will be a constantly shifting future society wherein the elements of college and career readiness are difficult to predict at best."[30] These opponents often argue against the standardization required by the Common Core, or they suggest that common standards will lead to school failure and subsequent privatization.[31] It would not be surprising if some of these teacher educators chose not to teach their students how to use the Common Core, which would of course limit the standards' potential impact.

Nevertheless, there are some opportunities for teacher education to begin to make stronger contributions to prepare teachers for this task. For one, there will be increasing pressure to do so, as teacher education programs are increasingly being evaluated using their graduates' value-added assessment scores. For another, students enrolling in teacher education programs may increasingly demand such training as *they* are evaluated on their classroom performance. Furthermore, there are hints that teacher education is responding to the Common Core. For instance, a special issue of *Journal of Teacher Education* is focused on this topic. Certainly there are challenges, but there is also the possibility that traditional teacher education may become a facilitator of standards implementation.

Supporting Professional Development and Curriculum Materials. A third requirement for effective standards implementation is professional development and curriculum materials that actively support the standards. We know that textbooks can differ dramatically in their effects on student learning.[32] One plausible hypothesis for this is that the more effective texts are those that are better aligned with the state standards and/or assessments. (Of course there are other plausible hypotheses, and textbook alignment is important regardless of the reasons for the differences in textbook effectiveness.)

While there has not been a systematic examination of the alignment of textbooks to state standards, there is evidence that the quality of textbooks is an impediment to standards implementation.[33] Under the No Child Left Behind Act, textbook companies responded to 50 different sets of state standards specifying dramatically different content expectations[34] by adopting a "kitchen sink" approach to selecting content, in which they included a wide range of content. This way, a single edition could be adopted relatively easily in any state, because it was guaranteed to include the content in that state's standards. And because there was no external body rating the alignment of textbooks to standards, claims of alignment went unverified. Thus teachers and district curriculum coordinators were left to either take text-book companies' claims of alignment at face value or attempt to determine textbook alignment themselves.

Unfortunately, there is little evidence that teachers and district curriculum coordinators have been able to simply read the standards and create aligned curricula. Teachers have not been able to create substantially aligned curricula, given the poor alignment of instruction with standards and assessments under NCLB.[35] Further, research shows that school district personnel responsible for creating curricula often interpret the language in state standards in ways not intended by the standards' authors. These inaccurate interpretations resulted in written curricula that differed substantially from the standards authors' intended approach to reform.[36] There is no reason to think that the capacity of district personnel to create aligned curricula has substantially changed, so the alignment of curriculum materials remains an issue of high importance.

There are at least a few promising developments in curriculum materials that may bode well for standards implementation. One of these is the collaboration of Pearson and the Gates Foundation to develop mathematics and English language arts curricula aligned with the Common Core. While other textbook companies have moved rapidly to tweak existing curriculum materials, this pairing is developing new, technology-integrated materials explicitly aligned to the Common Core. Another potentially promising development is the growth of online lesson-sharing sites (e.g., BetterLesson), which have an explicit focus on aligning lessons with standards. These aggregator sites allow for user-generated, crowd-sourced content to spread widely, potentially replacing some of the influence of textbook companies. Finally, the mere existence of the Common Core should reduce some of the "kitchen sink" incentives, as textbooks will only need to address one set of standards. While it will be important to verify the quality and alignment claims made by these contributors, there is nonetheless reason for cautious optimism.

In terms of professional development, states and districts are investing tremendous resources to create quality, aligned programs to support teachers. A recent survey indicates that all but one Common Core adopting state has plans in place for teacher professional development specifically related to the Common Core.[37] These plans are heavily featured and described in states' ESEA waiver applications, and there is the potential for great economies of scale given the common goals. Of course the quality of the professional development (PD) is paramount, and it is hoped that states and districts will learn from what we know about the features of effective PD in creating their programs.[38] It remains to be seen whether the PD will have its intended effects, but it is nonetheless important that states are paying attention to this issue and not merely assuming that the standards will be implemented by districts without support and training.

How the Common Core Can Complement Teacher Policies

Learning About Effective Pedagogy. One of the central goals of the current policy movement toward enhanced teacher evaluation is giving teachers feedback to help improve their pedagogy. Unfortunately, with the way instruction is currently practiced, it is very difficult to learn about effective pedagogical practices. The reason for this is because there is so much variation across classrooms in the content of instruction. When trying to pull apart which pedagogical practices lead to achievement gains, therefore, content is likely to be confounded with pedagogy in ways that make identifying meaningful pedagogical effects quite unlikely.

Even after years of standards-based reform there remain wide disparities in content coverage across U.S. classrooms. For instance, a study of eighth-grade mathematics instruction in 60 Midwest districts showed that content coverage varied dramatically across districts. In some districts, eighth-grade classes taught material that was typical of fifth-grade rigor, while in other districts, the average classes were at a seventh-grade level of rigor (none were at grade level or higher.)[39] These content coverage differences have been shown to have meaningful relationships with achievement differences across sites.[40] What would be much more desirable, from the standpoint of learning how to effectively teach core content, is if teachers generally taught the same content, but in different ways. This would allow researchers to determine which strategies were effective and which were not.

The Common Core may help address this issue. There is the hope that alignment of instruction with the standards will be greater in the Common Core era than in the NCLB era, and research offers some suggestions for how to improve alignment and where to target alignment efforts.[41] As I suggest above, however, improved alignment will only happen to the extent that the Common Core is supported with aligned assessments, teacher education, professional development, and curriculum materials.

If alignment is indeed improved, this will reduce the variation in the content of instruction that has plagued U.S. schools for years. Aside from the obvious equity effects of such a shift, it would also result in important benefits for teacher evaluation and improvement. To the extent that value-added model (VAM) scores are taken to represent differences in instruction in a better aligned system such as the one envisioned, these differences should represent differences in instructional quality and not be confounded with differences in content coverage. This will allow for more instructional improvement over time, and it will also create a clearer discernment of overall pedagogical quality in ways that can enhance teacher evaluation purposes.

Facilitating the Comparison of Teacher Education Programs. The movement to compare teacher education programs, particularly based on their contributions to teachers' classroom performance, may benefit considerably from the move to the Common Core. Perhaps most obviously, the Common Core will put teacher education programs in 45 states and the District of Columbia on a level playing field in terms of their desired goals. Under the NCLB system, programs within states could be easily compared—though they generally were not—but programs between states could not. Not only were programs across states preparing teachers to teach to different sets of standards (to the extent that teacher education programs actually prepare teachers for this task), but also the teachers' performance was measured using different assessments. With common standards and impending common assessments, it will be much easier to compare program effectiveness across states, at least insofar as those judgments are made based on teachers' contributions to student learning. To be sure, there may be barriers to cross-state comparisons; perhaps the most obvious of these is the difference in state accountability systems should the ESEA waivers persist.

On a related point, teacher education programs themselves will have clearer objectives under the Common Core than under previous sets of standards. This is particularly true for teacher education programs at institutions that draw students from many states (for example, some flagship state universities and private colleges). Under NCLB's state standards, these programs were able to choose whether to prepare teachers to teach their state standards or, perhaps, standards from professional organizations (e.g., the National Council of Teachers of Mathematics). But the former would only end up targeting those teachers who remained in the state, and the latter would not prepare teachers to teach any state's standards. Under the Common Core, it will be possible to prepare preservice teachers to address the nearly national standards against which they will presumably be evaluated. In principle, this clarity should enable teacher education programs to make meaningful gains in the quality of the preparation they provide to new teachers. In practice, there may be difficulties in improving teacher education programs, as discussed below.

Decreasing the Standards Churn. Standards-based reform has been around for two decades or more in many states. Thus the vast majority of teachers currently teaching in U.S. K–12 schools began teaching during the standards-based reform era (especially given the recent trend toward an ever-more-inexperienced teaching force).[42] In that time span, states have typically undergone two or three changes in standards; the typical duration for a set of standards to remain in place in a particular state is approximately 8 years.[43] This "standards churn," while perhaps necessary for improving the standards over the years, makes it difficult for teachers to make long-lasting instructional improvements. After all, by the time they adapt to new standards and assessments, the materials they are using to teach to these standards are often on their way out.

Historically, teachers have often been able to ignore many state and federal education policy reforms, as these reforms have often been cyclical and short-lived.[44] Earlier in the history of standards-based reform, teachers might have thought this would happen with standards, too. However, the Common Core clearly symbolizes the full commitment of state and federal governments to the long-term implementation of standards-based reform in schools and districts. While educators might have thought the standards-based reform era would pass after the failure of NCLB, it is apparent that policy makers still believe in standards-based reform. There is simply no evidence that standards-based reform is going away anytime soon. Moreover, the Common Core Standards themselves will likely be more stable than the state standards they are replacing. The stability of the Common Core seems likely for several reasons: (1) The development period was long and involved many stakeholders; (2) the standards are viewed by most as being of higher quality than most of the state standards they are replacing; (3) it will be more difficult to achieve consensus on revisions with more than 40 states working together; and (4) the supporting assessments and curriculum materials are still being fully developed and implemented.

Why does this stability have potential to positively affect teacher policy? First, the persistence of standards-based reform over several decades makes it harder and harder for teacher educators to ignore standards. Doing so would put their students and (depending on state accountability rules) themselves at a disadvantage. Second, reduced standards churn, coupled with the nearly national nature of the standards, decreases barriers for teachers to move across state lines. This can potentially enhance the market for quality teachers, though there are perhaps other barriers to cross-state moves (such as pension portability). Third, it is possible that decreased standards churn, combined with the great efforts being undertaken to develop quality assessments and curriculum materials, should make it easier for teachers to continually learn about the best ways to teach the Common Core content, rather than having to relearn and readapt their teaching practices to standards every few years. None of these benefits are guaranteed, but all are possible if the Common Core remains the relatively stable instructional target for the coming years.

CHALLENGES

None of these opportunities is guaranteed to materialize. Quite the contrary, without a robust series of implementation supports, we are unlikely to see the kind of meaningful change that is now widely expected. In this section I discuss some of the most serious challenges to the opportunities presented above. I focus on three that are perhaps the most salient: (1) the timing of standards rollout and teacher policy implementation; (2) a lack of seriousness about alignment; and (3) the politics of teacher policy.

The Implementation Timeline

Despite the potentially promising role of the new standards and assessments, the transition to the new assessments has the potential to be painful in the short run. And that pain may, in turn, affect support for implementation of the teacher evaluation policies. Given these potential pains, I believe states and districts should consider a moratorium on the use of Common Core assessment results for evaluating and making high-stakes decisions about teacher effectiveness for the next several years.

One reason that the transition is likely to be painful is that many states have adopted the Common Core Standards but are still using their old assessments, which were (or at least were intended to be) aligned with old state standards. Thus there is a very real fairness and validity issue in the short run, because teachers and students are being measured on tests that are not even good representations of the old standards, let alone the new ones. If the results from these old assessments are used for high-stakes decisions about individual teachers while teachers are working to implement the Common Core, it would not at all be surprising to see widespread dissatisfaction and even lawsuits against districts and states on basis of the poor alignment (and therefore weak validity) of these assessments. While such lawsuits have not been filed in the case of teachers, there is historical precedent for students. For instance, in *Debra P v. Turlington* in Florida, a student sued the state over its new high school graduation exam policy, arguing that she did not have the opportunity to learn the content on the exam (in the language of the court, "curricular validity").[45] Recent work suggests lawsuits by students or teachers in light of new teacher evaluation policies may become common and could very well be successful.[46] Both researchers and policy makers are concerned about these short-run implementation issues.[47]

Another way in which the transition timeline will be painful is that proficiency will almost certainly drop in many states as they transition to the Common Core. Kentucky is the first state to roll out Common Core–aligned assessments, and their recent assessment results showed a roughly 30 percentage point drop in proficiency.[48] While proficiency rates almost always drop when moving from one test to another, this trend may be exacerbated in the current case because many states have indicated in their ESEA waiver plans that they have chosen to set more ambitious proficiency targets on the Common Core–aligned assessments than on their old state assessments. Thus, for at least the few years after the new tests are rolled out, there will likely be instability and poorer-than-anticipated performance. This presents at least two problems. First, there is a logistical/technical problem: How can teachers' contributions to student learning be evaluated when moving from one assessment system to another? It is possible to calculate value-added or student growth percentile scores under these conditions, but these calculations are not transparent to teachers or the public. Second, there is a public support problem: How will the undoubtedly weaker proficiency results affect public and teacher support for continued expansion of teacher evaluation policies as well as the Common Core?

In short, the timing of the rollout of new teacher evaluation systems is especially inconvenient given these assessment implementation difficulties. States are scheduled to officially roll out the new assessments in 2014–15, but it would be advisable to hold off using these results to inform high-stakes decisions for teachers until another year or two after that, in order to reach a steady state. Given some of the challenges in using achievement data and observational ratings to estimate teacher effectiveness, including the weak relationships among measures and the instability of both value-added and observational measures of performance, caution is probably warranted here anyway. While most agree that the combination of assessment data with high-quality observations can provide useful evidence for helping improve instruction, moving too quickly could jeopardize the gains in public and teacher support that have been made in the past half decade.[49]

A Lack of Seriousness About Alignment

Under NCLB, state assessments were required to be aligned with their corresponding state content standards. There are several techniques that are accepted by the Department of Education as evidence of alignment. Unfortunately, the two main alignment techniques—one pioneered by Norman Webb, and the other by Andrew Porter—tend to produce different results. The most commonly used approach tends to produce results that say tests are reasonably well aligned with standards.[50] The second most commonly used approach tends to produce results that show poor alignment of tests and standards.[51] In part, these divergent findings represent somewhat esoteric differences in how alignment is defined. But given how central alignment is to the success of NCLB-style standards-based reform, and given the poor classroom implementation of state standards under NCLB, it is increasingly apparent that the research and policy community needs to move to a more rigorous consensus about what alignment means and how it is measured.

But it is not enough that we get serious about alignment of assessments with standards. Perhaps even more important is that we begin to meaningfully improve the quality and alignment of curriculum materials to support the standards. The poor quality and alignment of textbooks and curriculum materials should be among our foremost concerns, given how important these materials are in shaping teachers' instruction. There has never been a systematic examination of the alignment of textbooks to state standards; thus claims of alignment made by textbook companies have gone unverified. Conducting alignment analyses of textbooks and providing teachers and district personnel with alignment information is a relatively low-cost intervention, and it would go a long way toward helping teachers align their instruction. Without this kind of information, standards implementation will undoubtedly be weaker than desired, and the instructional and achievement effects of the Common Core will be diluted. Furthermore, variation across settings in the quality of instructional supports will contaminate efforts to estimate teacher performance from assessment data.

Politics

Perhaps the most serious challenge to the Common Core's influence on teacher policies is the role of politics. Given all of the above challenges, there are a number of reasons to think the next few years will be rocky ones. As teacher evaluation systems are rolled out, there will be growing pains in districts and states. These implementation issues include training observers, allocating time for them to conduct their observations, establishing reliability, and presenting results clearly to the public. Simultaneously, teachers are being expected to radically reshape their teaching strategies and content coverage. These reforms are not inherently linked with one another (e.g., it is not necessary to have common standards in order to initiate new teacher evaluation policies). However, the reforms are occurring at the same time, and both types of reforms were encouraged by President Obama's Race to the Top initiative and Elementary and Secondary Education Act waivers. Thus it would not be surprising if these two policy initiatives became politically entwined in ways that diminished the likelihood of either reform persisting and leading to meaningful change. Indeed, there are already signs on the left that the Common Core is being conflated with teacher quality reforms such as tenure and evaluation rules, and it is therefore acquiring some of the negative political stigmas associated with those teacher policy reforms. For instance, both issues have become cause célèbre among organizations, such as "Save Our Schools," seeking to push back against recent advances in standards, accountability, and choice policies. Save Our Schools' website has a page devoted to anti–Common Core editorials, with one arguing that "we are being seduced by the idea that a common set of standards and assessments to match will deliver equitable outcomes from our schools."[52]

There are also political difficulties on the right. Perhaps reacting to the Obama administration's perceived overreach in compelling states to adopt the Common Core through Race to the Top, a few Republican governors

and legislatures have toyed with repealing the standards adoption or pulling out of the assessment consortia. The American Legislative Exchange
Council (ALEC) also considered a resolution opposing the Common Core,
though it was ultimately defeated. The longer the standards are in place, the
less likely it is that states will return to their state-specific standards. But it
is clear that there is some pressure to return to more local control over what
is taught in schools. In short, with politics pushing from both sides, and
with the more politically contentious issues around teacher policy happening at the same time, the path for Common Core implementation may not
be perfectly smooth.

The political issues are further complicated by the uncertain future of
the Elementary and Secondary Education Act (ESEA). With the waivers issued to more than 30 states and the president reelected, it looks increasingly
unlikely that we will return to a federally designed accountability system
any time soon. But there are a number of states that do not have approved
waivers, and it is unclear what will happen in those states. This complicated
mess could certainly bleed over into either of these two policy areas, thus
undermining the success of both initiatives.

WHAT TO WATCH FOR

Both the Common Core Standards and the spate of teacher quality reforms
hold great promise for improving educational outcomes for students. These
two reforms have the potential to mutually reinforce one another, leading
to better aligned, more coherent, and more effective instruction. However,
if Common Core implementation is as poorly supported as was the case for
state standards under NCLB, that reform will not have the dramatic effects
policy makers envision. Similarly, if teacher quality policies are implemented carelessly, without consideration for the instability of most measures of
teacher performance, those policies could actually have dangerous negative effects. Some of these potentially dangerous effects include waves of
teacher lawsuits, increases in teacher turnover, and reductionist responses
from teachers that make instruction worse, not better. In short, the next
several years will be crucial for the success of these policies. Briefly, I offer
three suggestions for policy makers.

First, *take it slow*. Particularly given the confluence of new policies,
there is no reason to rush the use of assessment results for high-stakes decisions. Making decisions on the basis of bad data will inevitably result in
pushback from teachers and may well lead to the failure of these policies.
While it is true that kids shouldn't have to wait for good teachers, moving
too rapidly may create negative effects—such as those I mention above—

that will outweigh any benefits gained from improved teacher evaluation policies.

Second, *learn from previous mistakes*. There is near universal agreement that NCLB did not result in desired outcomes. There are many reasons for the law's failure, but perhaps the most obvious is that it had numerous, obvious design flaws that were identified from the earliest stages of implementation. Many of these same design issues apply to teacher evaluation reforms, so policy makers would be wise to learn from the mistakes of prior law. Three such suggestions are:

1. Accountability measures must be fair for all teachers. This means that these measures must not penalize teachers who teach in schools serving more disadvantaged students or who teach more difficult subjects. This means, among other things, choosing a growth model that controls for student characteristics and puts teachers on a level playing field, no matter which students they teach. Otherwise, the system will create incentives for teachers to avoid challenging placements.

2. Policy makers should take steps to improve the reliability of teacher evaluation measures. Both value-added models and observational scores are fairly unreliable from year to year, so policy makers should consider averaging across class sections or years in order to improve that reliability. Also, high-stakes decisions should not be made on the basis of a single year's data for such an unreliable measure.

3. Measures of achievement used in accountability policies should consider performance along the full distribution, rather than just above or below proficiency. This will create better incentives for teachers to focus on achievement gains among all students, rather than just the "bubble kids" right below the proficiency cut.

Third, *provide the necessary support*. From a policy standpoint, standards and accountability systems under NCLB were not designed to support effective implementation and response. Most glaringly, tests were poorly aligned to standards. Nor did states, teacher education programs, or school districts adequately support implementation through aligned PD or curricula. To address these issues, I would recommend several policies, some of which I have already suggested:

1. The assessment consortia should consider multiple approaches to alignment, and they should be absolutely sure that all the content in the standards is adequately assessed. Given recent flare-ups

      in Seattle over benchmark assessments (tests given throughout the year to measure students' progress toward the standards), districts might also be vigilant about the alignment of benchmark assessments to the curriculum teachers are supposed to be teaching.

2. States or districts, working together to leverage the tremendous economies of scale presented by the Common Core, should contract with researchers to rigorously study the alignment of curriculum materials with the standards. These can include textbooks from major publishers, as well as available online materials from popular sources such as Khan Academy. There is no reason to trust textbook publishers' claims about alignment.

3. States and teacher education programs should study the impact of preservice teacher education programs on teachers' practices and contributions to student learning. There is almost no good evidence in this regard, and any new evidence would undoubtedly have national significance and implications.

Overall, these are serious issues and are not easily addressed. But there is at least the possibility that these two policy reforms will have long-lasting and meaningful effects on teaching and learning in schools nationwide. If not supported in implementation in the ways I describe, however, they will likely fail to achieve their desired effects.

NOTES

1. National Council on Teacher Quality. (2012). *State of the states 2012: Teacher effectiveness policies.* Washington, DC: National Council on Teacher Quality.

2. Porter, A., McMaken, J., Hwang, J., & Yang, R. (2011). Common Core Standards: The new U.S. intended curriculum. *Educational Researcher, 40*(3), 103–116.

3. Weisberg, D., Sexton, S., Mulhern, J., & Keeling, D. (2009). *The widget effect: Our national failure to acknowledge and act on differences in teacher effectiveness.* New York: The New Teacher Project.

4. National Council on Teacher Quality, *State of the states 2012.*

5. Sawchuk, S. (2013, February 6). High ratings for teachers are still seen. *Education Week.*

6. Christie, K., & Zinth, J. D. (2011). *Teacher tenure or continuing contract laws.* Denver, CO: Education Commission of the States.

7. U.S. Department of Education. (2011). *Preparing and credentialing the nation's teachers: The secretary's eighth report on teacher quality based on data provided for 2008, 2009 and 2010.* Washington, DC: U.S. Department of Education.

8. Gansle, K. A., Burns, J. M., & Noell, G. (2011). *Value added assessment of teacher preparation programs in Louisiana: 2007–2008 to 2009–2010*. Baton Rouge, LA: Louisiana Board of Regents.

9. Beach, R. W. (2011). Issues in analyzing alignment of language arts Common Core Standards with state standards. *Educational Researcher, 40*(4), 179–182; Cobb, P., & Jackson, K. (2011). Assessing the quality of the Common Core State Standards for mathematics. *Educational Researcher, 40*(4), 183–185; Carmichael, S. B., Wilson, W. S., Porter-Magee, K., & Martino, G. (2010). *The state of state standards—and the Common Core—in 2010*. Washington, DC: Thomas B. Fordham Institute.

10. Floden, R. E., Porter, A. C., Schmidt, W. H., Freeman, D. J., & Schwille, J. R. (1980). Responses to curriculum pressures: A policy-capturing study of teacher decisions about content. *Journal of Educational Psychology, 73*, 129–141.

11. Polikoff, M. S. (2012). The redundancy of mathematics instruction in U.S. elementary and middle schools. *Elementary School Journal, 113*(2), 230–251; Schmidt, W. H., & Houang, R. T. (2012). Curricular coherence and the Common Core State Standards for mathematics. *Educational Researcher, 41*(8), 294–308.

12. Polikoff, M. S. (2012). Instructional alignment under No Child Left Behind, *American Journal of Education, 118*(3), 341–368.

13. Polikoff, M. S. (2012). The association of state policy attributes with teachers' instructional alignment. *Educational Evaluation and Policy Analysis, 34*(3), 278–294; Schmidt, W. H., Cogan, L. S., Houang, R. T., & McKnight, C. C. (2011). Content coverage differences across districts/states: A persisting challenge for U.S. policy. *American Journal of Education, 117*(3), 399–427; Schmidt, W. H., & McKnight, C. C. (2012). *Inequality for all: The challenge of unequal opportunity in American schools*. New York: Economic Policy Institute and Teachers College Press.

14. Schmidt, W. H., Cogan, L. S., et al., "Content coverage differences across districts/states."

15. Polikoff, "Instructional alignment under No Child Left Behind."

16. Polikoff, "The redundancy of mathematics."

17. Polikoff, M. S., Porter, A. C., & Smithson, J. (2011). How well aligned are state assessments of student achievement with state content standards? *American Educational Research Journal, 48*(4), 965–995.

18. Smith, M. S., & O'Day, J. A. (1991). Systemic school reform. In S. H. Fuhrman & B. Malen (Eds.), *The politics of curriculum and testing: Politics of education association yearbook*. Bristol, PA: Falmer Press.

19. Polikoff, "The association of state policy attributes."

20. Porter, A.C., Polikoff, M.S., Barghaus, K.M., & Yang, R. (in press). Constructing aligned assessments using automated test construction. *Education Researcher*.

21. Cohen, D. K., & Moffitt, S. L. (2009). *The ordeal of equality: Did federal regulation fix the schools?* Cambridge, MA: Harvard University Press.

22. Sykes, G., Bird, T., & Kennedy, M. (2010). Teacher education: Its problems and some prospects. *Journal of Teacher Education, 61*(5), 464–476.

23. Cochran-Smith, M., & Zeichner, K. M. (Eds.). (2005). *Studying teacher education: The report of the Aera Panel on Research and Teacher Education*. Mahwah, NJ: Erlbaum.

24. Cochran-Smith & Zeichner, *Studying teacher education*.

25. Schmidt, W. H., & Houang, R. T. (2012). Curricular coherence and the Common Core State Standards for mathematics. *Educational Researcher, 41*(8), 294–308.

26. Ma, L. (1999). *Knowing and teaching elementary mathematics: Teachers' understanding of fundamental mathematics in China and the United States*. Mahwah, NJ: Erlbaum.

27. Bushaw, W. J., & Lopez, S. J. (2012). Public education in the United States: A nation divided. *Phi Delta Kappan, 94*(1), 8–25.

28. Achieve. (2012). *Growing awareness, growing support: teacher and voter understanding of the Common Core State Standards & assessments*. Washington, DC: Achieve.

29. Thomas, P. L. (2010, August 11). Why common standards won't work. *Education Week*.

30. Burns, L. D. (2012). Standards, policy paradoxes, and the new literacy studies: A call to professional political action. *Journal of Adolescent and Adult Literacy, 56*(2), 93–97.

31. Apple, M. W. (2000). *Official knowledge: Democratic education in a conservative age* (2nd ed.). New York: Routledge.

32. Bhatt, R., & Koedel, C. (2012). Large-scale evaluations of curricular effectiveness: The case of elementary mathematics in Indiana. *Educational Evaluation and Policy Analysis, 34*(4), 391–412.

33. Schmidt, W. H., McKnight, C. C., Houang, R. T., Wang, H., Wiley, D. E., Cogan, L. S., & Wolfe, R. G. (2001). *Why schools matter: A cross-national comparison of curriculum and learning*. San Francisco, CA: Jossey-Bass; Spillane, J. P. (2004). *Standards deviation: How schools misunderstand education policy*. Cambridge, MA: Harvard University Press.

34. Porter, A. C., Polikoff, M. S., & Smithson, J. (2009). Is there a de facto national intended curriculum? Evidence from state content standards. *Educational Evaluation and Policy Analysis, 31*(3), 238–268.

35. Polikoff, "Instructional alignment under No Child Left Behind."

36. Hill, H. C. (2001). Policy is not enough: Language and the interpretation of state standards. *American Educational Research Journal, 38*(2), 289–318; Spillane, *Standards deviation*.

37. Education First and Editorial Projects in Education. (2013). *Moving forward: A national perspective on states' progress in Common Core State Standards implementation planning*. Seattle, WA: Education First and Editorial Projects in Education.

38. Desimone, L. M. (2009). Improving impact studies of teachers' professional development: Toward better conceptualizations and measures. *Educational Researcher, 38*(3), 181–199.

39. Schmidt, W. H., Cogan, L. S., et al., "Content coverage differences across districts/states."

40. Schmidt, W. H., McKnight, et al., *Why schools matter*.

41. Polikoff, "The association of state policy attributes"; Polikoff, M. S. (2013). Teacher education, experience, and the practice of aligned instruction. *Journal of Teacher Education.* (Published online ahead of print.)

42. Ingersoll, R., & Merrill, L. (2010). Who's teaching our children? *Educational Leadership, 67*(8), 14–20.

43. Polikoff, "The association of state policy attributes."

44. Tyack, D., & Cuban, L. (1995). *Tinkering toward utopia: A century of public school reform*. Cambridge, MA: Harvard University Press.

45. Madaus, G. F. (1983). *The courts, validity, and minimum competency testing*. Boston, MA: Kluwer/Nijhoff.

46. Baker, B. D., Oluwole, J. O., & Green, P. C. (2013). The legal consequences of mandating high stakes decisions based on low quality information: Teacher evaluation in the race-to-the-top era. *Education Policy Analysis Archives, 21*(5), 1–71; Hutt, E., & Tang, A. (in press). The new education malpractice litigation. *University of Virginia Law Review.*

47. Sparks, S. D. (2012, October 31). Caution urged on "value added" reviews. *Education Week.*

48. Ujifusa, A. (2012, November 7). Ky. road-tests Common Core. *Education Week.*

49. Bill & Melinda Gates Foundation. (2012). *Gathering feedback for teaching: Combining high-quality observations with student surveys and achievement gains*. Seattle, WA: Bill & Melinda Gates Foundation; Mihaly, K., McCaffrey, D. F., Staiger, D. O., & Lockwood, J. R. (2013). *A composite estimator of effective teaching*. Seattle, WA: Bill & Melinda Gates Foundation.

50. Webb, N. L. (2002). *Alignment study of language arts, mathematics, science, and social studies of state standards and assessments in four states*. Washington, DC: Council of Chief State School Officers.

51. Porter, A. C. (2002). Measuring the content of instruction: Uses in research and practice. *Educational Researcher, 31*(7), 3–14.

52. Cody, A. (2012, May 18). Critical questions about the Common Core. *Education Week: Living in Dialogue*. Retrieved from http://saveourschoolsmarch.org/issues-2/curriculum-creation-use-curricula/articles-common-core-state-standards/

CHAPTER 4

Will Charter Schools Lead or Lag?

Robin Lake
Tricia Maas

IN 45 STATES, the Common Core State Standards (CCSS) are coming. In theory, the Common Core simply provides a set of expectations about what students should know and be able to do in order to be ready to succeed in college and career. The standards have been lauded as a way to elevate the teaching profession and to focus student instruction on critical skills needed for college and career rather than rote knowledge, but have also been critiqued as an attempt to centralize authority over school curriculum. The CCSS have been viewed as both a cure-all and an end-all in public policy forums and in teacher lounges across the country.[1]

Ideologically, the push for tighter and better reins on what teachers teach could appear to be in direct opposition to charter school philosophy, which delegates decision making to the school level. Charter schools are publicly funded schools that accept increased accountability in exchange for increased autonomy in areas such as curriculum, staffing, and resource allocation. Charter schools tend to value and fiercely protect their independence. Early in the charter school movement, perceived threats to school autonomy, such as state standards and testing, stirred up significant resistance among charter leaders. Some observers, however, argued that charter schools and standards were, in fact, complementary ideas: Charter schools provide the avenues for innovation and flexibility, enabling schools to achieve ambitious standards, while standards and aligned assessments provide necessary accountability and performance targets for decentralized systems and loosely regulated entrepreneurs.[2]

The ongoing tension between the largely decentralized charter school movement and national and state movements toward centralized standards and accountability systems raises many questions for charter schools as Common Core implementation is deployed: Will Common Core implementation have any effect on the freedoms with which charter schools operate? Will the sector leaders see it as a threat or an opportunity? Are charter schools sufficiently informed about Common Core? And do they have sufficient resources to provide teachers with the necessary professional development to adjust their instruction?

To learn more about how the charter sector is approaching and preparing for the Common Core Standards, we interviewed over a dozen individuals, including leaders of major charter management organizations (CMOs), charter school association leaders, technical assistance providers, and charter school principals.[3] We asked about their hopes and fears for the CCSS, what it would take to make implementation successful, and how they thought the new standards might affect innovative developments in education. We also collected responses to a brief survey from 19 charter support organizations (CSOs—organizations that provide various kinds of assistance to new and existing charter schools) to learn how and to what extent these organizations are assisting charter schools in the CCSS implementation process, and reviewed CSO websites and publicly available documents from CSO Common Core workshops and trainings.

While our research produced some common refrains, charter leaders' views and approaches concerning the Common Core are as diverse as the sector itself. In this chapter we describe the various points of exuberant optimism, and other times, nearly paranoid concerns, at play among leaders in the charter school sector. In general, those we interviewed are enthusiastic that Common Core State Standards will, in themselves, set a more rigorous and meaningful set of expectations for the skills students are expected to have upon graduation than most current state standards. Especially among proponents of blended learning and technology-based instruction, prominent school and association leaders believe that CCSS will allow innovative ideas to expand more quickly across states. Many leaders of well-known high-performing charter management organizations praise the increased rigor of the standards, are enthusiastic about the opportunity to easily compare student test scores and materials across states, and do not worry that the Common Core will infringe on their schools' autonomies. In theory, charters will be in the same place that they are now: operating freely, while being held to government standards. The shift from state to federal standards, they say, *should* not have a discernible impact on charter school autonomy.

On the other hand, some in the charter sector have significant concerns that the rollout of Common Core will be watered down or underfunded by states. Some even contend that states and districts will slowly begin to erode charter school autonomy through new curricular or staff development requirements associated with the Common Core. If policy makers water down the standards or lower cut scores on tests, the Common Core will only be a dressed up version of a standards movement that we have already experienced. Others fear that the increasing universality of standards portends a move toward centralization that will ultimately impinge on the school-level decision making that charter leaders hold sacred and would all but defeat the purpose of charter schools.

What even the most optimistic and cynical agree on is that the details that will determine whose vision becomes reality are yet to be determined. If the history of state standards implementation is any indication of what is to come, the specific testing items put forth by the assessment developers, cut scores that determine student proficiency levels, consequences for failure to meet standards, and implementation supports (including teacher preparation programs) will have a significant impact on how the standards affect charter schools and all public schools.

Many national thought leaders in the charter field admit that they have put off thinking about the fast-approaching Common Core. National charter support organizations seem to be farthest behind in thinking about how to help charters prepare for the Common Core, but there are individuals and organizations at all levels of charter schooling that would benefit from thinking more deeply about how the charter and Common Core movements will interact. Leaders of CMOs, technical support organizations, and charter school associations sometimes speak about the Common Core as someone might talk about a line on the second page of their to-do list: a looming responsibility that they hope to push off for as long as possible. Some support organizations and CMOs planned, but had not yet begun, to develop tools for schools. Others trust that their most aggressive school leaders will take the lead and act as models and mentors for other principals.

For some, this hands-off approach to the Common Core in the charter sector may be symptomatic of a culture of deference to school-level initiative, independence, and expertise. As a result of this culture, many state charter school associations and technical assistance providers have, to this date, focused more on advocacy and business supports than instruction. Common Core, then, presents a challenge for them: how to provide high-quality classroom-relevant expertise on minimal budgets without re-creating the one-size-fits-all professional development that many charter schools have tried to escape.

At the same time, there are several new entrepreneurial efforts underway in state associations and in schools that offer innovative points of guidance for how the charter sector nationally could lead on Common Core implementation. Several state organizations are providing high-quality supports and are sometimes using technology and networks to deliver supports in a way that the diverse and fiercely independent charter sector finds effective (and that might benefit other public schools as well).

What's clear is that charter schools, with their flexibility over funds, staffing, and curriculum and their inclination toward creative solutions (for example, adopting new learning technologies), can either play a significant leadership role in CCSS rollout, reallocating resources to help prepare teachers, creating novel approaches to reaching small and rural schools, and participating in state and local implementation efforts, or the sector can sit back and let it play out, waiting to see how the superstars of the movement fare on the new tests and leaving it to district and state officials to supply most of the supports, whether they fit with unique charter approaches or not.

For better or worse, on the Common Core train that's coming down the tracks, the charter sector is like the little red caboose: a small force, easily forgotten but potentially significant. In the coming years, the sector will demonstrate whether it will create powerful new approaches to preparing schools to meet the standards or struggle to do its part and be left behind. We conclude this chapter with a set of cautions and recommendations to spark a national discussion about possible points of action for charter support organizations and other leaders in the sector. Central to those recommendations is a call for state and national charter sector leaders to take a more proactive role in the implementation decisions that are speeding down the track.

THE CHARTER LANDSCAPE

Overall, charter sector opinion leaders and practitioners, like other public school actors, are all over the place when it comes to the Common Core.[4] In general, they are cautiously optimistic about the potential for the Common Core to create more rigorous and meaningful standards, but many are conflicted and harbor some fears about how the Common Core will be rolled out, and that the national support organizations are not yet prepared to help. To successfully implement the Common Core, national and state support organizations need to pay attention to training and support and need to sound a wake-up call to get the attention of independent charter schools that are not already preparing for the CCSS. Charter leaders also need to be vigilant about defining bright lines around where their autonomy over curricular decisions lies.

Common Core as a Rorschach Test

In our interviews with charter leaders, we were struck by how much they seemed to see in the Common Core what they wanted to see—determined by their personality and background. CMO leaders as well as proponents of "blended learning" school models (models that combine online and classroom-based instruction) tend to see the Common Core as a real positive—both in terms of organizational efficiency and student learning. On the other side, there are many charter leaders who are fiercely independent, sometimes to the point of paranoia, and raise important questions about whether the Common Core will be implemented in such a way as to erode the autonomies that make charter schools unique.

We most commonly observed an attitude of cautious but genuine optimism and good will toward the Common Core State Standards. Although many national and state leaders admit that they have not made the time to learn about the nuances of the CCSS, most are firmly supportive of the Common Core as they understand it. They view it as a way to orient all states around college-ready standards, to move from fact-based to inquiry-based learning (a type of learning that most of our interviewees feel is lacking in most college prep, "no excuses" charter schools), and to create a common vocabulary around quality for all charter schools.

Much of this optimism, however, is based more on aspiration than information. Other than school-level leaders, most opinion leaders in the charter sector have not actually dug into the standards yet or tracked the likely test items. Several candidly admitted that they really did not know much about the Common Core Standards and how they might affect charter schools.

The varied perspectives at play in the charter sector are probably not very different from those in other public schools. But the charter sector is so varied and independently minded that it creates a complex picture for predicting how people will respond. As one leader of a charter school support organization said, "Charter schools are a messy lot." The charter sector's inherent lack of uniformity extends to how they are responding to the Common Core.

High Hopes Rest on Rigor and Scalability

Many in the charter sector hold extremely high hopes for the Common Core State Standards and assert that good will come of them in various ways. The most frequently mentioned virtue is rigor. Although some thought leaders admitted that they had not spent much time reviewing the standards, all of the 12 individuals we talked to had confidence that the CCSS are more rigorous than the state standards currently in place. Some like the idea that the standards are empirically aligned with college entrance skill requirements. Others appreciate that they place a higher value on students' ability to understand concepts than to memorize facts.

More than anything, principals and CMO leaders with whom we spoke believe that perceived legitimacy of the goals among teachers will, in itself, help schools make progress with student learning. Principals and other leaders told us that their teachers are enthusiastically embracing the standards and are actively working to align their curricula with them. One CMO leader we spoke with said 2 years ago their leadership team shared the Common

Core Standards with principals and teacher leaders and they "practically got a standing ovation."

CMOs, which benefit from the economies of scale from running multiple schools and have typically embraced the idea of standards and accountability for results, seem to be especially enthusiastic about the Common Core Standards. Indeed, the CMO leaders with whom we spoke believe that Common Core implementation will make it much easier for their organizations to expand across multiple states and maintain common quality control and support systems, mainly because the Common Core allows them to compare their schools' outcomes across states with a common metric rather than having to develop formative exams and quality control systems that are unique to each state's learning standards. The Common Core, then, is a boon for CMOs that are thinking about expanding outside of state lines.

Some blended learning advocates, many of whom run CMOs, go even further and say that common standards are *necessary* for their success. Models like Rocketship Education rely on a standardized curriculum across all of their schools to attract partnerships with tech-based curricula and diagnostic providers who find it too costly to operate if they have to adapt to several different sets of standards. Tom Vander Ark, a leading blended learning advocate, believes that the Common Core and shift to digital assessment are "coincidental and complementary." "Online assessment," says Vander Ark, "will respond to the need for better/cheaper assessments and will, in turn, accelerate the shift to digital [learning]."

Other observers are also optimistic that the Common Core will be a boon to innovators, including new charter operators. One longtime thought leader said, "I've always thought that innovators thrive in a marketplace where yardsticks and goals are very clear." Although we did not speak to all of our interviewees about how the Common Core might open up a space for new online curriculum providers, the seven leaders with whom we broached the subject agreed that the CCSS and associated economies of scale will provide an opportunity for the development of online curriculum and other technological advances.

One leader of a CMO that uses blended learning thinks the emergence of resources, videos, and the like could be very powerful, but he and others caution that charter leaders will have to become very savvy consumers in this marketplace. All providers, for example, will assert that their content aligns with the Common Core, but that will not always be the case. This leader thought some sort of "Consumer Reports" for Common Core providers and products would be extremely helpful to charter leaders. CSOs and CMOs could help leaders become wise consumers by fostering in-person and online communication between school leaders about the strengths and weaknesses of new curricula and instructional tools. The New York Charter Schools Association (NYCSA) has already begun to develop a system through which charter schools share feedback with NYCSA about vendors that they have used. NYCSA then organizes that feedback and dispatches it to their schools. This system could serve as a model for CSOs as charter schools move to adopt new programs and technologies. The National Alliance for Public Charter Schools and state associations could also host workshops to help school leaders learn how to assess the evidence on various providers.

Fears of Infringement on Autonomy, Under-Preparedness

To be sure, it would be politically difficult for sector leaders to do anything but support the adoption of higher standards—the sector has tried hard to brand charter schools as being for quality, not just change for change's sake. At the same time, some charter thought leaders seem a little conflicted, some even wary, about the implications of the Common Core for charter schools, primarily on the question of whether enthusiastic or rushed state and local implementation plans could erode the ability of charter schools to choose or develop their own unique approaches to curriculum and instruction.

Most of those with whom we spoke felt that the Common Core, in itself, was not a threat to charter school autonomy, noting that in many ways the Common Core represents nothing dramatically different from their own state standards. As one support organization leader noted, "Common Core is just a decent set of standards. What's new isn't really the standards, but the uniformity behind it." But many did raise concerns that if states or districts begin to set homogenous requirements for common curricula or staff development, charters could feel some infringement. For example, they might be required to send all of their staff through district staff development workshops or use district-approved curricula. Others worried that some charter schools will panic when new assessments are put into place and will attempt to adjust instruction by simply adopting a new textbook. By contrast, at least one charter principal and a charter support organization conveyed the feeling that effective implementation of the Common Core necessitates hard work around instructional innovation and piecing together a curriculum from various sources to meet the needs of a particular set of students.

It was often difficult for us to get charter leaders who feared infringement to give detailed examples of how these scenarios might play out, but some provided specifics. One CMO leader admitted that he worried the Common Core could end up taking away his teachers' freedom to use diverse options to meet student needs by forcing schools to teach certain standards in certain grades, at certain times of the year, or, eventually, by prescribing a curriculum. In line with the greater charter philosophy, the leader firmly stated, "One-size-fits-all doesn't work." A different charter school principal with whom we spoke echoed that charter schools were created to provide something distinct from district schools, and he viewed Common Core as a pressure toward "sameness." He stated, "If parents wanted common, they would just send their kids to neighborhood schools."

Most of those who feared infringement on charter autonomy felt that Common Core implementation could threaten "innovation" and diversity in the charter sector as a result of the assessments, not the standards themselves. The concern is that the assessments will, de facto, require schools to follow a prescribed course sequence and pacing schedule in order to perform well on the exams. Especially for blended learning schools designed to dramatically customize instruction for each student using technology, such constraints could limit the ability of schools to move students through online coursework designed to move students through learning progressions as soon as particular course content is mastered. Another concern is that the exams will lock states into one type of assessment for the next 10 years just as the assessment technologies are improving and changing rapidly. As just one example, the potential for course-embedded or game-based assessments, just emerging now, could transform how innovative charter schools measure mastery, creativity, and complex thinking. As one thought leader put it, "I'm worried that the testing consortia will produce the tests we should have had in 2003."

We encountered pockets of fairly intense opposition among those in the charter sector; there are many who distrust government or who do not value government-mandated testing. One principal told us he thinks that government standards serve to "establish a statement of quality that has little relevance to if a school is truly good." He thinks people writing "these reforms" see 50 decision-making bodies as a weakness in the education system, whereas he sees state-level decision-making power as a strength, allowing state education systems to be responsive to local needs. He also firmly believes that the CCSS is just the first step toward standardized curricula. He stated, "Without a doubt, it is the goal to bring about a national curriculum. People pretend that there's some debate about this; there isn't."

This low-trust perspective was shared by the head of one blended learning network who, despite an overall sense of optimism about the rigor of CCSS, worries that the Common Core is the "camel's nose in the tent" for imposing a broader set of requirements on charter schools. Regardless of their degree of concern, many agreed that the charter school sector would do well to continue to articulate that common standards are different than common curricula and to be preemptively outspoken about how common curricula would undermine the goals of the charter movement.

Some thought leaders mentioned that they would like to see high-performing charters have the option to file for an exemption from the Common Core in order to protect their instructional or curricular autonomy.

Schools able to demonstrate sustained high performance on another approved exam, for example, might apply for a waiver from their state board to bypass Common Core testing. Although multiple people raised Common Core waivers as an option, it is unclear how politically feasible such an exemption would be. Charter schools would likely have to make a strong case that the Common Core was impeding their ability to be successful. However, waivers for high-performing schools could loosen restrictions about the order in which students take specific subject tests and pardon schools from having to take any required formative assessments throughout the year.

Big Rollout Concerns: Some Unique to Charter Schools

In almost every interview we conducted, we heard a recognition that at this point, people know very little about what Common Core implementation will actually look like. Leaders acknowledged that most views are necessarily speculative, and that there are serious questions to be resolved. The most pessimistic interviewees raised ominous questions about whether states are prepared to handle the responsibilities of implementation. Many held a strong belief that in their rush to join the Common Core movement, many states didn't think through the necessary financial and technical commitments and underestimated the challenges ahead.

The most pessimistic prediction is that states that have been "seduced into thinking that this is coming at someone else's expense" will simply not have the money available to implement things well and the whole thing will "inevitably collapse." There are other, less dire, predictions that we have been down this road before with standards implementation and should realistically expect that states will repeat mistakes (such as misaligned assessments and lowered cut scores to give the illusion of improving performance) if nothing is done to prevent them from doing so. One leader from a charter support organization was less than hopeful about how states would handle Common Core implementation: "It's like, we tried high-stakes standards and testing once and it worked so badly that we decided to do it all over again."

Although it's unclear what implementation will ultimately look like, some leaders in the charter sector speculated possible scenarios about various ways Common Core implementation could go badly for public school improvement efforts and for charter schools. Some predict that, as was the case in many states under the last wave of standards and assessment, state cut scores will be adjusted after the first round of test scores come back to make it look like more kids are close to meeting the proficiency standard. In this scenario, differences between high- and low-performing schools—charter and traditional public alike—would be magnified for a short time, but would fade as it became easier for students to pass the test.

Others worried that when new tests come out, charter school performance will come under attack (as when NAEP charter scores first came out) because the early analyses will not account for different student populations. Because charter schools serve a disproportionate number of low-income students, on average, they would likely appear to perform worse than district schools. Advocates warn that charters that perform well compared to similar student populations—but not compared to the state as a whole—may have to defend their scores and should be prepared to fight that battle.

A third possibility is that charter schools that have used instructional techniques to prepare their students well for traditional tests may not do as well on Common Core assessments. Some of the CMOs that have received the most publicity, such as KIPP, Uncommon Schools, and STRIVE Preparatory Schools, tend to focus heavily on preparing students to do well on content and skills emphasized by current state exams. They have been criticized for doing so at the expense of instruction in critical thinking and analytic skills.[5] If such schools do not take steps to adjust their instruction, and if the CCSS do indeed emphasize less fact-based knowledge and more critical thinking skills, one observer warned that charter schools that have historically performed very well on state tests may take more of a "hit" than traditional public schools when the test scores come out.

Regardless of the scenario that plays out, most leaders we interviewed speculate that charter schools and their district counterparts can count on a messy rollout process, with states changing cut scores, shifting timelines, and setting unclear accountability requirements.

Show Me the Test Items

Even the Common Core enthusiasts with whom we spoke recognize that the rigor of the Common Core Standards is entirely dependent on what the test score items will be. They point out that while most of the policy discussion has been about the standards themselves, the tests being developed by Partnership for Assessment of Readiness for College and Careers (PARCC) and Smarter Balanced Assessment Consortium (SBAC) will really define what schools must focus on. As one leader of a charter support organization said, "The Common Core is not mandatory; the assessments are."

One skeptic warned that the standards themselves may look great to teachers, but the assessment writers will have to pick and choose competencies to measure and will have to choose items that can be measured reliably. In his view, this makes it likely that the tests themselves will look a lot like most existing state exams, which rely on multiple-choice questions and other assessment techniques that minimize subjective grading. In the end, the components of the standards that address higher order thinking—

perhaps the most commonly praised aspect of the Common Core—may be the hardest to measure objectively and therefore least likely to end up in the assessments.

Further, because states have the ability to set their own "cut scores" to determine how they will define proficiency, the level of rigor promised in aspirational standards may never make its way into classrooms—at least not in the long term. If states end up lowering cut scores to make statewide performance look better, standards (ambitious, but in and of themselves unmeasurable) will become meaningless. A leader of one high-performing charter network opined that states will ultimately determine how rigorous the CCSS actually are: "After all the dust has settled, if people don't hold the line in terms of the assessment, this will all be wasted."

What's more, states will likely have to reset any existing accountability requirements to give schools a chance to adjust to the new standards, giving low-performing schools continued license to exist. Alternately, states could start holding schools and students accountable for test score achievement without giving schools and teachers sufficient time to adjust their practices to the new standards and tests, a scenario one CMO leader deemed "educational malpractice." Based on past implementation of state standards and tests, it seems most likely that states will take varied approaches. Some will likely push hard to maintain momentum on state accountability ratings and school interventions, but many others will bow to political pressure from interest groups to slow down and give schools safe harbor from interventions for some extended period.

Because the actual test items are not yet developed and states have not defined cut scores, it is impossible to know if these scenarios will play out as critics suggest. For the charter sector, however, the need to prepare for these contingencies and participate in relevant state and local implementation conversations is evident.

Show Me the Money

Charter school thought leaders are of different minds when it comes to the expenses associated with implementation. What most agree upon is that some states and types of charter schools will have a harder time coping with the financial burden of implementation than others. People believe that charter schools in higher spending states, those associated with CMOs, or who have good access to district resources will be much better positioned to prepare teachers for the new requirements of the Common Core.

One CMO leader worried that states like California, which have been implementing deep budget cuts for several years, will say, "that's great. It's just too expensive," referring to the thoughtful and thorough implementation of the Common Core. States that do not feel they have adequate resources to invest in the Common Core may only partially implement supports for the standards. For charter schools, finding funds for intensive staff development training, curriculum alignment, and other schoolwide preparations will not be easy in California and other thin budget states.

In some areas the tight financial situation has already created such a sparse resource environment that curricular changes may not require schools to replace textbooks or software. As one California-based support provider observed, right now the curriculum in many charter schools is "coming out of the copy machine," so the cost for Common Core implementation will mostly be in staff development time. This development and planning time, however, is not trivial, especially in some high-performing charter schools, which have a reputation for already demanding long hours of their teachers. Asking teachers to work even longer hours to prepare, while denying raises or actually cutting pay, is going to be hard, no matter what.

But even for especially cash-strapped states and stand-alone charters, most of those we interviewed felt that while additional funding would be nice, schools do not necessarily need it. The schools will simply have to make smart decisions about how to best invest in curricular materials and prepare their staff to teach the Common Core Standards. Some charter leaders warn that the charter sector will not serve itself well by complaining they don't have the funds to implement the Common Core. Such protests may sound like whining from the charter sector, whose "I can do it myself" ethos has often nettled those in the traditional system. As one CMO leader said, "Everyone cries out that they don't have enough money to implement Common Core, but if that happens 'shame on us' for not preparing and budgeting properly." He says, even in California, "The money is there." It's a question of allocation.

In this sense, it may be that charter schools will actually be *better* positioned to prepare teachers than traditional public schools because their autonomy to spend their money as they please will allow them to make allocation decisions quickly as Common Core implementation rolls out and inevitably changes. As a charter school principal in Colorado said, "We [don't have the money] to just throw away all of the math books and buy new ones," but she also noted that as a charter school, she felt that she was at an advantage because her school has the ability to allocate money and provide professional development in the ways it thinks best.

The most positive take on the tight fiscal environment in which the Common Core will be implemented is that all schools, charter and district, will be forced to rely on innovative, flexible, and scalable technology-based resources rather than new textbook adoptions. The flexibility and creative capital already present in some schools may be more necessary than ever and, more than ever, may act as an effective model for other schools.

Although most CMO and charter school leaders with whom we spoke feel that they will have sufficient money and resources to implement the Common Core, many expressed worries about whether the stand-alone "mom and pop" charters will be prepared and have access to implementation support. One longtime charter advocate and observer noted that states and districts are notorious for failing to include charter schools in guidance documents, trainings, and other notifications, especially if they are not sponsored by a school district. He wondered, if states and districts do offer high-quality supports, "Will charter schools get the e-mail?" Even if districts provide trainings, however, many charter leaders say they would not want to be required to take part, as they distrust that the method and style of professional development would meet their unique missions.

Leaders and Laggards

If charter schools don't trust states and districts to provide the support they need, the sector will have to provide most of those supports itself. But the support infrastructure may not be ready. Based on our discussions with those in the charter sector, some leaders are moving full speed ahead while others are all but ignoring the Common Core.

In general, national charter supports seem to be lagging. The national support organizations, like the National Alliance for Public Charter Schools and the National Association of Charter School Authorizers, are still working on understanding what kind of supports charter schools need from a national level and what role national support organizations will play. A lot of the high-level policy actors we spoke with conveyed that when it comes to Common Core implementation needs, they are "not mentally there yet."

State-level CSOs appear to be more engaged with the Common Core, but their efforts sit on a broad spectrum. The Arkansas Public School Resource Center provides extensive mentoring and technology-based resources to charter and district public schools. The Colorado League of Charter Schools offers a number of workshops and training resources. And New York City has developed a cross-sector collaboration between district and charter schools to support Common Core implementation (for more detail, see Figures 4.1–4.3). Although most state-level CSOs that responded to our survey reported dedicating substantial resources to supporting charter schools in Common Core implementation, a quarter of our survey respondents reported that they have provided no supports around the unrolling of the Common Core Standards.

FIGURE 4.1. The Arkansas "Achieving By Changing" Initiative

In 2012 the Arkansas Public School Resource Center (APSRC) created a 3-year initiative to help rural and charter schools implement the Common Core. Funded by a grant from the Walton Family Foundation, Achieving By Changing (ABC) works to leverage the existing resources of partner schools. Schools that choose to join ABC are grouped into regions. An instructional coach assigned to the region makes monthly visits to each school and leads monthly "hub" meetings for all schools in a region, which involve networking activities, professional development modules, information gathering, and presentations on the latest information about the Common Core.

Technology is a key component of the ABC Initiative. The program uses an educational social networking site called Edmodo and eDoctrina to facilitate the sharing of resources such as unit or lesson plans. In addition, ABC schools receive at least two technology-based professional development modules each month and teachers are expected to implement techniques and skills presented in the modules. Although technology plays a major role in ABC, APSRC's overarching expectation is that teachers will use available tools to restructure their instructional practices to reflect a more rigorous and relevant curriculum.

FIGURE 4. 2. New York City Charter School Center's Cross-Sector Collaborations

With funding from the Bill & Melinda Gates Foundation's District-Charter Collaboration Compacts, the New York City Charter School Center will partner with a local school support network, New Visions, over the next 3 years to build the capacity of middle schools to integrate the new Common Core standards. Specifically, New Visions will work with four district schools and four independent charter schools to provide in-depth, inquiry-based curricular and assessment support. The partnership aims to create and disseminate Common Core–aligned lesson modules and formative assessments for schools throughout the city and the state to adopt.

The Charter Center will also partner with Coro, New York City's Leadership Center, and the New York City Department of Education to deepen the city's teacher and leadership pipeline. Coro will bring together a diverse cohort of 20 secondary school leaders and high-potential teachers—from all types of public schools—to form a leadership collaborative. This group will establish a learning community to provide peer mentorships, strategy sessions with experts in the field, and guidance on the development of school change projects designed to support students' college readiness.

The CSOs that have offered supports around the Common Core have approached the task in different ways. The Ohio Alliance for Public Charter Schools has supported schools in a traditional way, offering professional development through training sessions and workshops. Several workshops on the standards have sold out and now the Ohio CSO plans to provide professional development on the PARCC testing, which they anticipate will also have high attendance. By contrast, a CSO in Connecticut has taken a

FIGURE 4.3. Colorado League of Charter Schools

Some Colorado principals with whom we spoke felt very confident about their school's transition to the new standards, in large part because of the support that they had received from the Colorado League of Charter Schools. The League has worked with 16 teachers from nine schools to author a publicly available document outlining how Core Knowledge content aligns to the new standards for each subject from kindergarten through eighth grade[6] and has hosted seminars and webinars for charter schools on various aspects of moving to the Common Core. These seminars and webinars have offered school leaders specific action steps that they can immediately take and spotlighted potential program vendors for principals. Although the Colorado League has offered support and suggestions, one principal emphasized that the League did not encourage her to buy an off-the-shelf "perfect curriculum" (as she said she would have been tempted to do without their support). Instead, the League supported her and her team in digging into the standards and piecing together a curriculum that made the most sense for her staff and students.

more hands-off approach, providing most of its support by facilitating communication and resource sharing between schools.

Other support organizations have backed even farther away from assuming an expert role in the nuances of instruction, instead managing tools and helping to develop policy. For example, the New York Charter Schools Association (NYCSA) has acted as a "Consumer Reports" for its schools, annually providing a list of vendors, which NYCSA adjusts the next year in response to school leaders' feedback. The D.C. Association of Chartered Public Schools has been a political actor, participating on a state team (District of Columbia) in discussions and revisions of PARCC, and has relayed outcomes of these meetings to charter school leaders.

CMOs' and principals' varied engagement with the Common Core mirrors that of charter support organizations. Some CMO executives seem confident in their ability to shift quickly to Common Core assessments and align their curriculum, but many are also relying heavily on principals to experiment and determine best practices, which they can then spread to other principals and schools in the network. Other CMOs, however, feel that their internal standards already align well with or surpass the Common Core and are making only minor adjustments to prepare for the coming change of guard.

We interviewed principals who said, "Everything we do is tied to the Common Core right now . . . for us it's a priority." Other principals, however, say they are actively resisting the Common Core or just seem to be taking a minimalist approach, providing minimal training for teachers until the timeline for implementation of assessments gets closer.

One charter school principal in Colorado noted that she was able to receive good professional development in the district where she is located and from the Colorado League of Charter Schools, so she felt that she had "the best of both worlds." She didn't feel that she lacked support, but thinks that some charter schools—particularly rural schools—might struggle to get enough support just as rural district schools might. Another Colorado charter principal says he all but ignores standards because he is confident that his school's curriculum and program surpasses both current standards and the Common Core. He recognizes, however, that schools that are not as strongly anchored by their own vision will feel burdened by the change to the Common Core and will feel a need for extra supports.

Some schools are not taking advantage of the help that state CSOs are offering and will likely ignore the Common Core as long as possible. CSOs don't necessarily view their role as getting principals and teachers to pay attention. A challenge for state and local CSOs is to maintain open lines of communication with schools about what they need, while avoiding a paternalistic or directive role. One support organization leader wants to (but has not yet) put together a basic toolkit around the Common Core that charters can use when and how they like. Other than that, the organization was not sure what kinds of support schools want or need. In all, there seem to be some leaders and some laggards at the state charter school support level.

Part of the challenge for charter support organizations at the national and state levels is figuring out ways to provide workshops and coaching relevant to the wide variety of charter school models from Core Knowledge to Waldorf and everything in between. At the moment, most workshops provide basic information on deconstructing the new standards, understanding the assessments, and how to best deliver content aligned to the CCSS. Workshops vary in price and depth, ranging anywhere from free webinars and symposia to conferences spanning multiple days, costing $700 or more per person.

In many ways, this is the charter sector's first major attempt to provide widespread teaching and learning supports, an area that has generally been considered something that schools themselves should take care of. Authorizers and support organizations walk a fine line—in some ways they assume the role of a district, providing administrative support to schools with limited staff and capacity. However, they differ from districts in that they should allow charter schools make their own decisions for their unique set of students.

The charter sector faces a new challenge as the support infrastructure determines whether and how to best provide access to teaching supports without falling back on the generic district workshop models that they eschew.

MOVING FORWARD

Before specific test score items are released and states move forward with new supports and requirements, people see what they want to see. Right now, thought leaders in the charter sector exude both irrational exuberance for the Common Core and a vague paranoia, as well as a variety of legitimate hopes and concerns. What is clear is that their defining attributes (e.g., autonomy, flexibility, and accountability) position charter schools well to take advantage of the opportunity the Common Core presents.

Charter schools have the flexibility to be early adopters or originators of new technology-based instructional supports, the nimbleness to adapt quickly and reallocate resources, and the ability to take innovations to scale by opening new schools with similar models. Charters stand ready to take advantage of the opportunity for scaling up effective practices that common standards make possible. The ease of comparing schools across state lines provides an opportunity for funders, aspiring CMOs, and researchers to demonstrate and learn how different designs work in different contexts and to track what kinds of innovations charter schools invent in response to the Common Core opportunity.

There is a lot of good will, optimism, and even enthusiasm for the potential for CCSS to increase the rigor of schooling and to create college-going expectations. CMOs that built their reputation on closing the achievement gap readily admit that the deeper instruction the Common Core demands will be a welcome way for them to improve student outcomes. Charter leaders could strategically leverage enthusiastic supporters with strong track records to help skeptics understand the opportunity the Common Core represents for student success.

At the same time, there are also important vulnerabilities (also owing to their autonomy and disconnectedness to the status quo) with which the charter sector has not yet fully come to terms. The first is that there is likely a significant portion of charter schools that are not at all plugged in to a high-quality support network to help them prepare. There is also a significant portion that may actively resist or postpone using available supports. If these schools continue to ignore the Common Core, they may not fare well on the state exams. Second, if, as some fear, early test score analyses don't take growth or student demographics into account, the charter movement could lose political ground and be forced to exert valuable resources on damage control and correcting misconceptions. Third, it will cause headaches for authorizers trying to hold charter schools accountable for results if the schools can assert they did not have time to prepare for the Common Core and therefore cannot be held accountable.

State and national groups should also play an active role in creating and supporting implementation via online resources and networks to make sure that charters are as prepared as possible for the first rounds of testing. The worst possible scenario is for the charter sector to appear unprepared (or less prepared than district schools) for Common Core implementation, especially given the reputation for "high quality" that many in the sector have worked to achieve. The charter community could, in fact, make a concerted effort to prove that it is innovative, not just around school design, but also around supports for school improvement. It could lead the field in responding to schools' requests for specific kinds of professional development and collaboration without dictating solutions, promoting high-tech curricula options, and developing a national platform to help school leaders be wise consumers of online Common Core–aligned curricula.

A good start would be for national charter support organizations to begin to identify the best state association implementation resources in the country and see if they can be scaled nationally or adopted in other states. As is the case in New York City, the charter sector would also do well to look for opportunities to collaborate with districts or district schools to share effective strategies and tools.

To avoid unfair comparisons of charters and traditional public school performance, charter advocates should preemptively commission high-quality research that analyzes charter school performance on Common Core assessments, taking student demographics into account. Charter school authorizers should also begin discussions now with schools under their purview to determine how accountability agreements will be adjusted with the new standards and assessments.

Some of the resistance to the Common Core is rooted in the fear that Common Core implementation will lead to intentional or de facto infringement on charter school autonomies. In fact, even many strong supporters of the Common Core and some of the most promising school providers hold this concern. If state assessments are too rigidly tied to particular course progressions and grade levels, Common Core may make it impossible for some of the most innovative blended learning models to demonstrate whether mastery-based or game-based assessments can improve outcomes for students. Others fear that the test will simply not be as rigorous as the standards, and that states will play with cut scores. Guidelines for how CCSS could be deployed in states might help allay these fears, especially if they were accompanied by some watchdog efforts and creative proposals for waivers from grade-specific exams. This is something that the National Alliance for Public Charter Schools could take on effectively in tandem with state associations. Such efforts could proactively spell out the distinction between standards and curriculum and give examples of what appropriate and inappropriate implementation might look like.

Of course, no amount of preparation internal to the charter sector has the ability to prevent states from doing the things that many charter leaders fear will happen: backing off of high standards by decreasing cut scores, and holding schools accountable for results on new assessments before teachers and schools have had an adequate opportunity to adjust their practice to the new standards and tests. Although those we interviewed did not raise it, another looming issue is the need for strong teacher preparation programs to help teachers impart the higher order thinking skills prioritized in the Common Core, while still being able to maintain classroom order and remediate basic skills in the high-poverty urban neighborhoods that many charter schools serve.

Representatives from the charter sector would be wise to stay actively involved in all of these policy and implementation discussions to demonstrate leadership and to be involved in key decisions.

In the end, the Common Core is a set of aspirations tied to a wave of implementation and policy changes that would allow those aspirations to be realized. There have been similar sets of aspirations in the past that produced very little in the way of improved student outcomes. Standards—even great standards—in and of themselves cannot create better teachers or get more students to excel in college.[7] Any good they can do depends entirely on what people in schools and the people who support and oversee schools do to respond to the opportunity. The charter sector can play a powerful role in driving the necessary changes that will result in better outcomes, but only pockets of the charter sector are currently positioning themselves to do so. What's more, too few charter leaders are playing watchdog to make sure that the very autonomies that ought to position charter schools to craft creative curriculum designs in response to the aspirations of the Common Core are not undermined by overzealous and overly prescriptive state implementation requirements. We hope the ideas presented here can be a jumping-off point for a set of discussions and actions to change that.

NOTES

1.   Darling-Hammond, L. (2010/11, Winter). Soaring systems: High flyers all have equitable funding, shared curriculum, and quality teaching. *The American Educator, 34*(4), 20–24; Johnson, F. (2012, February 29). Common Core's good, bad, and ugly [Web log post]. *National Journal.* Retrieved from http://education. nationaljournal.com/2012/02/common-cores-good-bad-and-ugly.php#2170794; Banchero, S. (2012, May 8). School standards pushback. *Wall Street Journal.*

2.   Hill, P. T., & Lake, R. J. (2002). *Charter schools and accountability in public education.* Washington, DC: Brookings Institution Press.

3.   We anonymously quote and paraphrase the opinions of the individuals we interviewed throughout the chapter.

4. Throughout this chapter we use phrases like "opinion leaders" and "leaders in the charter sector" to refer to the broad set of individuals with whom we communicated. Our interviews and surveys included leaders of major CMOs, charter school association leaders, technical assistance providers, and charter school principals. Together, these actors have substantial influence over the direction of the charter movement.

5. Rud, A. G., & Zeichner, K. (2012, December 11). How to get Washington's charter schools to work. *Seattle Times*.

6. The Colorado League of Charter Schools. (2011). *Core knowledge alignment to the new revised Colorado content standards.* Retrieved from https://www.coloradoleague.org/uploaded-files/Core-Knowledge-Alignment-2011.pdf

7. Loveless, T. (2012). The 2012 Brown Center report on American education. *Brown Center on Education Policy at Brookings, 3*(1).

CHAPTER 5

Accountability: A Story of Opportunities and Challenges

Deven Carlson

THE EDUCATION COMMUNITY currently faces the reality of integrating the Common Core State Standards—the latest large-scale education reform initiative—with existing policies, many of which had themselves been the *reform du jour* in earlier years. Among the most prominent of these existing policies is school accountability. Effectively nonexistent only 25 years ago, today all 50 states have implemented policies that sanction—and, more recently, reward—public schools and districts based on their standardized test scores, test participation rates, attendance levels, and graduation rates, among other metrics.

These accountability systems first began to appear in the early 1990s. By 2001, the year that No Child Left Behind (NCLB) was passed by Congress, 30 states had implemented some sort of school accountability policy.[1] The passage of NCLB immediately elevated accountability from a state-level agenda item to a national reform initiative. Among other features of the law, NCLB required all 50 states as well as the District of Columbia and Puerto Rico to implement high-stakes accountability systems by the 2003–04 school year.

Multiple studies have concluded that accountability has been somewhat successful in raising standardized test scores, but most observers agree that accountability is the latest in a long line of reforms to fail to live up to initial expectations and promise.[2] Indeed, as accountability has matured beyond infanthood and into adolescence and middle age, its imperfections have become increasingly clear. Existing accountability systems have been criticized on a number of grounds, including that they rely on low-quality assessments, narrow the curriculum, and employ methods that fail to separate school effectiveness from the characteristics of students attending the school. Consequently, enthusiastic support for the reform has given way to calls for creating "smarter" accountability systems.

The process of integrating the Common Core Standards with existing state accountability systems will undoubtedly give rise to a number of challenges, but it will also present several opportunities. Policy makers' responses to these challenges and opportunities will play a significant role in determining the eventual success or failure of the Common Core reform effort. This chapter identifies and discusses four major accountability-related issues that policy makers will confront as they work to implement the Common Core Standards. Specifically, the discussion to follow will focus on (1) aligning the Common Core Standards with the content of the associated standardized tests; (2) redefining proficiency in terms of the Common Core Standards; (3) the opportunity for increased comparability across states; and (4) how the NCLB waivers issued by the U.S. Department of Education affect the relationship between the Common Core Standards and accountability systems.

ENSURING ALIGNMENT OF STANDARDS WITH TESTS

State accountability systems vary widely in their design, but they all incorporate standardized test results to one degree or another. As this is unlikely to change in light of Common Core implementation, it is important to ensure that the new tests used to assess students' mastery of the Common Core Standards are well aligned to the standards. Put another way, the tests need to provide a valid and reliable measure of whether students possess the knowledge and skills that the standards say they should.

Although this point may seem obvious, past experience with state accountability systems has demonstrated that achieving high levels of alignment between standards and tests can be a challenging task. Moreover, there are reasons to believe that these challenges may be exacerbated in the context of the Common Core Standards. For one thing, the Common Core Standards are not in any way designed to dictate the content that teachers should teach or the manner in which content is taught.[3] Rather, they are solely intended to identify the body of knowledge and skills that students need to be successful in the modern economy. If this is the case, then the tests used to assess students' mastery of the Common Core Standards should reflect this; it must be possible—within reasonable limitations—for students receiving a variety of content through any of several instructional techniques to perform equally well on the assessments.

Historically, standardized tests underlying state accountability systems have not rewarded variable content and multiple instructional techniques;

school and district officials are fully aware of the specific content—and the particular instructional strategies used to deliver that content—that is likely to maximize scores on assessments. This is evidenced by the intense test preparation sessions that many schools and districts employ in the weeks leading up to administration of the state assessments. Critics of both these test preparation sessions and standardized testing more generally have expressed concerns that this content and these instructional strategies differ from those that would maximize students' long-term success in life. This perceived disconnect is at least partially responsible for the negative perception of "teaching to the test."

There are two primary conditions that would need to be met in order for "teaching to the test" to be viewed positively. First, we would need to identify—and reach consensus on—the body of knowledge and skills that are necessary for students to achieve outcomes we deem important. Second, tests would have to provide a valid and reliable assessment of students' mastery of these standards and would need to be designed in a manner such that they do not privilege any specific content or instructional practices. If these two conditions were met, then teaching to the test would be a good thing. In fact, under this scenario, teaching to the test would likely be considered synonymous with high-quality teaching.

The first condition has been achieved. The Common Core Standards represent the most visible effort to identify this body of knowledge and skills, and their widespread adoption suggests there is broad political consensus on the content of the standards. However, it remains to be seen whether this second condition will be met. The responsibility for developing the requisite high-quality assessments was intended to reside primarily with the two assessment consortia—the Smarter Balanced Assessment Consortium (SBAC) and the Partnership for Assessment of Readiness for College and Careers (PARCC)—that were created using federal Race to the Top dollars and charged with developing "second-generation assessments" for the Common Core Standards.[4]

Although the two consortia are designed to be primarily responsible for the overall character of the assessments, they will contract with private test vendors to develop specific test questions. To illustrate what these second-generation assessments might look like, SBAC and PARCC released sample items to testing vendors and other stakeholders in the summer of 2012. These sample items provide some encouraging signs for the quality of the second-generation assessments that will accompany the Common Core Standards. In response to the sample items, a former state assessment director was reported by *Education Week* as stating, "These are very high-level kinds of tasks that students are going to be asked to do. It is significant that all kids are being asked to do this sort of thing."[5] Such reactions are indicative of the general agreement that the sample items move beyond current assessments and require students to possess significantly more depth of understanding and substantially greater subject knowledge. For example, a sample mathematics item for fifth-grade students released by SBAC shows a video of five swimmers competing in a race and presents each swimmer's time, rounded to the nearest hundredth of a second. The item then asks the student to describe how the results of the race would change if the race relied on a clock that rounded results to the nearest tenth of a second. The correct answer is that there would have been a three-way tie for first place and a two-way tie for fourth place. Such an item compares favorably to multiple-choice tests today, in which students would likely be asked to determine the number of swimmers that would have tied for first place if the race clock rounded results to the nearest tenth of a second.[6]

In a blow to the optimism of the previous paragraph, it is important to acknowledge that, by relying on items requiring greater subject knowledge and depth of understanding, the second-generation assessments will also place greater demands on test vendors. The current tests underlying accountability systems do not require vendors to develop very complex items. It remains to be seen how successful vendors will be at adapting their practices to align with what the assessment consortia envision.

ACCELERATED TIMELINE AND OTHER HURDLES

The task outlined above will be made even more difficult by the accelerated timeline for development and implementation of the assessments underlying the Common Core Standards. The two assessment consortia were developed during the 2010–11 school year, and full implementation of the assessments is scheduled for the 2014–15 school year. This would be an aggressive timeline for developing, field-testing, and implementing a "current-generation" assessment, to say nothing of an assessment as novel and innovative as what they are intending to develop. In addition to the new item paradigm discussed above, the second-generation assessments are also designed to utilize computer adaptive testing (CAT). Under a CAT approach, which is used for the GRE and other assessments, the specific test questions that students see are partially determined by their responses to previous questions. As a stylized example, if students answer a question correctly, then they will next see a more difficult question. If they answer it incorrectly, then they will see a less difficult question.

Transitioning to a CAT approach is likely to produce two major challenges. First, it is unclear how well the assessment consortia and the associated test vendors will be able to integrate second-generation assessment items into a CAT approach. On their face, complex assessment items and CAT do not seem to be naturally compatible. Complex assessment items often require students to construct a response, as opposed to simply selecting the answer from a list of choices. Whether these constructed responses can be graded in a valid and reliable manner within a CAT context remains unclear. Second, there will be logistical challenges related to assessment administration that need to be addressed. Many districts currently administer all accountability-related assessments using pencil-and-paper tests. Assessments administered through a CAT approach will require technological infrastructure and resources that many districts simply do not currently possess.

Moreover, the two consortia are completely funded by federal grants that expire in 2014. Looking ahead, it is not clear how these expensive endeavors will be financed after their respective grants expire. SBAC has assembled a Sustainability Task Force to develop recommendations for maintaining the consortium in a manner that allows states to continue procuring and maintaining their assessment systems, but there is little certainty about the structure, or even the existence, of these entities going forward.

If all aspects of the assessments intended to accompany the Common Core Standards work entirely as designed, it seems likely that they will completely revolutionize test-based accountability. However, this is not the first time that we have been promised "new and improved" assessments, and most people would agree that these previous promises have been largely unfulfilled. Although we hope this time will be different, the manner in which policy makers and practitioners respond to forthcoming challenges will be a crucial determinant of the extent to which these second-generation assessments achieve their promise. Indeed, past experience in many policy domains has demonstrated that the ultimate success or failure of a policy is largely determined by the quality of its implementation.[7]

DEFINING PROFICIENCY LEVELS

Regardless of the quality of the assessments that ultimately accompany the Common Core Standards, states will be faced with the task of setting proficiency levels (*Basic, Proficient, College and Career Ready,* or any other label they want to attach to a specific level of test performance) on those assessments. This process is a small part science, a small part art, and a large part politics. The scientific part of the process comes from the reliance on experts in determining the specific level of test performance that corresponds to a particular level of mastery of a body of knowledge and skills. These experts generally employ well-validated and systematic methods to help reach these determinations, but there is also an undeniable element of subjectivity and judgment in the process—this is the artistic element. Indeed, even the most systematic and expert-driven approach to setting proficiency levels does not definitively identify a single scale score that corresponds to a level mastery of knowledge and skills that renders a student *Proficient* or *Advanced*. Instead, such an approach typically generates a range of scale scores that could serve as valid cut points, and experts must then use their experience and judgment to identify the precise scale score to serve as the cut point.

For better or worse, policy makers never rely solely on expert analysis when making policy-related decisions. Indeed, political considerations play an important role in almost every policy decision, and the process setting of proficiency levels is no exception. In general, there are two competing constituencies pressuring policy makers responsible for setting proficiency levels.

On one side, there are individuals and groups that see this process as an opportunity to impose aggressive and rigorous expectations for the levels of knowledge and skills that students should possess. These groups generally argue that U.S. students need to be equipped with high-level math, science, and reading skills in order to compete and succeed in the 21st-century economy. They often cite the National Assessment of Educational Progress (NAEP) as an example of a high-quality and respected assessment that successfully employs a rigorous definition in which only 30–40% of students are deemed proficient.[8] Such individuals and groups often look to Massachusetts as a model—it has challenging standards and equally rigorous proficiency thresholds.

Other individuals and groups are more skeptical of setting rigorous proficiency levels such as those used by NAEP. The objections against NAEP-like proficiency levels are grounded in three main types of arguments—technical, comparative, and political—although the lines separating these argument types are blurry at times. Many of the technical arguments trace their origins to a National Academy of Sciences (NAS) evaluation conducted in the 1990s that concluded the process for setting NAEP achievement levels was "fundamentally flawed" and listed several technical arguments in support of this conclusion.[9] The comparative arguments typically rely on studies such as a comparison of the 1999 TIMSS administration and the 2000 NAEP administration. This study found that in only the two highest scoring countries—Chinese Taipei and Singapore—would the average student score at a level deemed proficient under the NAEP science assessment.

The general logic underlying political arguments holds that, because of their unrealistic nature, setting proficiency thresholds similar to NAEP's is ultimately counterproductive. Critics argue that the inability to achieve the proficiency thresholds will contribute to the development of a culture permeated by a perception of failure, and often cite how NCLB's measure of Adequate Yearly Progress (AYP) lost nearly all credibility because of its unrealistic goal of 100% of students achieving proficiency in math and reading by 2013–14.

There are two potential negative effects when such classifications are imposed on schools that are widely perceived as being high-quality and successful in nature. First, a classification of "failure" may negatively impact the culture of a school that previously—and perhaps accurately—perceived itself as being successful. Second, classifying well-regarded schools as "failures" may bring the credibility of the policy that imposes the label into question. To illustrate this point, imagine a suburban school district that has historically prided itself on the quality of its schools. How would parents, teachers, and other stakeholders react if 60 or 70% of students in the district were suddenly deemed to not be proficient in math or reading? It is more likely that there would be an outcry about the policy than the quality of schooling in the district.

Of course, supporters of rigorous proficiency levels could argue that NAEP has been operated under rigorous proficiency thresholds for 2 decades and never experienced a level of blowback. However, this can be primarily attributable to the fact that NAEP has never had any significant stakes attached. Once high stakes are attached to an assessment—as they would be under an assessment used for accountability purposes—the whole game changes.

When it comes to setting proficiency thresholds on the assessments accompanying the Common Core Standards, policy makers will be forced to walk a tightrope. On one hand, they have to set the thresholds at a high-enough level to ensure that they cannot be criticized for failing to support educational reform or for promoting the "soft bigotry of low expectations." Such political pressures are very real and are illustrated by comments made by Joanne Weiss, who is the chief of staff for U.S. secretary of education Arne Duncan. In reference to an August 2011 study on the rigor of state proficiency thresholds, Weiss was quoted by *Education Week* as saying that "low expectations are the norm in way too many states in the country."[10] She continues, noting that allowing states to determine their own proficiency thresholds is "lying to parents, lying to children, lying to teachers and principals about the work they are doing." In response to this sort of pressure, several states—including Wisconsin, Oklahoma, and Mississippi—raised their proficiency thresholds in recent years.

On the other hand, policy makers will be pressured not to set thresholds so high that they are effectively unattainable, as doing so may undermine the validity of a policy and generate political pressure for change, pressures to which policy makers may respond. South Carolina, for example, had historically been recognized as having some of the most rigorous proficiency standards, but state policy makers ratcheted down proficiency thresholds in the late 2000s in response to pressure generated by the high proportion of students classified as nonproficient. States' previous experience with setting proficiency levels can lend some useful insight into the set of potential resolutions. As is the case in many policy areas, past is prologue.

LEARNING FROM PAST EXPERIENCES

Implementation of the Common Core Standards will not be the first time that states have been confronted with the task of setting proficiency levels for assessments to be used for accountability purposes. Indeed, states were faced with a very similar task when they were required to define the proficiency levels for the tests underlying the accountability systems mandated by NCLB. The law set a target of all students being classified as *proficient* by the 2013–14 school year, but it granted states full discretion over both the assessment they would use to measure proficiency as well as the proficiency threshold.

There are two primary lessons that we have learned from states' go-round. First, we know that states—when left to their own devices—will produce substantial variance in the rigor of their proficiency thresholds. Currently, the variance in proficiency thresholds across states is somewhat masked by the fact that states use different assessments that are scored on different scales. However, a series of studies by the National Center for Education Statistics (NCES) has endeavored to provide cross-state comparability in proficiency thresholds, taking advantage of the fact that the NAEP is administered in all 50 states. Using the results of these two assessments, the authors employ well-validated techniques to estimate the NAEP scale score that corresponds to the threshold for the *Proficient* level for each of the 50 states and the District of Columbia.

The variance in states' proficiency thresholds is illustrated by Table 5.1. As an example of the variation, consider the proficiency thresholds set by Tennessee and Massachusetts in fourth-grade reading; these two states had the lowest and highest respective proficiency thresholds at the time the study was conducted. Table 5.1 demonstrates that a student in Tennessee only needed to earn a score equivalent to a 170 on the NAEP scale in order to be deemed proficient. In Massachusetts, on the other hand, a student needed to earn a score equivalent to a 234 on the NAEP scale to be considered proficient. It is useful to think of this 64-point difference in standard deviations (the proficiency threshold in Massachusetts is over 1.8 standard deviations higher than in Tennessee) or percentile terms. In Tennessee, a student could earn a score equivalent to about the 8th percentile of all students who took the fourth-grade NAEP reading assessment in 2009 and be considered proficient, while a student in Massachusetts would need to earn a score equivalent to approximately the 65th percentile of all students who took the fourth-grade NAEP reading assessment in 2009 to receive the same proficiency designation. Any way you characterize it, the difference in proficiency thresholds across these two states is immense.

The second lesson emerging from states' initial experiences with setting proficiency thresholds is that proficiency is a fluid concept—at least in terms

TABLE 5.1. Estimated NAEP Scale Equivalent Scores for State Proficiency Standards, by Grade, Subject, and State: 2009

State	Grade 4		Grade 8	
	Reading	*Math*	*Reading*	*Math*
Alabama	179	207	234	246
Alaska	183	218	231	268
Arizona	193	212	241	266
Arkansas	200	216	241	267
California	202	220	259	–
Colorado	183	202	228	256
Connecticut	208	214	243	251
Delaware	199	220	236	269
District of Columbia	205	217	244	258
Florida	206	225	262	266
Georgia	178	218	209	247
Hawaii	203	239	241	286
Idaho	186	213	218	261
Illinois	198	207	234	251
Indiana	203	229	255	273
Iowa	194	221	248	263
Kansas	186	217	236	265
Kentucky	205	223	253	273
Louisiana	192	221	243	263
Maine	207	234	253	284
Maryland	187	208	237	271
Massachusetts	234	255	249	300
Michigan	194	200	236	253
Minnesota	204	233	259	287
Mississippi	210	223	254	264
Missouri	229	246	267	287
Montana	198	235	246	285
Nebraska	Not available			
Nevada	202	225	246	269
New Hampshire	211	237	256	281
New Jersey	221	231	244	272
New Mexico	207	236	246	277
New York	200	207	247	249
North Carolina	204	220	246	253
North Dakota	203	225	253	278
Ohio	192	219	251	265

TABLE 5.1. Estimated NAEP Scale Equivalent Scores for State Proficiency Standards, by Grade, Subject, and State: 2009, Continued

State	Grade 4		Grade 8	
	Reading	Math	Reading	Math
Oklahoma	211	228	249	269
Oregon	177	214	250	266
Pennsylvania	206	218	245	272
Rhode Island	209	231	252	275
South Carolina	194	215	245	270
South Dakota	199	224	254	271
Tennessee	170	195	211	229
Texas	188	214	201	254
Utah	196	225	235	275
Vermont	214	236	259	282
Virginia	186	213	229	251
Washington	205	243	253	288
West Virginia	206	225	249	270
Wisconsin	189	219	232	262
Wyoming	208	226	259	278

Source: Bandeira de Mello, V. (2011). *Mapping State Proficiency Standards Onto the NAEP Scales: Variation and Change in State Standards for Reading and Mathematics, 2005–2009* (NCES 2011-458). National Center for Education Statistics, Institute of Education Sciences, U.S. Department of Education, Washington, DC: Government Printing Office.

of measurement. Table 5.2 presents the change from 2007 to 2009 in the estimated NAEP scale score corresponding to the proficiency threshold on states' fourth- and eighth-grade math and reading assessments. The table demonstrates that most states exhibited very little change in the estimated NAEP scale score corresponding to proficiency thresholds. A few states, however, exhibited dramatic changes from 2007 to 2009 in the estimated NAEP score corresponding to the proficiency threshold, typically in response to the pressures described previously. For example, in South Carolina the proficiency threshold dropped by the equivalent of nearly 30 points in fourth-grade math and reading between 2007 and 2009; the declines in eighth-grade proficiency thresholds were even larger in the state. On the other end of the spectrum, states such as Oklahoma and Mississippi significantly increased their fourth-grade proficiency thresholds between 2007 and 2009, particularly in reading.

So what does this discussion imply for Common Core implementation? At a basic level, it seems safe to say that the process of setting proficiency thresholds will be a contentious one. All states will face the competing pres-

TABLE 5.2. Estimated Change in NAEP Scale Equivalent Scores for State Proficiency Standards, by Grade, Subject, and State: 2007–2009

State	Grade 4		Grade 8	
	Reading	Math	Reading	Math
Alabama	0.2	1.3	0.0	-6.7
Alaska	-0.5	1.3	-1.7	3.3
Arizona	-4.7	-1.2	-3.9	-1.7
Arkansas	-13.1	-12.8	-7.7	-9.5
California	-8.1	-5.1	-2.9	–
Colorado	-3.7	0.8	-2.1	-2.7
Connecticut	-5.2	-6.4	-2.0	-1.1
Delaware	-3.8	-4.9	-3.3	-3.3
District of Columbia	Not available			
Florida	-2.8	-4.9	0.1	-0.6
Georgia	-7.1	4.5	-6.9	4.0
Hawaii	-8.8	1.1	-3.3	-8.0
Idaho	-10.7	-4.7	-14.5	-3.5
Illinois	-1.5	-0.8	-1.9	0.4
Indiana	4.0	1.6	4.1	6.7
Iowa	-4.5	1.3	-3.7	-1.4
Kansas	-5.8	-1.6	-4.9	-5.2
Kentucky	0.3	-5.8	1.6	-5.8
Louisiana	-0.8	-2.0	-3.2	-3.9
Maine	-6.4	-1.5	-8.4	-1.6
Maryland	1.4	1.3	-12.5	-6.8
Massachusetts	1.9	0.6	-3.1	-2.2
Michigan	16.0	-3.9	-1.8	-7.3
Minnesota	-11.1	-4.9	-5.9	0.8
Mississippi	46.5	18.5	3.4	1.5
Missouri	1.9	0.6	-4.7	-1.7
Montana	-5.0	0.8	-4.4	3.4
Nebraska	Not available			
Nevada	-4.6	1.6	-1.7	2.4
New Hampshire	0.6	-2.4	-2.1	-1.2
New Jersey	19.9	11.1	-8.1	-0.2
New Mexico	-2.7	3.6	-2.5	-8.3
New York	-9.2	-11.9	-12.6	-23.5
North Carolina	21.8	-10.9	29.3	-17.0
North Dakota	1.3	-0.6	2.3	-0.6
Ohio	-6.2	-5.2	11.6	0.3

TABLE 5.2. Estimated Change in NAEP Scale Equivalent Scores for State Proficiency Standards, by Grade, Subject, and State: 2007–2009, Continued

State	Grade 4		Grade 8	
	Reading	Math	Reading	Math
Oklahoma	39.6	14.7	16.8	19.8
Oregon	-8.2	-6.4	-0.7	3.5
Pennsylvania	-5.5	-5.2	-0.4	0.9
Rhode Island	-1.3	-4.4	-1.5	-4.2
South Carolina	-28.9	-29.8	-36.3	-42.4
South Dakota	13.4	-0.2	5.4	0.8
Tennessee	-4.3	-2.7	0.0	-5.3
Texas	0.9	-2.6	-21.0	-13.8
Utah	-1.2	1.7	0.8	19.2
Vermont	-0.1	-3.4	-4.6	-1.4
Virginia	-5.1	-6.4	-10.0	-7.7
Washington	2.6	3.6	0.0	2.2
West Virginia	24.2	8.6	20.4	16.5
Wisconsin	-3.9	-3.7	1.7	-0.3
Wyoming	3.6	9.4	12.1	-1.5

Source: Bandeira de Mello, V. (2011). Mapping State Proficiency Standards Onto the NAEP Scales: Variation and Change in State Standards for Reading and Mathematics, 2005–2009 (NCES 2011-458). National Center for Education Statistics, Institute of Education Sciences, U.S. Department of Education, Washington, DC: Government Printing Office.

sures outlined above, and will be predisposed to resolve these tensions in different manners. Policy makers sought to address this challenge by including a provision in the grants underwriting the SBAC and PARCC assessment consortia requiring all member states to reach consensus on the assessments' proficiency thresholds. Whether such agreement will come to pass remains very much an open question. It is certainly possible that all states in each of the two assessment consortia will reach agreement on rigorous thresholds that truly indicate whether a student will be "college and career ready." However, it is also possible that states will be unable to reach consensus on rigorous thresholds. As a result, some states may exit the assessment consortia—as Utah and Alabama have already done for different reasons—but it is perhaps more likely that states will agree on a proficiency threshold less demanding than that employed by NAEP, and thus less rigorous than many initially desired. Such an outcome could satisfy all relevant requirements while minimizing the political blowback resulting from large numbers of nonproficient students.

A second major implication of this discussion involves the evolution of proficiency thresholds. Indeed, the initial thresholds set by SBAC and PARCC member states are unlikely to be permanent. Moreover, the sole formal mechanism driving SBAC and PARCC member states to agree on common proficiency thresholds could effectively disappear when the federal grants underwriting the assessment consortia expire in 2014. SBAC and PARCC member states could act strategically by initially setting somewhat "low" proficiency thresholds and slowly raising them over time in response to mounting political pressures. Such a strategy would minimize the initial political blowback that could stem from heightened failure rates, while allowing the consortia to appear proactive as they increase the proficiency thresholds over time. Of course, this strategy would also undermine the stated goal of having the thresholds represent what it truly means to be *Proficient* or *College and Career Ready*, but this would certainly not be the first time that operative proficiency thresholds failed to correspond to the intended level of knowledge and skills. Much uncertainty remains, but it is clear that a good deal of hard work on the part of state policy makers, the assessment consortia, and educators will be required to resolve these difficult and contentious issues in a manner that allows the Common Core Standards to succeed.

COMPARABILITY ACROSS STATES

Our governmental structure and historical development has produced strong support for local control of education throughout the United States. This reality represents a substantial hurdle that supporters of more uniform education policy—such as the Common Core Standards—encounter in their reform efforts. NCLB navigated this hurdle by mandating that states implement school accountability systems, but allowed them a fair amount of discretion in determining the details of those systems. Consequently, school accountability in the United States is currently characterized by 50 distinct state systems—systems that are based on different standards for what students are expected to know and be able to do, different assessments that are scored on incomparable scales, and different proficiency thresholds, among other features.

Whether by design or accident, the variation in state accountability systems makes cross-state comparability quite difficult. This means that cross-state comparisons are made with relative infrequency. Indeed, comparisons in education—particularly those based on the outcomes of accountability systems or accountability-related assessments—are almost always within-state in nature. We routinely see urban student achievement compared to suburban student achievement within a single state, but we rarely see urban student achievement in one state compared to urban student achievement in another state. The comparative ease in making intrastate, relative to interstate, comparisons lends implicit support to—and also grew out of—the view that education is an issue best addressed at the state and local levels.

Moreover, this situation provides an incentive to make invalid cross-state comparisons. For example, individuals or groups who want to compare student achievement in two states will likely compare the percentage of students who score above the proficient level in the first state to the percentage of students who score above the proficient level in the second state. Specifically, policy makers may make cross-state comparisons to highlight the success of a policy they support, to demonstrate the need for additional resources, or any number of other reasons. Although the value of such a comparison ranges from, at best, meaningless, to at worst, counterproductive, it is almost inevitable that these comparisons will be made, primarily for political purposes.[11] Consequently, there is a reasonable argument to be made that—given the near inevitability of cross-state comparisons—future policy action should make an effort to facilitate valid comparisons.

Regardless of one's view on the value of cross-state comparisons and the ability—or lack thereof—to make them, it is undeniable that the Common Core Standards provide an opportunity for easier cross-state comparability. However, this may not translate to future cross-state comparability in terms of proficiency thresholds, sanctions, and other features of future accountability systems. As discussed in the previous section, there will be significant pressure on states to reach a common resolution on these issues, which will need to be reconciled with strong support for local control of education in many quarters of the United States. As a consequence of the uncertainty over the ultimate resolution of this issue, it is important to consider the implications of both potential scenarios: (1) cross-state consensus on all inputs to future accountability systems and (2) interstate differences with respect to any or all of these inputs.

The most visible consequence of states reaching a consensus on the specifications of their accountability systems and the inputs into those systems would undoubtedly be the ability to make simple, straightforward, and valid comparisons of student performance across states. It would become significantly easier to identify the states in which students are performing well and those in which they are performing poorly. NAEP currently provides meaningful evidence on this issue, but such interstate comparisons based on the Common Core assessments have the potential to have an even more powerful effect because the states will have identical standards of knowledge and skills. With NAEP-based comparisons, states can—and often do—reasonably argue that their lower scores are partially attributable to the fact that their standards are not as closely aligned with NAEP; such an argument would be invalid for comparisons based on the Common Core assessments.[12]

A related consequence of cross-state comparability is the potential for increased competition between states. States are generally quite sensitive to neighboring states' policy actions and outcomes; a significant number of studies in political science demonstrate that a state's consideration and adoption of a given policy is influenced by its geographic proximity to other states that have adopted that policy.[13] In the specific context of proficiency thresholds, Peterson and Hess (2008) note at least some degree of geographic similarity with respect to these thresholds—they conclude that northeastern states generally have the most rigorous thresholds, southern and midwestern states have the lowest, and western states fall somewhere in between.[14] The ability to make direct cross-state comparisons of student achievement has the potential to make policy makers more aware of how their state is performing in relation to others and—if they are performing poorly—spur them to make policy changes intended to improve educational outcomes.

This basic approach was used to encourage states to adopt the Common Core Standards. Specifically, Common Core proponents noted that Massachusetts had both rigorous standards and high NAEP scores, while many states with low standards had low NAEP scores. An example of this argument can be found in the Thomas B. Fordham Institute report, *The State of State Standards—and the Common Core—in 2010*. The report states:

> But when great standards are combined with smart implementation, policy makers can move mountains. That's the lesson we take from Massachusetts, with its commendable expectations, well-designed assessments. . . . It should surprise no one that the Bay State now tops the charts of the National Assessment of Educational Progress (NAEP) in reading and math in both fourth and eighth grades, or that it's posted solid gains for its neediest students.[15]

For better or worse, facts like these are used as evidence to support the argument that all states should adopt rigorous standards. This comparative argument in support of Common Core adoption was effective from a political standpoint. Similarly structured arguments would likely become more commonplace if the Common Core Standards are adopted and implemented in a manner that facilitates easier cross-state comparisons.

The polar opposite of a completely uniform set of state accountability systems is a scenario in which each state has a uniquely designed system. The consequences of such a scenario are fairly easy to predict because it is essentially the status quo. Such a scenario is characterized by limited cross-state comparability, a greater level of local control, and all of the consequences of these features that are discussed above.

Another possible outcome is cross-state adoption of the Common Core Standards, as well as the accompanying assessments—either SBAC or PARCC—and proficiency thresholds, but different rewards, sanctions, or other features of the accountability system. In fact, this might be the most likely outcome. In this case, states could operate under identical—or at least similar—standards and assessments, but administer different rewards and sanctions for a given performance level. For example, imagine a situation in which there are two schools that are identical in all respects—demographics, socioeconomic composition, achievement outcomes, and all other factors that matter for state accountability systems. If accountability systems develop in the way described above, there is a very real possibility that these two schools would face different sanctions or rewards for their (identical) performance, a difference based solely on the state in which the school is located. Perhaps even more illustrative of the potential sensitivity of this issue is a scenario where—for an identical level of teacher or principal performance—two jurisdictions reach different decisions with respect to hiring, firing, or salaries. Of course, schools and educators across states are not held to the same standards under the current system, but this fact is effectively masked by the difficulty of making valid cross-state comparisons.

The impending adoption of the Common Core Standards and related assessments would make this differential treatment quite transparent, thus making it likely to emerge as a point of contention. However, just because an issue is likely to become contentious does not mean that it is bad or should not be done. Indeed, the point here is not to argue that schools and educators should be held to the same standards in every state, but simply to flag the issue as one that would be likely to gain some publicity and to alert policy makers to the necessity of thoughtful engagement on the issue.

NCLB WAIVERS AND ESEA REAUTHORIZATION

Looming behind all of the issues discussed above is the possible reauthorization of the Elementary and Secondary Education Act (ESEA) or—what seems to be the more likely scenario—the continued issuance of waivers from the requirements of the law. NCLB was authorized for 5 years when it was signed into law in January 2002, and was scheduled for reauthorization in 2007. However, there has been minimal progress toward revising the law over the past 5 years.

The legislative paralysis, coupled with the continuously growing dissatisfaction with NCLB, contributed to the Obama administration's decision to take the unilateral—and highly controversial—action of inviting states to apply for waivers to specific components of NCLB. This invitation, which was announced in September 2011, was accompanied by the Department of Education's detailed application guidance that instructed states to develop (1) college- and career-ready expectations for all students; (2) a system of differentiated recognition, accountability, and support for schools and districts; and (3) a system to support effective instruction and leadership. At this point, the Department of Education has approved waivers for 40 states and the District of Columbia, and several other states have submitted applications and are awaiting word on their approval. Therefore, in a very real sense, the NCLB waivers represent a reauthorization of the law—one that emanates solely from the executive branch, rather than from the more conventional approach of the legislative and executive branches exercising their respective constitutional powers.

The Department of Education identified differentiated accountability as the overarching principle that should guide states in developing their accountability systems.[16] That is, the Department of Education wanted states to develop accountability systems where schools were not just classified as "failing" or "not failing"—the approach taken in NCLB—but systems with several different performance levels into which schools can be classified. Unlike NCLB, which classified schools based on reading and math scores, the waiver guidance encourages states to use several outcome measures, including graduation rates and progress toward closing achievement gaps. States have taken several approaches to developing differentiated accountability systems, but the two most common approaches are numerical indexes and A–F school grading systems.

So what are the implications of the NCLB waiver process for the development of future state accountability systems that will need to be integrated with the Common Core Standards? First, it has become clear that the Department of Education is encouraging states to propose rigorous and challenging proficiency thresholds in their waiver applications—thresholds comparable to those used by NAEP. As evidenced by the large number of waiver applications submitted, states are eager to gain release from the shackles of NCLB, and they are willing to take a wide variety of actions—including setting rigorous proficiency thresholds—to gain such release. In addition, this federal encouragement provides effective cover for state-level supporters of such proficiency definitions. For better or worse, arguments that begin with "The feds want . . ." or "ED (the Department of Education) says we have to . . ." are often powerful ones in state-level policy debates.[17] Overall, the incentive for states to set NAEP-like proficiency thresholds, coupled with the fact that the vast majority of states seem likely to soon be using one of two tests, has the potential to lead to significantly greater cross-state comparability—and all the associated opportunities and challenges discussed above—on Common Core–related assessments.

The fact that the NCLB waiver process seems likely to lead to greater cross-state assessment comparability does not necessarily imply that it is also likely to lead to greater cross-state comparability on accountability systems more generally. Although the waiver requirements are fairly prescriptive, they are not completely determinative; states are allowed some discretion in determining the specific inputs and design of their accountability systems. The Common Core assessments are clearly one required input, but states are free to identify others and this freedom is likely to reduce cross-state comparability. Further inhibition of cross-state comparability is likely to come from the fact that states have freedom to choose the metric they will use to differentiate schools. For example, some states have adopted A–F grading systems, while others have created a numeric index on which to score them. Clearly, these different metrics—coupled with potentially different inputs—complicate cross-state comparisons.

Taken as a whole, the NCLB waiver process encourages similarity in proficiency thresholds across states—an encouragement formalized in the terms of the grants funding the assessment consortia—but is likely to have little effect on the cross-state comparability of accountability systems more generally. Of course, it is important to recognize that the preceding discussion could be rendered wholly irrelevant if NCLB is formally reauthorized in the near future and the terms of that reauthorization differ from those that have been used in the waiver process. If reauthorization were to occur, the accountability provisions in the new law would govern the design of states' accountability systems, and the systems developed through the waiver process could instantly become invalid. It seems unlikely, though, that reauthorization would have any notable effects on the assessments accompanying the Common Core Standards. However, as noted above, there seems to be little likelihood of formal NCLB reauthorization occurring anytime in the near future.

CONCLUSION

To this point, the Common Core Standards have advanced as far as they have on the policy-making agenda because different constituencies and interest groups have reasonably been able to see and defend them in different ways. On one hand, supporters of more centralized education policy are enthusiastic about the fact that the Common Core Standards specify a single body of knowledge and skills that students in 45 states and the District of Columbia will be expected to possess, and they are willing to accept the fact that the Common Core Standards are not formal federal policy. On the other hand, individuals and groups generally supportive of local control of education have no principled opposition to rigorous standards and support the Common Core because their adoption and implementation can reasonably be viewed and defended as state-driven in nature.

The malleable view of the Common Core Standards has been instrumental because everyone can find political cover for their support of the Common Core. A reduction in this malleability seems imminent, however, as policy makers will soon be forced to make concrete choices regarding the standards that will have readily discernible impacts for educators, students, and other stakeholders. The nature of these choices will play a large role in determining the ultimate success or failure of the Common Core State Standards, in general, and their integration with existing accountability systems, in particular.

This chapter produces three main lessons for our understanding of the likely future of the Common Core Standards and their integration with state accountability systems. First, the discussion of proficiency thresholds—and the assessments more generally—suggests that interstate tensions are likely to arise relatively soon after Common Core implementation. Some of these tensions have already begun to develop and have manifested themselves through the 2012 state superintendent election results in Indiana and the withdrawal of Utah and Alabama from the assessment consortia. As discussed in greater detail below, the nature in which these early tensions are resolved will be very important to the Common Core's future. Second, because of the differences in states' educational cultures, disagreements are unlikely to go away over time. If anything, they are likely to become more pronounced. Maintaining the integrity of the Common Core Standards will require continued attention and effort. Third, educational cultures, like any type of culture, are difficult to change. It has taken more than 2 decades, but accountability systems—unlike the Common Core—have become part of the educational culture in the United States. This implies that any conflict between accountability systems and the Common Core Standards is likely to be resolved in favor of maintaining accountability systems.

Given these lessons, there are two major actions that policy makers and practitioners can take to facilitate successful implementation of the Common Core Standards and their integration with accountability systems. First, policy makers should recognize that they are not likely to be successful in changing state educational cultures in the short term, and should instead resolve to maximize the reform's effectiveness within the constraints of existing state educational cultures. In practice, this likely means devolving Common Core–related decisions—including those regarding accountability systems—to the lowest possible level without undermining the intent of the reform effort. It is important to recognize that the optimal level for making these decisions will vary according to the issue at hand. For example, given the conditions of the grants underwriting the assessment consortia, decisions regarding proficiency thresholds should probably be made at that level, at least initially. In contrast, the design of accountability systems is best left to the states, while curricular decisions should occur at the district, or even school level. This will clearly be a delicate balancing act, but it is imperative to achieve that balance if the Common Core is to be successful. Second, when interstate differences arise over the direction of the Common Core—as they surely will—policy makers should not just reach a superficial solution to the issue. Rather, they should attempt to address the underlying structural causes of the difference. This could take several forms. For example, if there were disputes among states within an assessment consortia over proficiency thresholds, policy makers could seek to rearrange the assessment consortia to make them more homogenous with respect to educational culture. As currently constituted, there seems to be little rhyme or reason to which states are members of each assessment consortia. Similarly, with respect to issues that may arise because of cross-state comparability, policy makers could permit states to design their own accountability systems—and even set their own proficiency thresholds—but develop a system that, given this diversity, facilitates the types of cross-state comparisons that scholars, policy makers, and educators might value. Failure to address underlying structural causes will simply ensure that the issue will arise again in the future, most likely in an even more difficult and menacing manner.

The extent to which policy makers are able to take advantage of the opportunities and successfully navigate the challenges when integrating the Common Core with state accountability systems will help resolve whether the relationship between these two reforms is one of synergy or friction. The nature of the relationship will be partially determinative of whether we move the quality of education in the country forward or whether these reform efforts—like so many previous ones—simply fizzle out.

NOTES

1. For a table specifying the year in which states adopted their accountability policy and summarizing other scholars' perceptions of the strength of the accountability program in each state, see Dee, T. S., & Jacob, B. (2011, Summer). The impact of No Child Left Behind on student achievement. *Journal of Policy Analysis and Management, 30*(3), 418–446.

2. Dee & Jacob, The impact of No Child Left Behind; Hanushek, E. A., & Raymond, M. E. (2005). Does school accountability lead to improved student performance? *Journal of Policy Analysis and Management, 24*(2), 297–327; Camoy, M., & Loeb, S. (2002, Winter). Does external accountability affect student outcomes? A cross-state analysis. *Journal of Educational Evaluation and Policy Analysis, 24*(4), 305–331; Tyack, D., & Cuban, L. (1995). *Tinkering toward utopia: A century of public school reform.* Cambridge, MA: Harvard University Press.

3. Common Core State Standards Initiative. (2012). *Frequently asked questions.* Retrieved from http://www.corestandards.org/resources/frequently-asked-questions

4. Presently, 25 states are members of the SBAC while 11 states and the District of Columbia are members of PARCC.

5. Gewertz, C. (2012, August 22). Consortia provide preview of common assessments. *Education Week.*

6.   Additional sample assessment items can be found on the SBAC website (http://www.smarterbalanced.org/sample-items-and-performance-tasks/) and the PARCC website (http://www.parcconline.org/samples/item-task-prototypes).

7.   Pressman, J. L., & Wildavsky, A. (1984). *Implementation: How great expectations in Washington are dashed in Oakland; or, why it's amazing that federal programs work at all this being a saga of the Economic Development Administration as told by two sympathetic observers who seek to build morals on a foundation of ruined hopes* (3rd ed.). Berkeley: University of California Press; Bloom, H. S., Hill, C. J., & Riccio, J. A. (2003). Linking program implementation and effectiveness: Lessons from a pooled sample of welfare-to-work experiments. *Journal of Policy Analysis and Management, 22*(4), 551–575.

8.   Peterson, P. E., & Hess, F. M. (2008). Few states set world-class standards. *Education Next, 8*(3).

9.   For a full exposition of these arguments, see Pellegrino, J. W., Jones, L. R., & Mitchel, K. J. (1999). *Grading the nation's report card: Evaluating NAEP and transforming the assessment of educational progress.* Washington, DC: National Academies Press.

10.   Joanne Weiss, quoted in Sawchuk, S. (2011, August 24). Analysis finds states strengthening rigor of student exams. *Education Week.*

11.   Cross-state comparisons are often made to support or refute an argument that a state should take or not take some particular policy action. Specifically, an advocate or opponent of some policy will look to some other state that implemented the policy in question and make an argument that it did or did not work.

12.   On its face, misalignment between a state's standards and the contents of NAEP may seem like a negative mark for a state. However, owing to the tradition of local control of education in the United States, many state-level policy makers do not view any misalignment in a negative manner. Such policy makers often do not believe that the federally determined content of NAEP is necessarily what should be taught in schools in their state.

13.   Berry, F. S., & Berry, W. D. (1999). Innovation and diffusion models in policy research. In P. Sabatier (Ed.), *Theories of the policy process* (2nd ed.). Boulder, CO: Westview Press.

14.   Peterson, P. E., & Hess, F. M. (2008). Few states set world-class standards. *Education Next, 8*(3).

15.   Carmichael, S. B., Martino, G., Porter-Magee, K., & Wilson, W. S. (2010). *The state of state standards—and the Common Core—in 2010.* Washington, DC: Thomas B. Fordham Institute. p. 2

16.   The U.S. Department of Education specified seven specific features that these systems must contain. First, the system must be based on both graduation rates and student growth in reading and math achievement for all students, as well as all subgroups of students. Second, states must set ambitious, but achievable, annual measurable objectives (AMOs) with respect to reading and math achievement growth and measure progress toward these AMOs using assessments in Grades 3–8 and once in high school. Third, the system must identify "reward schools," and the state education agency (SEA) must provide these schools with recognition or awards. Fourth, the system must identify at least the bottom 5% of schools as "pri-

ority schools," and the SEA must assist the schools in implementing a federally approved turnaround strategy. The accountability system must also contain criteria for determining when a school exits priority school status. Fifth, at least an additional 10% of schools must be classified as "focus schools," and the SEA must ensure that interventions are implemented in those schools. As with priority schools, there also need to be criteria for determining when a school exits focus school status. Sixth, the accountability system must provide incentives and supports to other Title I schools that are not meeting their specified AMOs. Finally, the system needs to contain strategies for building school, district, and state capacity to improve student learning in all schools and in low-performing schools in particular.

17. Mehta, J., & Teles, S. (2011). Jurisdictional politics: A new federal role in education. In F. M. Hess & A. P. Kelly (Eds.), *Carrots, sticks, and the bully pulpit: Lessons from a half-century of federal efforts to improve America's schools.* Cambridge, MA: Harvard Education Press.

CHAPTER 6

The History of History Standards: The Prospects for Standards for Social Studies

Peter Meyer

WHEN STUDYING HISTORY with any degree of seriousness, one quickly realizes that it is equal parts art and science, as much constant debate as settled truth, and, done well, can be a rousing good time. Indeed, the teaching of history is fraught with much of the same ferment and drama as daily life, a wonderful way of introducing children to other worlds and times—and a perennial problem for educators trying to write history curricula. Add to the mix the fact that history has been folded into the field of "social studies," and the curricular challenges mount. And this is just the beginning of the question of whether we will ever see Common Core State Standards (CCSS) in social studies.

What we will learn later in this story, is that the urge for a *common* curriculum is as American as apple pie. But it has never happened. It's "the 'third rail' of education policy," says education journalist Robert Rothman, "touch it and you die."[1] Until now. We now have common standards in math and English language arts in 45 states and the District of Columbia, as close to a common *national* curriculum as we've ever been. Does that mean we may have national social studies standards? Have the leaders of the Common Core movement figured out how to deactivate the third rail?

THE KEY TO NATIONAL SELF-IDENTITY

History has taken a number of beatings in our schools over the years, in part because it comes with baggage: We refight the battles of the past. It isn't that there aren't plenty of rules of research and professional standards for sorting truth from fiction, which is why we can be fairly certain that George Washington was our first president and Abraham Lincoln our 16th. But just as the events that history documents are often contentious, so too the arguments persist. Is Washington better than Lincoln? Did the South secede because of states' rights or slavery? Did Franklin Roosevelt save the union or sow the seeds of debilitating socialism? And that doesn't begin to answer questions about whether Christopher Columbus was a pioneer of enlightened discovery or a demon colonialist.

It's an old problem. Take Plutarch and Herodotus, two of the world's most famous historians (the latter sometimes called "the father of history"). "Nearly two thousand years ago, Plutarch denounced Herodotus, saying he had slandered the greatest Greek cities, not least Thebes, which was in Plutarch's native region of Boeotia," write Gary Nash, Charlotte Crabtree, and Ross Dunn in their brilliant 1997 book *History on Trial: Culture Wars and the Teaching of the Past.* There are always disagreements about the past, which is not surprising considering that history is meant to describe a present no longer with us. We know what "the present" is like. Napoleon considered Tacitus, another noted historian, an "unjust slanderer of humanity," relate Nash et al., while the same man earned praise from Thomas Jefferson and John Adams, who associated "the morality of Tacitus" with the "morality of patriotism."[2] And speaking of Jefferson, in 2012, some 186 years after the revered third president's death, the *New York Times* ran an op-ed essay by a visiting professor of legal history at Duke, a respected institution, under the headline "The Monster of Monticello." Indeed, according to this reading of history, Jefferson was a "creepy, brutal hypocrite."[3]

But if there is so much disagreement, what do we make of George Santayana's famous remark, "Those who can't remember the past are doomed to repeat it"?

It is already troublesome enough, in many educators' eyes, that history, once an indispensable part of our school curriculum, got shrunk and is now just another piece of the "social studies" pie—defined by the National Council for the Social Studies (NCSS) as an interdisciplinary field "drawing upon such subjects as anthropology, archaeology, economics, geography, history, law, philosophy, political science, psychology, religion, and sociology, as well as . . . the humanities, mathematics and natural sciences."[4]

The important thing to note, for the moment, is that history itself—more properly historiography—is a constant argument not just about the events which have led to our current predicament or, as we shall see, to our national character, but about our ways of knowing such stuff. It is nothing if not an argument, but does that mean we can't *know* something? Can't teach something? Jefferson said the key to a successful democracy is an *informed* public. Informed about what? About the present, which is a cacophony of voices? Or the past, which is only slightly less jarring in its squabbles? But the question for educators and policy makers today is whether we should be frightened off by the disputes and disagreements about our past—not to mention the quarrels embedded in the other social sciences. Talk about an ontological mess. What would Sartre say? And if we can't agree what to teach our students, do we teach them nothing and risk driving those students—and the country—off the Santayana cliff?[5]

DON'T KNOW MUCH ABOUT HISTORY

Whether viewed as a national and nation-building truism or as a personal and individual uplifting motto, the yoking of current identity to memory—history—is a significant principle of education. We teach things past not just to improve individual self-esteem, but that of the nation.

In the face of these existential disagreements, do we stop teaching history? Or have we already stopped? Jay Leno has made a staple out of the *Tonight Show*'s man-on-the-street interview. Who was the first president? Roosevelt. When did the Civil War start? 1790. The National Assessment of Educational Progress (NAEP) report, considered the gold standard of such things, does not provide a much more optimistic view than Leno about our children's knowledge of history: "At grades 4 and 8, the percentages of students at or above proficient in 2010 were not significantly different from the percentages in 2006, but were higher than the percentages in the first assessment in 1994. At grade 12, the percentage of students at or above proficient was not significantly different from the percentages in previous assessment years." That may sound like good news: Things have not gotten a lot worse. Unfortunately, the bad news is that less than one quarter of students performed at or above the proficient level in 2010.[6]

It is not that history is an imprecise (social) science; it is that real life is imprecise. Journalists are considered authors of the first draft of history—or *were*, until the Internet age; sometimes they get it wrong and sometimes getting it right doesn't matter.[7] We may think we live in a concrete present; in fact, real life is messier than history precisely because there are fewer filters in our daily lives than our historical ones—and this is why we should teach history before trying to teach current events. Withstanding the test of time, as Tacitus and Jefferson have, suggests that our children have more to learn from them about eternal verities than from the local mayor.[8]

The best argument for history in our classrooms is that the argument—about the social contract, about how we get along, about who said what and when—encompasses so much of our lives, then and now, that it would behoove our students to know more about the people and events that have "withstood the test of time" than those who are on the cover of *People* magazine or the front page of the local *Ding Herald Express*. After all, how many of those cover personalities will be remembered even 5 years after the fact? What does it mean that we remember Homer several thousand years after he died? Or do we? Our lives are so much more history than math—though STEM boosters would no doubt disagree. Can we plausibly disregard discussion of *The Federalist Papers* in the study of civics? Or, to state it differently, do we learn more about civics from James Madison or James "The Former Fireman" Mayor? Would we rather hear from our local congressman about the meaning of government? Or from Alexander Hamilton? Or from the "Monster of Monticello"—who happens to be the primary author of the Declaration of Independence?

IN SEARCH OF A COMMON CURRICULUM

In his brilliant history of American education, *The Making of Americans: Democracy and Our Schools*, E. D. Hirsch captures the inherent—or so it would seem—urge to a have a common curriculum, suggesting that it's a necessity if we are going to be a single country. It is an argument for a national self-identity not unlike an argument for an individual identity. "Not just Webster," Hirsch writes, "but *all* of our earliest educational thinkers argued that *precisely because we were a big, diverse country of immigrants, our schools should offer many common topics to bring us together* [emphasis added]; if schools did so, they felt, we would be able to communicate with one another, act as a unified republic, and form bonds of loyalty and patriotism among our citizens."[9] *E Pluribus Unum*. From the many, one.

The belief that common knowledge is the currency of communication—and nation-building—is as old as the country itself. Hirsch describes an early competition (1795) sponsored by the American Philosophical Society, offering a prize for the best essay describing a system of education "adapted to the genius of the United States." There were two winners, writes Hirsch, "both of whose essays advocated a national core curriculum." Concludes Hirsch, "this idea of commonality in the early curriculum was far from a radical idea in 1797. . . . It was already the consensus view of such earlier writers as Jefferson and [Benjamin] Rush," the latter, who had written a 1786 essay called "Thoughts upon the Mode of Education Proper in a Republic," arguing for "one general and uniform system of education" to "render the mass of the people more homogeneous and thereby fit them more easily for uniform and peaceable government."[10]

Though the idea of "commonality" would fade by the end of the 19th century (shaken by the trauma of Civil War, writes Hirsch, a sudden antipathy for "mindless rote learning," and a celebration of "the child-centered school"), prior to the 1890s, history courses in American public schools

were still fairly consistent, dominated by Greek and Roman mythology, heroes of the American Revolution, and narratives designed to inspire patriotism and moral conviction.[11] According to Ronald Evans's 2004 book *The
Social Studies War,* these "standards" were usually taught by formal ora-
tion and basic recollection of factual information such as names, dates, and
places.[12] In practice, the information transmitted was disorganized and varied widely depending on variables such as geographical location, heritage,
and personal conviction. In 1884, the American Historical Foundation was
founded and a movement toward a professional standard began.[13] It was an
intellectually eventful period—if we are to believe our historians.

In 1893 the Report of the Committee of Ten on Secondary School Studies advocated an interdisciplinary approach to the subject of history. In 1916
the National Education Association (NEA) recommended that "social studies" be the name of the content area. In 1918 the Commission on the Reorganization of Secondary Education endorsed a curriculum that emphasized,
along with traditional history, "current issues, social problems, and recent
history, and the needs and interests of students." That same year, the Cardinal Principles of Secondary Education called for the unified study of subject
areas that previously had been taught separately. Its main goal would be to
cultivate citizens.[14] Thus the birth of what we now call "social studies."

Of note, however, is that history and social studies, as part of the core
course of studies in our public schools, were always seen as nation-building
and citizen-making endeavors. In fact, citizenship education was one of the
main missions of the National Council for the Social Studies, which was
formed in 1921. Even today, according to the NCSS, "the primary purpose
of social studies is to help young people make informed and reasoned decisions for the public good as citizens of a culturally diverse, democratic
society in an interdependent world."[15]

But almost from the beginning, the new discipline had its detractors. In
1924 Ross Finney, who headed the Committee on the Teaching of Sociology for the American Sociological Association, wrote in *The School Review*
about a recommended social studies course called *Problems of Democracy:*

> Emphasis on the sore spots in society has a certain morbid effect on the minds
> of young persons. It makes them imagine that they ought to be agitators,
> radicals, reformers, philanthropists, social workers, or something of the sort.
> It tends to fill their heads with queer immature ideas, with increased danger
> that they may fail to function normally in the staple relations and fundamental
> institutions of society. And that is likely to do far more harm than good.[16]

The debates on social studies continued through the 1920s and 1930s,
but by the 1940s the social studies curriculum had become an accepted
hodgepodge of subjects, focusing less and less on traditional history and
geography. During World War II, historian Allan Nevins wrote in the *New*

York Times Magazine that requirements in American history and government were "deplorably haphazard, chaotic, and ineffective."[17]

By the 1980s, history requirements in most schools had dwindled to trivial levels. In a 1988 national test, only a minority of high school seniors showed even a general sense of the chronology of events in America's past or were familiar with the Declaration of Independence.[18] In at least half the states, high school students needed only a single year of U.S. history to graduate.

THE GROWTH OF THE SOCIAL STUDIES MESS

We can skip over most of the battles between the *Social Studies Report* of 1916 and the fights through the 1950s because what happened between 1990 and 1995 sums up the modern war with near-perfect pitch—and sets the stage, for better or worse, for the challenges of writing common—or "national" or "American"—standards today. And this doesn't even count the controversies over social studies itself.[19] In fact, the standards fight of the 1990s sums up both the social studies battles of the 1920s and 1930s and the culture wars that broke out in the 1960s (the latter battles included major revisions of American history lessons; the most jarring, perhaps, was the transformation of Christopher Columbus from a hero of discovery and enlightenment—the famous 1892 Chicago World's Fair, also known as the Columbus Exposition, celebrated the 400th anniversary of the Italian explorer's "discovery" of the "new world"—to a demon of colonialism).[20]

These revisionist histories, as is the nature of history, were not only shaped by current events—race riots at home and an unpopular war abroad—but by the continuing research of professional historians who unearthed new evidence and new witnesses. Multiculturalism waxed ascendant and textbooks began rewriting history—to more argument—to reflect racial inequities if not historically significant inaccuracies. But as such revisionism trickles down to our textbook companies and our schools, the dreaded "politically correct" problem also asserted itself.[21]

Then came 1987. It's rare for books on education to hit the best-seller lists, but that year two did exactly that: *The Closing of the American Mind: How Higher Education Has Failed Democracy and Impoverished the Souls of Today's Students* by Allan Bloom, and *Cultural Literacy: What Every American Needs to Know* by E. D. Hirsch. At one point, *Cultural Literacy* rose to number two on the *New York Times* Best Seller list for nonfiction, just behind *Closing of the American Mind*. Both authors urged a return to traditional teachings, though in very different ways and for very different reasons. As for social studies, Hirsch lamented a field gone astray—fragmented and devoid of content.

But this was the "cafeteria style" time in American education, as Hirsch would point out, when you got to choose the education you wanted. Most kids, not surprisingly, chose *easy*, setting in motion a race to the bottom unprecedented in American education. As American society—and the teaching of social studies, and a watered-down history—became increasingly balkanized, "child-centered" as many educators believed, Hirsch advocated an objective, content-rich, grade-by-grade curriculum that students from diverse backgrounds could and should learn. By this time, however, his was such a radical view of education as to make him a status quo pariah even as the book climbed the bestseller charts. As early as 1983, Hirsch had been lamenting the effects of cultural fragmentation, arguing that a literate society depends upon shared information:

> The dominant symbol for the role of the school was the symbol of the melting pot. But from early times we have also resisted this narrow uniformity in our culture. The symbol of the melting pot was opposed by the symbol of the stew pot, where our national ingredients kept their individual characteristics and contributed to the flavor and vitality of the whole. This is the doctrine of pluralism. It has now become the dominant doctrine in our schools, especially in those subjects, English and history, that are the closest to culture making. . . . No culture exists that is ignorant of its own traditions. In a literate society, culture and cultural literacy are nearly synonymous terms. American culture, always large and heterogeneous, and increasingly lacking a common acculturative curriculum, is perhaps getting fragmented enough to lose its coherence as a culture.[22]

A CALL FOR NATIONAL EDUCATION GOALS

Just 6 years later, in 1989, president George H. W. Bush declared that "the time has come, to establish national performance goals, goals that will make us internationally competitive, second to none in the 21st century."[23]

In his second State of the Union address, in 1990, Bush proposed a National Education Goals initiative,[24] appointing a bipartisan group of governors and administration officials to a new, congressionally chartered National Council on Education Standards and Testing, carrying "the unfortunate acronym 'NCEST,'" writes Robert Rothman.[25]

The decision to make Lynne Cheney, then head of the National Endowment for the Humanities (NEH), chair of NCEST's history task force turned out to be fateful. Cheney, wife of Dick Cheney, a former chief of staff in the Ford administration and a longtime conservative congressman from Wyoming, was a formidable conservative in her own right (she would serve as a senior fellow in education and culture at the American Enterprise Institute). She and education secretary Lamar Alexander quickly announced that the NEH and the U.S. Department of Education (USDOE) would provide $1.6 million to UCLA to create a National Center for History in Schools, appointing UCLA professors Charlotte Crabtree (education) and Gary Nash (history) as director and associate director of the program, respectively, with a mandate to develop national history standards for Grades 5–12.[26] (There were also plans to complete a similar set of standards for world history.) The project would come to involve 200 historians and educators from every historical discipline and every political stripe. Over the next 32 months the group produced 6,000 drafts of history standards.[27]

ACHIEVING CONSENSUS, MAYBE

Despite the sticking points (mostly about multiculturalism and world history), the project moved forward and in September 1992 a first set of drafts was sent to USDOE and the NEH, which both endorsed and commended the progress being made. The endorsement also included another $1 million in additional funding. Stakeholders were optimistic that a strongly supported set of standards would be released in the near future.[28]

In June 1993 NCEST approved the final version of criteria that would guide the writing of the standards. By May 1994, with the standards virtually written, NCEST and the National Forum for History Standards offered extensive praise for the standards including documents for both U.S. and world history, and the writing group met for the last time in a hotel ballroom in Crystal City, Virginia, to celebrate what it believed to be a job well done.[29] Wrote Karen Diegmueller and Debra Viadero in *Education Week*:

> One by one, the men and women gathered around the conference tables offered final words and praise for the American history documents that were nearly completed. "Bravo," said a representative from a private schools' group. "Extremely admirable," enthused the American Federation of Teachers' liaison to the project. "Commendable," offered a historian.[30]

If this sounded too good to be true, it was.

POLITICAL FALLOUT

Eight months later, write Diegmueller and Viadero, "the plaudits heard around that hotel ballroom had been replaced by scorn." And 2 weeks before the scheduled unveiling of the standards, on October 20, 1994, in what Diegmueller and Viadero called "a pre-emptive strike," the *Wall Street Journal* published an op-ed by Lynne Cheney, who had been out of the loop since inauguration day in 1993 and had not seen the history standards until that fall. Ominously, her essay was titled "The End of History." The first two sentences were devastating:

> Imagine an outline for the teaching of American history in which George Washington makes only a fleeting appearance and is never described as our first president. Or in which the foundings of the Sierra Club and the National Organization for Women are considered noteworthy events, but the first gathering of the U.S. Congress is not.

Cheney continued in that vein, noting that traditional American heroes, such as Ulysses S. Grant, Alexander Graham Bell, Thomas Edison, Albert Einstein, Jonas Salk, and the Wright brothers were not mentioned at all, while Harriet Tubman was named four times.[31]

Conservative talk show hosts, led by Rush Limbaugh, leapt into the debate, denouncing the history standards. But even moderate voices such as Diane Ravitch, who had been an assistant secretary of education under Bush and a promoter of the standards, and historian Arthur Schlesinger Jr. criticized the proposals. Then, early in 1995, by a vote of 99 to 1, the U.S. Senate adopted a nonbinding resolution that condemned the standards as irresponsible. Nonbinding though it may have been, the Senate resolution put the nail in the coffin of the last attempt to adopt national history standards.[32]

It didn't much matter that in November of that year USDOE released results from the 1994 National Assessment of Educational Progress (NAEP) test in history showing that nearly three fifths of 12th-graders could not even reach the "basic" level of achievement. The fourth- and eighth-graders who took the exam did not fare much better.[33] By that time, however, even Bill Clinton, who had been a part of the genesis of the Goals 2000 initiative, withdrew his support.

Lessons Learned

The fact that proponents of the Common Core have gotten as far as they have in the wake of the NCEST disaster is a good indication that the CCSS group learned some important lessons.

One, most assuredly, is that you have to stay in the game. Unlike Cheney and Diane Ravitch, who left in the middle of the process, many standards supporters, like Chester "Checker" Finn Jr. and his Thomas B. Fordham Institute, have been deeply committed to the Common Core endeavor—and are still in the game. More problematic, perhaps, is that David Coleman, called the "chief architect" of the Common Core, though still a sought-after speaker on behalf of CCSS, is now president of the College Board.[34]

Second, the leaders of the CCSS movement were acutely aware of the need to ensure that the process was driven by the states, not the federal government. Support for common standards by the Council of Chief State School Officers (CCSSO) and the NGA was "overwhelming," writes Robert Rothman, but much of that support came because of a deep respect for the belief that "local communities should set their own standards."[35] Critics see this as a smokescreen, hiding what they believe is a "nationalized" curriculum, an argument made much stronger when the Obama administration tied Race to the Top funds for states to their acceptance of the CCSS.[36] But whether USDOE's funding carrots make it a federal program or not, there is no doubt that the initial impetus for Common Core Standards was state-driven. "It was very clear people did not want the federal government setting standards," former North Carolina governor James Hunt, a major leader of the national standards movement, told Robert Rothman.[37] "These new standards have not been *imposed* on states. They have *emerged* from states, much as the United States did almost 225 years ago when the Constitution and Bill of Rights were adopted."[38]

A third lesson would seem to be an appreciation for bringing professional standards to the task of studying social studies—to keep ideological cants to a minimum. When it comes to history, and, by extension, most of the other social studies, it's nearly impossible to separate historical facts from people's opinions and political points of view about those "facts." Perhaps the worst of the culture wars are over[39] as much as the CCSS leaders wanted to avoid "the specter of a federally led effort," recalls Michael Cohen, president of Achieve Inc., one of Common Core's major promoters, "There needed to be a different way to talk about it."[40] Maintaining professional standards in these subjects—there are just as many opinions about what and how to teach math and science as there are opinions about economics and history—is a must. There is some consensus that, despite the controversy over "informational texts," the ELA standards aspire to a higher standard of academic knowledge and skills.

Fourth, fly under the radar. At one point during a telephone interview with Jack Jennings, founder and former president of the Center of Education Policy who for 27 years before that worked for Congress as the staff director for the elementary and secondary education subcommittee in the House and then as general counsel for education for the House's full Committee on Education and Labor, I asked what he thought of David Coleman. "Who's that?" asked Jennings.[41] If one of Washington's most seasoned education policy makers hasn't heard of Coleman (who has since become much more visible), no doubt the public knows little of the endeavor.[42] And it is clearly intentional, as a visit to the Common Core's website proves: The wizard is hidden. To this day (as of this writing), more than 2 years after the CCSS project began, the names of those responsible for it cannot be found on the program's official website (http://www.corestandards.org/voices-of-support).

Finally, CCSS proponents seem to have learned that you need to keep the dialogue going. According to Ronald Evans, professor of teacher education at San Diego State University, the most important lesson from the history wars of the 1990s is the need for a truly open, public discourse on the issues. He doesn't explain why the process of that time wasn't open or public in his account, *The Social Studies Wars*, but he emphasizes the need for a rejection of the "propaganda, scapegoating, and interest group financing" that seemed to dominate the national discussion of the issues.[43] The fact there continues to be dialogue about the CCSS, despite critics seeing such discussion as the effort's death knell, could save the effort from the do-or-die dilemma.

WILL WE SEE SOCIAL STUDIES STANDARDS?

With the dust hardly settled on the train wreck of the NCEST history standards, are the folks at CCSS whistling past the graveyard in thinking they can sell the states on social studies standards? The success of the math and ELA standards (at least, as of this writing) suggests that they've learned from the 1990s debacle. Have they learned enough?

We have seen almost no improvement in student performance in any social studies measures in the last 10 years, so there continues to be ample reason to ramp up the standards.[44] Can we overcome partisanship and find a professional standard that might improve our children's knowledge of social studies (history, civics, economics, anthropology, geography, religion, political science, and so on)?

Only if Chester "Checker" Finn can hold his fire. Says Jack Jennings, "If Checker wants to, he could set back the cause or at least severely damage it."[45] Jennings pays appropriate tribute to Finn, a former assistant secretary of education in the Reagan administration, a onetime chair of the NAEP board, and founding president of the influential education policy think tank, the Thomas B. Fordham Institute (at which this writer is a policy fellow). When an early "framework" for the social studies standards was released in the fall of 2012, Finn leveled a shot over the bow:

> The cumbersome, inscrutable title is the first clue that something is not right: "Vision for the College, Career, and Civic Life (C3): Framework for Inquiry in Social Studies State Standards." Welcome to the social studies follies. We might thank the Council of Chief State School Officers . . . for ensuring—so far, anyway—that this jumble is not portrayed as "national standards" for social studies. Instead, it's the beginning of a "framework" for states intending to rethink their own academic standards in social studies, a hodgepodge part of the K–12 curriculum.[46]

"I heard Chester talk about National Standards in the 1980s," Jennings, now semiretired, says, "and so it takes a degree of self-restraint on the part of policy people and political people in order to achieve national standards. It took that restraint on the part of many people with [the CCSS] reading and math standards."[47]

THE FIVE QUESTIONS

One doubts that conservatives will show much restraint. And as of this writing, though 45 states and the District of Columbia had signed on to the Common Core math and ELA standards, there is pushback—from both sides of the political spectrum.[48] A full-throated debate began in the fall of 2012, and by February 2013 Andrew Ujifusa reported in *Education Week* that

Opponents of the Common Core State Standards are ramping up legislative pressure and public relations efforts aimed at getting states to scale back—or even abandon—the high-profile initiative, even as implementation proceeds and tests aligned with the standards loom.[49]

In April 2013 Randi Weingarten, head of the American Federation of Teachers and an early proponent of the Common Core, earned headlines for calling for a moratorium on tying Common Core tests to teacher evaluations.[50] This is anything but the firestorm following Lynne Cheney's *Wall Street Journal* jeremiad, but it is giving many people pause about whether we will see Common Core State Standards in other subjects.

As part of my research for this paper, I asked a number of key players to answer five questions exploring the odds of ever seeing a CCSS in social studies.[51] The respondents included E. D. Hirsch, the godfather of the "content counts" movement, which energizes the current ELA Common Core, who was an early critic of the CCSS but is now a supporter;[52] Chester Finn, as noted earlier, a former assistant secretary of education in the Reagan administration, now president of the Thomas B. Fordham Institute; Kate Walsh, president of the National Council on Teacher Quality; Robert Rothman, the education journalist, currently a senior fellow at the Alliance for Excellent Education; Christopher Cross, an assistant secretary of education in the George H. W. Bush administration and former president of the Maryland State Board of Education;[53] Michael Cohen, another former assistant secretary of education (Clinton administration), and president of Achieve Inc.; and Dane Linn, former director of the education division of the NGA's Center for Best Practices and a key player in bringing the ELA and math Common Core Standards to fruition.

Perhaps the most surprising reply came from Linn, whose appraisal of the social studies standards was blunt, "The process is a mess and it's going nowhere and nowhere fast."[54] In fact, most of the respondents were more modulated.

Has the fight over the ELA and math Common Core State Standards impacted the chances of introducing similar standards in other subjects, specifically social studies? Robert Rothman doesn't agree that the ELA and math standards process was a "fight." "There have been some disagreements about particular standards," he says, "such as the issue that has emerged recently about the proportion of nonfiction in the ELA standards, and there have been some objections to what people consider (erroneously) federal standards, but all attempts to derail the standards thus far have failed."

Christopher Cross says that "the fights over ELA and math will not have a significant impact on other standards. Science may be a bigger flashpoint because of issues like creationism."

Rothman agrees. "The experience with the Common Core makes it more likely that there might be common standards in social studies," he believes. "States generally agree that the process produced better standards than they could have produced on their own."

Hirsch and Walsh are not so sanguine. "It isn't so much the fight that is preventing the development [of social studies standards] (and I would argue that the fight hasn't been all that bad)," says Walsh, "but just the chaos the standards have created in the states."

"The ideological battle lines are drawn," says Hirsch. "The opponents of the multistate standards would be even fiercer with this topic." In other words, if we thought ELA was hard, social studies will be harder. Walsh believes that it is "highly unlikely that there will be any movement on social studies standards, as much as they are needed, until some of the dust [from the ELA and math standards] settles in the states."

The dust-settling may take a while. "We need to roll out ELA and math and get the assessments working," says Walsh.

"I'm far from convinced that national social studies standards are a good idea in the first place," adds Finn. "And the version that seems to be in the process is becoming absolutely awful, worse than none."

Is there political will to introduce national-level social studies standards? "I know some serious supporters of the Common Core (for ELA and math) who believe that even the possibility of national social studies standards will weaken the political base of the existing Common Core itself," says Finn. "I think there is no political will to find consensus on this one."

Rothman too is doubtful that there will be enough energy to work on social studies. "As long as accountability systems focus solely on reading and math, there is little pressure for social studies standards," he says. "And the political battles over social studies soured a lot of people on the attempt."

This suggests a serious diminution in the will to press for social studies standards. Despite the efforts to create a social studies "framework," Cohen agrees that "developing high-quality, rigorous social studies standards that would stand a strong chance of being adopted in many states would be a very difficult political lift, and they would most likely be subject to close scrutiny, if not strong attack, almost immediately."

"Personally, I would argue that there should be standards in the specific disciplines—history, geography, economics, and so on—rather than having things lumped as social studies," says Cross. "I believe that will be the greatest fight, unless this issue is resolved prior to the release of anything else."

Hirsch believes that "the opponents of CCSS are much more emotionally engaged than the proponents," but most of the opposition was directed at nonacademic issues. "Where to turn one's energies and attention (having run out of reform ideas)?" he says. "Let's turn our attention to the fed takeover."

Given the terrible battles over social studies standards in the 1990s, even if CCSS tackles social studies, is there any chance that the standards will have any content? "What do you mean, will they have content?" asks Rothman. "The history standards of the 1990s, the ones that ignited heated battles, had plenty of content. It was the content that people fought over. If you are suggesting that people will want to paper over differences by watering down the standards, that's what some critics of the Common Core thought, and they were proved wrong."

Christopher Cross also believes that it's possible to write serious standards and that, in fact, they did that in the late 1990s, after the NEH effort crashed and burned. The Council for Basic Education, where Cross was then CEO, convened panels of experts and that led to a revision in the history standards. "We actually cross-referenced areas where standards crossed disciplines. For example, learning about something like Newton is both science and history. Learning about a country such as Russia involves learning about things that involve history, geography, music, art, and political science."

Cohen thinks that the emphasis on informational texts "will strengthen social studies instruction, not give educators and policy makers a pass on it. Informational text is all about content, so if students read complex history, are expected to draw evidence from it and develop and write clear, logical, evidence-based essays, social studies instruction could become more rigorous and effective."

Will the emphasis on "informational" texts in the CCSS ELA tempt educators—and policy makers—to look the other way on social studies standards? Either by not tackling them or by making them vague enough to be palatable to all groups? "I don't think the emphasis on informational text is enough to put off a discussion of standards," says Rothman. "The literacy standards say nothing about what the content of social studies should be." Finn agrees, but believes that "vagueness in this field means the absence of specific content, which is so serious a problem as to make the entire venture impossible."

Hirsch, on the other hand, believes that the informational text issue "has offered a point of attack against CCSS. It's a terrible, soulless phrase." His argument is that "a coherent, knowledge-based curriculum is the foundation for reading everything including fiction and poetry. The aims of good fiction and nonfiction are the same—truth in substance and pleasure in form."

And Finn offers this interesting take on what happened after Lynne Cheney ended the last effort. "We must remember that the 'National History Standards' of the 1990s, though denounced by the NEH chairman and the U.S. Senate, nevertheless infected social studies education in a lot of places."

This would seem to suggest that the choice is not between standards and no standards, but between worse and better. "Just about every state has social studies standards," adds Cohen, "requires school systems to teach social studies, and requires students to take a mix of history, civics, and related courses (e.g., economics) to earn a high school diploma. I think that the emphasis on informational texts in the CCSS—including in social studies/history—has helped."

And if you believe social studies standards are not possible or unlikely to survive politically, will the Common Core's focus on reading and math lead teachers to neglect untested subjects? "This is already a problem under NCLB and will remain so as long as state and/or federal accountability pressures are associated only with reading and math," says Finn. "But that's not a consequence of the Common Core per se. It's a consequence of narrowly cast accountability and assessment rules developed by state and national governments."

Rothman believes that "untested subjects might be neglected whether there are standards or not. It all depends on what schools are accountable for."

"Yes, it will so lead," argues Hirsch. And this is why he advocates "curriculum-based passages on reading tests, and a rule that at least one of the passages has to be about the civics taught in that grade."

SOCIAL STUDIES STANDARDS MOVING FORWARD

The Common Core may be one of the most important restructurings of America's public education school system that no one knows anything about.[55] But, as even Dane Linn suggests, "We're a long ways from social studies standards. We haven't even tested the math and ELA standards yet."[56]

As we have seen, there are any number of lessons to be learned from the failure to reach a consensus about national history standards in the 1990s, not to mention lessons learned from NCLB and Race to the Top, many of which have been alluded to by our respondents above and incorporated into the Common Core initiative, notably the attempt to keep the feds out of it. It may very well be that it is impossible to have national standards of any kind. But we are certainly on a powerful national standards train at the moment, and it is certainly worth considering whether we can do for social studies what CCSS proponents are attempting to do for English and math.

Jonathan Zimmerman, professor of education at New York University, believes that the examination of differences in the United States is precisely what is holding us together—and moving us forward.[57] He points out that differences in opinion on these matters are largely the result of differing worldviews, an opinion shared by Linda Symcox, who says that the debate is generally based on political or ideological backgrounds, and that "people will always differ on what they perceive to be the purpose of education and the best way to achieve its goals."[58]

Clearly, the way forward will be anything but smooth. As Chester Finn wrote about the social studies "framework" draft that was floating around at the end of 2012: "Did you spot the missing words? I'll bet you did. They are the verb 'know' and the noun 'knowledge.' As best one can tell, the present social studies project cares not a whit about whether kids end up with any of the familiar 'knowledge' of social studies."[59]

This no doubt would please some standards skeptics. But since there were very few voices on the left opposing the CCSS in ELA or math, and since the pendulum has been swung so far left for so long—toward inquiry and project-based social education curricula—with such dismal academic performance results, it is hard to believe that social studies standards writers could move the pendulum so far toward discipline- and content-focused curriculum as to alienate the left. Longtime standards champions like Finn have much more to lose in the Common Core fight and thus, as Jennings surmised, have much more leverage in the derailing process.

"I think that there are several keys to the survival of social studies," says Michael Cohen. "The first is having the public and the education system recognize the importance of studying social studies. I don't see any immediate obstacles to maintaining support for required instruction in social studies. Second, and related, is that states and local districts must continue to require social studies to be taught, and students to take the courses at the high school level in order to graduate. Third, if states implemented state social studies assessments at key grade levels, that too would ensure that the discipline continues to be taught. Note that none of these factors require common state standards in social studies, though good, clear, well-written standards would surely be helpful."

This is similar to Chester Finn's view that whether we have Common Core Standards or not, we will still have standards. Which brings us back to the question: What kind of standards will they be?

As Ronald Evans writes, "The primary pattern has been this: toward traditional and discipline-based curricula during conservative times; toward experimentation, child-centered and inquiry or issues-oriented curricula during liberal times. If you don't like the current direction of curricular reform, take heart, it may not last."[60]

Are these liberal or conservative times? Surely, if Barack Obama's second inaugural and 2013 State of the Union addresses are any indication, more government ("smarter government," as the president promised) is on the horizon. And the president's universal pre-K initiative earned initial support from both sides of the aisle.[61] But while the fiscal cliff may have focused the collective education mind, the ideological baggage brought to the history and social studies table may also freeze the collective education mind.

Linda Bevilacqua, president of the Core Knowledge Foundation, sees "six traps that could snare the Common Core," including the continuing allure of a "skills-based approach to assessing reading comprehension."[62] If the CCSS fail to reinsert content into our school curricula, the effort may be wasted. As David Steiner, dean of Hunter College's School of Education, says, "learning has to be about something in particular, not nothing in general."[63]

"It is very, very hard to agree on content in social studies," says Kate Walsh. "That's why no one is being taught history any more. Nevertheless, I am eternally optimistic that we will ultimately do the right thing. The emphasis on nonfiction provides an opening, helping to make sure that history is not neglected. Unfortunately, though, without state standards, there won't be much coherence to the content that is taught. But it is better than where we are now."[64]

The question for policy makers, including those contemplating common core social studies standards, is whether they will deny our students the opportunity to know the rich, elegant, confounding, and edifying history that shapes their country just because it is hard work to create it for them. One thing seems certain: We don't teach our children their history at their—and their country's—peril.

NOTES

1.   Rothman, R. (2011). *Something in common: The Common Core Standards and the next chapter in American education.* Cambridge, MA: Harvard Education Press, p. 53.

2.   Nash, G. B., Crabtree, C., & Dunn, R. E. (1997). *History on trial: Culture wars and the teaching of the past.* New York: Knopf, p. 22.

3.   Finkelman, P. (2012, November 30). The monster of Monticello. *New York Times.* Retrieved from http://www.nytimes.com/2012/12/01/opinion/the-real-thomas-jefferson.html

4.   National Council for the Social Studies. (2013). *About National Council for the Social Studies.* Silver Spring, MD: National Council for the Social Studies. Retrieved from http://www.socialstudies.org/about

5.   As David Steiner, dean of Hunter College School of Education, put it in a letter to the editor of the *New York Times,* "learning has to be about something in particular, not nothing in general." Steiner, D. (2013, April 25). Letters: Are common standards the answer? *New York Times.* Retrieved from http://www.nytimes.com/2013/04/26/opinion/are-common-learning-standards-the-answer.html?partner=rssnyt&emc=rss

6.   National Center for Education Statistics (NCES). (2011, June). *The Nation's Report Card: U.S. History 201. National Assessment of Educational Progress (NAEP).* Washington, DC: NCES. Retrieved from http://nces.ed.gov/nationsreportcard/pubs/main2010/2011468.asp#section4

7.   The *New York Times*' media columnist David Carr offers a refreshing reminder of why we need professional journalists in a fun story about how Matthew Hansen, a columnist at *The Omaha World-Herald,* solved the mystery about a photo that had gone viral on the Internet. See Carr, D. (2013, February 18). Logging off to trace a web photo to its source. *New York Times.* Retrieved from http://www.nytimes.com/2013/02/18/business/media/in-omaha-manhole-fire-photo-logging-off-in-search-of-some-clues.html?pag

8.   For one of the most powerful arguments for the study of history, see Bill Moyer's interviews with Joseph Campbell, author of the acclaimed book *The Power of Myth.* Campbell could surely make an argument, were he still alive, that the current emphasis on STEM (Science, Technology, Engineering, Math) is misplaced. See Moyers, B. (1988). *Joseph Campbell and the power of myth* [Television series]. Retrieved July 6, 2013, from http://billmoyers.com/spotlight/download-joseph-campbell-and-the-power-of-myth-audio/

9.   Hirsch, E. D. (2009). *The making of Americans: Democracy and our schools.* New Haven, CT: Yale University Press, p. 21.

10.   Ibid., pp. 21–22.

11.   Ibid., p. 25.

12.   Evans, R. W. (2004). *The social studies wars: What should we teach our children?* New York: Teachers College Press.

13.   Increasing concern over curriculum gave birth to a multitude of committees, for example, The Committee of Seven and The Committee of Ten, both of which had a great deal of influence on the history curriculum.

14.   Berson, M. J., Cruz, B. C., Duplass, J. A., Johnston, J. H., & Adler, S. A. (2013). *Social studies education: Overview, preparation of teachers.* StateUniversity.com. Retrieved from http://education.stateuniversity.com/pages/2433/Social-Studies-Education.html; Evans, R. W. (2006, September). Social studies wars: Now and then. *Social Education, 70*(5), 317–321; Adams, J., & Ginsberg, R. (2013). *Education reform: Overview, reports of historical significance.* StateUniversity.com. Retrieved from (http://education.stateuniversity.com/pages/1944/Education-Reform.html

15.   National Council for the Social Studies. (2013). *National curriculum standards for social studies: Executive summary.* Silver Spring, MD: National Council for the Social Studies. Retrieved from http://www.socialstudies.org/standards/execsummary

16.   Ross Finney, quoted in Evans, R. W. (2004). *The social studies wars.* New York: Teachers College Press, p. 31.

17.   Allan Nevins, quoted in Evans, *Social studies wars: Now and then,* p. 85.

18.   The battle over history standards: A survey of recent articles. (1995, Fall). *Wilson Quarterly, 19*(4).

19.   Taking up the existential question raised by Ross Finney, Michael Beran, writing in *City Journal,* calls the introduction of social studies to the school curriculum "a revolution in the way America educates its young. The old learning used the resources of culture to develop the child's individual potential; social studies, by contrast, seeks to adjust him to the mediocrity of the social pack." Beran, M. K. (2012, Autumn). Abolish social studies. *City Journal, 22*(4). Retrieved from http://www.city-journal.org/2012/22_4_social-studies.html

20.   A random Google search picks up the thread: "Christopher Columbus was a demon. Yeah. He was a fraud who murdered and enslaved thousands of Native Americans. But that's not the only reason I hate him. It's also personal. Columbus is why I have to tell people I'm Indian from India" (http://bitterseafigtree.tumblr.com/post/34686698803/christopher-columbus-was-a-demon-yeah-he-was-he). Does this mean we should not teach Christopher Columbus in our schools? For more on the view of Columbus in 1892, see Jones, J. O., & Meyer, P. (2010). *The pledge: A history of the Pledge of Allegiance.* New York: Thomas Dunne Books/St. Martin's Press.

21.   This is often reflected in the wholly nonprofessional and nonacademic practice of history by quota. In a recent page-one story in the *New York Times* about school books for Hispanics reporter Motoko Rich praises textbook publisher Houghton Mifflin for being "ahead of trade publishers" and "allocate[ing] exactly 18.6 percent of its content to works featuring Latino characters." Rich, M. (2012, December 5). For young Latino readers, an image is missing. *New York Times.*

22.   Hirsch, E. D. (1983, Spring). Cultural literacy. *American Scholar, 52*(2), 159–169.

23.   Nash et al., *History on trial,* p. 149.

24. Bush, G. (1990). *Address before a joint session of the Congress on the state of the union.* Retrieved from http://www.presidency.ucsb.edu/ws/index.php?pid=18095

25. Rothman, R. (2011). *Something in common: The Common Core Standards and the next chapter in American education.* Cambridge, MA: Harvard Education Press, p. 35. See also Nash et al., *History on trial.*

26. "A short history of the standards," 1995. *Education Week.* Retrieved from http://www.edweek.org/ew/articles/1995/11/15/11hist3.h15.html?r=1372207710

27. Diegmueller, K., & Viadero, D. (1995, November 15). Playing games with history. *Education Week.*

28. Symcox, L. (2002). *Whose history? The struggle for national standards in American classrooms.* New York: Teachers College Press.

29. The Forum represented constituencies that were broader than the Council and Focus Groups and included Afrocentrists on the left and neoconservatives on the right.

30. Diegmueller & Viadero, "Playing games with history."

31. Cheney, L. (1994, October 20). The end of history. *Wall Street Journal.* Retrieved from http://www-personal.umich.edu/~mlassite/discussions261/cheney.html

32. Wilentz, S. (1997, November 30). Don't know much about history [Review of the book, *History on trial*, by G. B. Nash, C. Crabtree, & R. E. Dunn]. *New York Times.* Retrieved from http://www.nytimes.com/books/97/11/30/reviews/971130.30wilentt.html

33. Diegmueller & Viadero, "Playing games with history."

34. Goldstein, D. (2012, October). The schoolmaster. *The Atlantic.* Retrieved from http://www.theatlantic.com/magazine/archive/2012/10/the-schoolmaster/309091/

35. Rothman, *Something in common,* pp. 59, 62.

36. Finn, C., & Greene, J. (2012, June 12). Should all U.S. students meet a single set of national proficiency standards? *Wall Street Journal.* Retrieved from http://online.wsj.com/article/SB10001424052970204603004577269231058863616.html

37. Rothman, *Something in common,* p. 56.

38. Hunt, J. B. (2011). Foreword. In R. Rothman, *Something in common: The Common Core Standards and the next chapter in American education.* Cambridge, MA: Harvard Education Press.

39. Many believed that the Common Core science standards (see http://www.corestandards.org/ELA-Literacy/RST/introduction) unveiled in April 2013 would be sunk by disputes over evolution and global warming. Though not without its critics, the reception to it has been muted. See Robelen, E. (2013, June 10). Common science standards make formal debut. *Education Week.* Retrieved from http://www.edweek.org/ew/articles/2013/04/09/28science_ep.h32.html

40. Cavanagh, S. (2010, January 7). U.S. common-standards push bares unsettled issues: Familiar themes emerge in resurgent debate. *Education Week.* (Published in print as Resurgent debate, familiar themes. *Education Week, 29*(17), pp. 5–6, 8–11.)

41. J. Jennings, personal communication (phone interview), December 6, 2012.

42. Goldstein, "The schoolmaster."

43. Evans, R. W. (2004). *The social studies wars.* New York: Teachers College Press, p. 178.

44. National Center for Education Statistics. (2011, June). *The nation's report card: U.S. history 2010.* Retrieved from http://nces.ed.gov/nationsreportcard/pubs/main2010/2011468.asp#section4

45. J. Jennings, personal communication (phone interview), December 6, 2012.

46. Finn, C. E. (2012). Social studies follies [Web log post]. *Flypaper* (Thomas B. Fordham Institute). Retrieved from http://www.edexcellence.net/commentary/education-gadfly-daily/flypaper/2012/social-studies-follies.html. Finn's criticism had an impact: The draft of the framework was removed from CCSSO's website.

47. J. Jennings, personal communication (phone interview), December 6, 2012. Finn was also part of the National Council on Education Standards and Tests, which "issued a ringing endorsement of standards" (Rothman, *Something in common*), p. 35.

48. Layton, L. (2012, December 2). Common Core sparks war over words. *Washington Post.* Retrieved from http://articles.washingtonpost.com/2012-12-02/local/35584536_1_informational-text-middle-school-teacher-english-teachers

49. Ujifusa, A. (2013, February 6). Pressure mounts in some states against Common Core. *Education Week.* Retrieved from http://www.edweek.org/ew/articles/2013/02/06/20commoncore_ep.h32.html

50. Anand, A. (2013, April 30). Weingarten: Common Core should stay, but stakes should go. *Gotham Schools.* Retrieved from http://gothamschools.org/2013/04/30/weingarten-common-core-should-stay-but-stakes-should-go/. See also Hernandez, J. C. (2013, April 30). Union chief recommends delay in use of test scores. *New York Times.* Retrieved from http://www.nytimes.com/2013/05/01/nyregion/postpone-use-of-new-test-scores-teachers-union-leader-says.html?hpw&_r=1&

51. Except for those of Jack Jennings and Dane Linn, the comments in this section are from e-mails to the author between September and December of 2012.

52. Rothman, *Something in common*, pp. 68, 72.

53. For Cross's defense of the Common Core in a letter responding to a George Will critique of the standards, see Cross, C. (2012, March 16). U.S. did not force states to adopt national educational standards [Letter to the editor]. *Washington Post.* Retrieved from http://www.washingtonpost.com/opinions/us-did-not-force-states-to-adopt-national-educational-standards/2012/03/14/gIQANsEDHS_story.html

54. D. Linn, personal communication (phone interview), December 11, 2012. Except for Linn, the comments in this section are from e-mails to the author, from September through December of 2012.

55. So many education reforms have been described as historic that I hesitate even to use the word *important.*

56. D. Linn, personal communication (phone interview), December 11, 2012.

57. Zimmerman, J. (2007). *Whose America? Culture wars in the public schools.* Cambridge, MA: Harvard University Press.

58. Symcox, *Whose history?*, p. 165.

59. Finn, "Social studies follies."

60. Evans, "Social studies wars, now and then," p. 25.

61. Chester Finn summed up the situation succinctly, making the point that Obama had the right ideas about education—for a governor, not a president. See Finn, C, (2013, February 15). Obama for governor. *Education Next.* Retrieved from http://educationnext.org/obama-for-governor/

62. Bevilacqua, L. (2013, February 28). Six traps that could snare the Common Core Standards [Web log post]. *The Core Knowledge Blog.* Retrieved from http://blog.coreknowledge.org/author/linda-bevilacqua/

63. Steiner, Letters.

64. K. Walsh, personal communication (e-mail), December 5, 2012.

CHAPTER 7

Technology

Taryn Hochleitner

Allison Kimmel

THE WIDESPREAD ADOPTION of the Common Core State Standards brings with it an unprecedented opportunity to integrate technology into K–12 schooling. A nationwide movement toward digital learning is already well underway, and has been growing with increasing momentum for the past decade. Schools are buying, calibrating, and integrating laptops and tablets into their classrooms, purchasing digital content in lieu of textbooks, and wiring buildings with Internet access to allow students to spend part of their day learning online. More and more, teachers are relying on web-based platforms to share lessons and instructional resources. Digital learning advocates trumpet the advantages of such a transition. Beyond cost savings and developing "21st-century readiness," they affirm that new technological tools will help teachers differentiate their lessons to better cater to students' diverse needs.

At the same time, 45 states and the District of Columbia have adopted the Common Core Standards and have launched implementation efforts. The standards both rely on and encourage the existing shift toward digital education, especially because they explicitly require students to learn math and English language arts skills using technology and multimedia. The standards specify that kindergarten students must "explore a variety of digital tools to produce and publish writing," while older students in Grades 11 and 12 should "use technology, including the Internet, to produce, publish, and update individual or shared writing products."[1] As Chris Minnich, executive director of the Council of Chief State School Officers (CCSSO), has explained, technological literacy is part of being "college-and-career" ready.[2]

There is widespread agreement that making the shift to the Common Core in time for the fall 2014 testing deadline will require substantial and expensive changes in schools and classrooms, most drastically in three areas: learning materials, instructional strategies, and assessments. Considering the growing enthusiasm for new education technology, it is not surprising that many of these resources are coming in digital form. Publishers are leaving paper textbooks behind to create new online-only Common Core curricula, and new education-oriented start-up firms are providing platforms for teachers to share lesson plans, formative assessments, and instructional strategies virtually. Most notably, the two testing consortias' assessments to evaluate student progress in meeting the standards will be delivered entirely online.

If the new standards and the pursuant learning materials, instructional strategies, and assessments rely on technology, it is essential that both reforms work in tandem. In that sense, making sure that the Common Core delivers on its promise has more to do with bandwidth, infrastructure, and technological training than it does with curricular scope and sequence. As education technology experts John Bailey, Carri Schneider, and Tom Vander Ark write, the marriage of the Common Core with the growing prominence and availability of education technology has the potential to "fundamentally shift the education system to personalize learning around the individual needs of every student."[3] But finding harmony between the digital learning movement and the Common Core may present challenges.

To better understand the opportunities and challenges presented here, we interviewed several leaders in the digital learning community, asking them to tell us their most pressing concerns about the relationship between the Common Core and technology. How is the Common Core accelerating the shift to digital learning? How prepared are states to adopt the standards and their accompanying assessments? What is the likelihood that states and districts will meet the device and infrastructure specifications before the testing deadline? What are the practical implications when it comes to this intersection that Common Core and digital learning advocates have overlooked?

All in all, the responses were split. Many argued that technology and the Common Core are mutually beneficial. In particular, the demand for technological advancements in instruction and assessment may motivate schools to make much-needed updates in infrastructure and bandwidth. But others were more skeptical, asserting that the onerous requirements related to online testing, new demands on teachers, and unforgiving price tags on infrastructure and materials will lead to the Common Core's undoing. Ultimately, while they came to the conclusion from different angles, our respondents generally agreed: *Whether or not states are willing and able to incorporate new technology in schools could make or break the Common Core.*

In this chapter we wrestle with two separate but interacting strands of the reform agenda—Common Core implementation and the increasing use of technology to deliver learning. In short, how will the Common Core Standards' reliance on technology affect districts' ability to adopt the standards sustainably and with fidelity? To answer this, we take a look at how technology will interact with three areas touched by the Common Core:

- Content and instructional materials
- Instructional skills and strategies
- Assessments

Next, we highlight the advantages and disadvantages of using technology to enable Common Core–related changes to each of these areas for states, districts, and schools.

Before we conclude, we reflect on the other, less visible side of the equation. How will Common Core–related specifications affect the future of the digital learning movement? Many who support digital learning maintain that it entails more than replacing textbooks with iPads; it's about using technological tools to enable changes to traditional practices that improve learning. The Common Core excites many education technology enthusiasts because it presents the opportunity to funnel hardware and wireless capabilities into otherwise skeptical or unwilling districts. At the same time, hastily procuring new technologies solely to meet new specifications risks stifling the opportunity that technology presents to improve learning and fundamentally redesign schooling altogether.

This chapter will draw on these concerns in order to anticipate how both strands of the education reform movement will fare as they move forward simultaneously. It will close with recommendations for policy makers and practitioners tasked with implementing and reconciling the Common Core in an increasingly digitized school environment.

NEW CONTENT AND INSTRUCTIONAL MATERIALS

The Common Core has the potential to increase competition between major publishers, and therefore improve the quality of textbooks and resources. Moreover, because of increasing demand, lower costs, and the ability to publish at scale, many new "Common Core–aligned" materials are coming in digital form. While these changes can prove advantageous to states, districts, and schools, they also present many roadblocks.

A National Market

In the BCC (Before Common Core) era, states were on their own to obtain instructional materials aligned to their particular standards. As education historian Diane Ravitch points out in her 2003 book *The Language Police,* this led the larger states, most notably Texas and California, to dominate the market.[4] Textbook manufacturers, supplemental material authors, and professional development resources often included content or supplemental sections that would satisfy other states' standards, but small states struggled to find appropriate instructional materials.[5]

The Common Core will ostensibly alleviate these concerns. A widely shared set of standards creates a national market for instructional materials. As Susan Patrick, president and chief executive officer of the International Association for K–12 Online Learning (iNACOL) explains, "Economies of scale can be realized in the content, professional development, and assessments developed and aligned to the Common Core."[6] For instance, Khan Academy, an online video lesson provider, makes it easy for users to find videos aligned with particular standards. These opportunities are likely to increase the number of schools implementing what has now become known as "blended learning," in which students spend part of the day learning online and part of the day learning in the traditional fashion with an instructor.

A widely shared set of standards also increases the market and demand for existing digital tools, inviting more entrepreneurs to enter the education space. One such entrepreneurial enterprise is DreamBox Learning, an adaptive online mathematics program founded in 2006, which advertises a Common Core–aligned curriculum. DreamBox allows students and teachers to receive feedback reports including detailed, line-by-line assessments of which standards each student has mastered so that teachers can target particular students and remediate accordingly.

Beyond this, the Common Core will present the opportunity to move education-related materials from print to digital form. Tom Vander Ark, venture capitalist and former school superintendent, predicts that in 5 years "half of states and districts will stop buying print textbooks and will shift to customizable digital texts and open education resources."[7] Indeed, from 2010 to 2012, more than a dozen states changed their policies or launched initiatives to encourage the use of digital content and, in some cases, open educational resources instead of print textbooks.[8] There are many factors driving this shift, not the least of which is the possibility to lower costs. Vander Ark found, "The roughly $8 billion spent annually on textbooks amounts to about $150 for every student, the price of a tablet computer running Google's Android operating system."[9]

Traditional textbook publishers have been slow to ditch paper and ink for computer screens, as evidenced by the acquisition of McGraw-Hill by private equity firm Apollo Global Management in late 2012. McGraw-Hill cited the transition to digital materials and the "massive changes in what employees do and how products are sold" as a reason for the split.[10] Others have welcomed the shift; Pearson, for example, has developed a Common

Core–based curriculum designed specifically for tablets and unavailable in print, the first of its kind for the company. As Luyen Chou, chief product officer for K–12 technology at Pearson Education, says of the new product, "it will be born digital."[11]

The Wild, Wild West

Advocates, such as the Alliance for Excellent Education, have argued that the Common Core will create the opportunity for states to work together and utilize a "wisdom of crowds" approach to buying instructional materials.[12] Though a larger marketplace has many upsides, it does present challenges when it comes to vetting materials. We have very little information about which instructional materials are being used in schools, and which are most effective.[13] This problem will only be amplified as the number of products that claim to be aligned to the Common Core multiplies without any mechanism to separate the wheat from the chaff. John Bailey, executive director of Digital Learning Now, suggests, "There is no sort of guidance as to who has the final authority to say that a product or a software system, or a book is aligned, or not aligned. And so, it's become a bit of a wild, wild west."[14] Further, because the assessments will not be available until 2014, it will be difficult to test whether these products are successful in the meantime. In addition, states have not taken advantage of the opportunity to work together when it comes to procuring and vetting resources. Bailey explains that some states, like Tennessee, are copyrighting their materials, making resources even more difficult to share.

Whether or not states decide to purchase digital or paperback content, procuring the necessary materials will be expensive. New York City, for example, estimated the cost of buying textbooks and other materials aligned to the Common Core will be $56 million.[15] Instead of marketing all new materials to cash-strapped districts, some textbook companies are busy retrofitting older curricula—begging the question of whether the transition to the Common Core will bring about fresh content or merely incentivize providers to put new covers on old books. Further, districts will need to anticipate future changes in the standards and allow the flexibility to adjust their curricular offerings accordingly.

It would appear that the increasing need and desire for digital instructional materials would find a natural complement in a new national marketplace for such resources. But the cost of buying new materials, and the difficulty determining which are the best to choose, are challenges with which states, districts, and schools will continue to wrestle.

INSTRUCTIONAL STRATEGIES

A 2012 Scholastic survey of over 10,000 teachers found that almost a third felt unprepared to teach the Common Core.[16] It is true that teachers will need to adjust their instruction to sync with the transition to common standards, not only to teach new content, but also to fully utilize new digital tools. While technology can provide a more convenient and robust platform to help teachers share instructional strategies, using these tools will require that teachers receive adequate preservice education and support through professional development.

Sharing New Strategies Online

Technology can be a useful tool to help teachers adapt their instruction to meet new standards. New entrepreneurial organizations such as Better-Lesson, Share My Lesson, and LearnZillion have created online platforms that allow teachers to share lessons and resources specifically aligned to particular Common Core standards. BetterLesson houses over 300,000 lesson files uploaded from teachers across the country, available for free to all teachers. Similarly, LearnZillion has created a "Dream Team" of exceptional teachers to provide high-quality, Common Core–aligned lesson plans. Finally, teachers can capitalize on resources like Mastery Connect, which provides a platform for teachers to share their assessments and track student mastery of various standards, including the Common Core.

An expanded Common Core–driven marketplace has attracted new interest in creating online professional development tools. Startup Bloomboard, for example, has created a platform for districts to use their observation and planning tools for professional development. Educators can learn new strategies by watching videos of others teaching Common Core–aligned lessons. Other organizations such as America Achieves and Student Achievement Partners have published resources on their websites to help teachers understand the Common Core and adapt their practices to teach to the new standards.

Increasing use of technology in conjunction with the Common Core will also grant teachers access to new data about student performance. Spurred in part by the Obama administration's Race to the Top competition, 20 states now require that student performance is a significant criterion in teacher evaluations.[17] John Bailey sees this shift as crucial for increasing teacher demand for timely student data and online professional development tools. He explains, "Teachers are going to be more open to data analytics systems and formative assessments, and more early warning signs if kids are on track or off track. They'll become must-haves pretty quickly when your job is on the line."

Teachers and Technology

Though technology can be helpful to teachers' practice, the Common Core's emphasis on technology does not come without concern. Most teachers recognize the benefits that new technology presents; Scholastic's 2012 survey found that 88% of veteran teachers agree that properly integrated technology in the classroom has a strong impact on improving academic achievement.[18] But including technology in their daily instruction can be a challenge for teachers.

Specifically, teachers may fear that technology will limit or place undue stress on their daily routine. First, teachers may worry that technology will replace their traditional role in the classroom. If so, teachers unions will fight against it to protect teacher jobs. As Idaho Education Association president Penni Cyr explains, "We know that online providers, as they have done in the past, will continue to use fewer teachers to teach more students. . . . That equates to a loss of teaching positions if you are requiring online courses."[19] Further, teachers feel that learning how to use technology in the classroom has added more stress to what is already a challenging job. In a 2013 nationwide survey of Advanced Placement and National Writing Project Teachers, 75% said that the Internet and other "digital tools" have added new demands and have increased the range of content and skills needed to teach. Forty-one percent say these tools create more work on their part.[20]

Moreover, many teachers argue that they do not receive adequate training in both teacher education institutions and professional development to prepare them to use new technologies in the classroom, leading them to resent the new tools. Education analyst Andrew Rotherham explains, "Many teachers are not familiar with technology or how to use it in the classroom, and high-quality training programs—either in schools of education or as part of a teacher's ongoing professional development—are rare."[21] A recent study from Blackboard Inc. and Project Tomorrow found a gap between principals' expectations for how teachers should integrate technology and the training those teachers received in order to do so. For instance, 45% of principals want teachers to incorporate student-owned mobile devices into their classrooms, but only 19% of aspiring teachers know how to do this.[22] With the Common Core nudging education technology into more classrooms, institutions that prepare teachers may feel more pressure to adapt to a changing teaching role.

Beyond improvements to preservice education, schools and districts will need to provide Common Core–oriented professional development to the more than 3 million teachers already in classrooms. Former executive director of the Council of Chief State School Officers Gene Wilhoit has written, "Nothing could be more critical to immediate success of the Common Core than professional development. . . . [Teachers] know this transition will be challenging and they're looking to states for guidance."[23] Unfortunately, both policy makers and practitioners have long regarded professional development as ineffective, so making meaningful improvements through this medium will be a challenge.[24]

ASSESSMENT

While the aforementioned issues present their own formidable challenges, the transition to online assessments might be the greatest hurdle the Common Core must overcome. Though computer adaptive testing may provide a more reliable and affordable measure of student knowledge and ability, preparing for the transition from paper-and-pencil to digital tests will introduce serious obstacles for many districts.

At the time of this publication, two consortia, the Partnership for Assessment of Readiness for College and Careers (PARCC) and the Smarter Balanced Assessment Consortium (SBAC), are developing assessments to measure student progress on the Common Core Standards. The computerized tests, both summative and formative, have been developed using $330 million in federal money, and have been lauded as an improvement over their oft-maligned standardized peers. For instance, when the federal grant application for the Race to the Top Assessment Program was released, Secretary of Education Arne Duncan referred to them as "an absolute game-changer in public education."[25]

In many ways, technology and testing make a promising pair. As Tom Vander Ark explains, "Online assessments are at the heart of the promise of digital learning." Why? They allow for more rapid feedback, providing "real time diagnostics that identify learning levels and gaps."[26] Here, the online nature of the assessments is a win for practitioners. Both PARCC and Smarter Balanced expect a quick turnaround for test results of approximately 2 weeks, and will employ an online reporting system and digital resource library.[27] Thus, instead of receiving a report at the end of the year, teachers can obtain feedback about student progress much more readily, which will be useful for designing individually targeted interventions.

Smarter Balanced is developing computer adaptive tests, meaning they cater questions of varying difficulty to individual test takers in order to discern the most accurate measure of a student's knowledge and skills. For instance, a student who answers the first question wrong will receive an easier question than a student who answers it right. They are seen as a vast improvement over the No Child Left Behind era exams that clustered the vast majority of questions around a benchmark for proficiency and had little sensitivity to determine student performance at either end of the scoring spectrum.[28] The tests will also include a significant amount of writing, which will be scored using computerized "intelligent scoring." As Vander Ark says, performance tasks that ask students to research and analyze information will "power the future of customized learning" and produce higher level, more reliable tests.[29]

But while online tests come with many advantages, they bring with them many practical challenges.

Given that the underlying logic of the Common Core is to allow for the ability to compare results across states, guaranteeing that the assessments are fair and reliable is crucial. To that end, PARCC and Smarter Balanced have designated certain device specifications and a time frame in which the tests must be issued. There are also certain infrastructure conditions necessary to carry out testing, including the amount of available bandwidth. It is important to understand each of these conditions, and their complications, in depth.

Device Specifications

First, both PARCC and Smarter Balanced require testing devices to have at least a 9.5-inch screen. This includes all desktops, laptops, and most tablets, but rules out smartphones and the iPad mini. Smartphones are becoming more prominent in classrooms; in fact, according to a 2013 nationwide survey of Advanced Placement and National Writing Center teachers, 73% allowed students to use smartphones to turn in assignments or complete work.[30]

The consortia also have rules about security and device add-ons. For example, PARCC requires headphones and microphones for students to take the tests, as well as external keyboards if a tablet is being used as a testing device.

Other specifications govern device operating systems. These requirements are disconcerting because some operating systems will become obsolete in a few years, imposing new burdens on cash-strapped districts. For example, according to the most recent National Council on Educationn Statistics (NCES) data, 84% of districts are using Windows XP Service Pack 3, an operating system allowable under both consortia's "minimum requirements."[31] Though these machines will be passable (though not "recommended") by consortia standards, districts will have to shift to new operating systems relatively quickly, as Microsoft will stop supporting the program in April 2014.

Many schools will have difficulties making these upgrades. Take Ohio's Union Local School District in rural Appalachia, for example, which has just 100 computers for its 1,000 students. District superintendent Kirk Glasgow says, "I hate to even admit to this, but we have some computers that are still operating on the Windows 95 operating system. That's terrible. Windows 95 will not operate with these tests." With the district having recently cut 17% of its $12 million budget, it won't be able to afford new devices or upgrades.[32]

Some providers have responded to the consortia's specifications by creating and marketing new devices at lower costs. Amplify, a company that produces K–12 education technology products, has created a tablet designed specifically for middle schools with a 10-inch screen. The tablet comes equipped with applications that allow teachers to check for understanding and access millions of Common Core–aligned lessons. Apple is selling iPads and other devices in packs of ten to make technology more affordable during this time.

Testing Window

With paper-and-pencil tests, an entire grade could conceivably take the same test simultaneously. Now, with each student having to use an approved testing device, scheduling could become much more complicated. The PARCC assessments encompass nine sessions, five for the performance-based assessments (PBA), and four for the end of the year component (EOY). PARCC estimates that students will need between 8 and 10 hours to complete each of the sessions in total (4–6 hours for the PBA and 3.5–4.5 for the EOY) each year, depending on the grade. Schools have a maximum of 20 school days to administer the PBA and 20 for the EOY.[33] Administrators will need to determine how many devices they will need in order to ensure all students can take the tests in the allotted time period. Staggered testing also introduces the possibility that some students will be taking the tests 4 weeks later than others, complicating security and reliability.

When it comes to making sure all students have the capability to take the test during a specified period of time, schools like Burlington High School in Massachusetts, which has adopted a one-to-one iPad program, are generally all set. However, for others with fewer computers, calculating the number of devices needed per student can get tricky. How many hours in an average 6-hour school day can be devoted to testing? What if one of the computers malfunctions and the ratio of students to devices must be adjusted? PARCC offers resources to help schools figure out how many devices they need for assessments, depending on the number of students in each grade, the number that can be tested simultaneously, and the school's available bandwidth.[34]

These testing window calculations may spur districts to buy more devices. Take the Sioux Falls School District in South Dakota, for example, which plans to spend $7 million over a 2-year period to buy Google Chromebooks. As the Associated Press reported, "District administrators long have been interested in providing each student with a computing device, but the shift to online tests gave them reason to do it sooner rather than later."[35] In planning for the testing window, Louisiana found that schools would need a 7 to 1 ratio of devices to students in order to administer the tests. The state estimates it will need to procure more than 35,000 new devices or upgrade some of the 100,000 current devices that fail to meet specifications in order to meet the requirements.[36]

However, other districts with fewer computers than students will struggle to orchestrate the process during the window allotted. Oklahoma's Hilldale Elementary school has only 43 computers for 400 students. Hilldale Public Schools superintendent Kaylin Coody told *Education Week,* "With the current financial constraints facing Oklahoma public schools, I do not see how most of us will be able to provide adequate hardware and prepare staff to manage the level of testing being planned, especially in a short testing window."[37]

Bandwidth and Connectivity

Ultimately, connectivity and bandwidth may be most critical in determining district capacity to take Common Core–aligned tests. Bandwidth represents the amount of data traveling across a network at a given time.[38] Rather than a set number, the level of bandwidth required for a school district depends on the number of students simultaneously taking the test. For example, Smarter Balanced reports that 2Mbps (megabits per second) can support 200 students.[39] As the State Education Technology Directors Association (SETDA) notes, "Most K–12 districts in the U.S now provide their students and teachers with some level of Internet access, but too often the speeds of those connections fall short of what's appropriate for learning."[40] SETDA has released a report to help district officials understand their level of readiness, but according to executive director Doug Levin, the speed districts think they have is often less by the time it reaches the classroom and other factors such as traffic in the school and the wider Internet are taken into account.[41]

When it comes to testing, it is not just about having speed, it's about having the capacity to allow all users on the network to perform at that speed. As EducationSuperHighway, a nonprofit working to provide better Internet infrastructure to schools, estimates, the typical school has the same Internet access as a typical home, with 100 times more users.[42] Having many users on the network at once strains the connection. Even schools that are used to digital learning are worried about bandwidth capacity during testing. Dennis Villano, director of Technology Integration at Burlington Public Schools in Massachusetts, oversaw the school's transition to one-to-one iPad classrooms. He explains that the network is an easy thing to forget about, but is critically important: "The biggest thing is not so much the device when it comes to test days—we're mostly concerned about infrastructure, wireless, and making sure the network is running. The network is the key, and then the devices really just connect to the network."

Cash-strapped districts often turn to the E-Rate program, a $2.3 billion federal program that helps districts and schools obtain discounts on telecommunication services via reimbursement. Joe Kitchens, superintendent of Oklahoma's Western Heights independent school district, says that the typical number of students online at one time is around 400. In order for all 3,700 students to take the Common Core tests, the district will have to double or triple its online capability. The district has applied for $30,000 of E-Rate funding to double its bandwidth, and $475,000 to improve internal networks and connect classrooms.[43] However, E-Rate is often unable to fund all applicants; in FY 2011 the program was only able to fund about half of the $4 billion demand.[44] What's more, E-Rate often doesn't allow for the high-speed services schools will need.[45] In June 2013, President Obama called on the FCC to make major changes to the program to help alleviate these issues, but whether there will be enough political support to make the changes remains to be seen.

AN UNCERTAIN FUTURE

Even districts that are more accustomed to working with new technology in the classroom recognize the challenge of implementing new Common Core assessments. North Carolina's Mooresville Graded School District has been using laptops in classrooms for 5 years now, but chief technology officer Scott Smith acknowledges it's tricky to prepare for the online tests. As he says, "You've got so many different variables to deal with. You've got to know the state of your wireless infrastructure and whether it's going to work based on your devices. You can do your best to simulate testing with some pilots and different groups, but it's very different when 1,600 kids at my high school all log in and do something at the same time." In some ways, it will be difficult to know whether districts are able to handle the new assessments until the first testing day arrives.

All of this culminates in the ultimate hurdle: money. Regardless of the timing, the deals, or the federal assistance, implementing the requirements associated with rolling out Common Core assessments will be expensive. The Pioneer Institute, which has been notably skeptical of the Common Core, offers a gross estimate of $6.9 billion in increased local district technology-related costs for those planning to implement assessments under the consortia.[46] That parses out to $2.8 billion in one-time up-front costs, $326 million in additional costs during the first year of operation, and $624 million in

costs for maintenance for the remaining 6 years. But the decidedly pro–
Common Core Thomas B. Fordham Institute reminds us in its 2012 report
on Common Core implementation, "It is nearly impossible to calculate the
cost of upgrading to a particular level of technology capacity because the
starting point varies from state to state, from district to district within a
state, and even among schools within a district."[47]

Indeed, all of the testing requirements rely on states, districts, and
schools being willing and able to pay for the necessary upgrades in hardware, infrastructure, and software—not only for the 2014 deadline but for
maintenance for years to come. Some districts, like Mooresville, have a budget line item to allow for technology costs every year, but other schools
don't have that luxury. According to 2008 (prerecession) data, more than a
third of districts do not have a formal computer replacement program built
into their budgets, and only 22% have an asset recovery program for at least
some of their computers.[48] Finding space to allow for long-term planning
will require a lot of political will, especially as school budgets have been lean
in the years following the recession. With the backlash surrounding standardized testing lately, it seems unlikely that districts will be able to claim
that testing is more important than, say, saving teacher jobs.

So how prepared are states to manage the implementation of these tests?
Our Magic 8 Ball says: "Outlook hazy." A few states, like Louisiana and
Florida, have done their own needs assessments. The results of these haven't
been optimistic. For instance, Louisiana found that only two districts met
both device and network readiness requirements.[49] Former Florida education commissioner Tony Bennett has mentioned devising a Plan B in case
the state is not ready for the Common Core assessments by the 2014 deadline. Those that have speculated from outside seem doubtful: In February
2013, Whiteboard Advisors reported that three quarters of its "Education
Insiders," a small, anonymous group of influential players in the education
world, feared schools lacked the necessary devices and bandwidth to be able
to meet consortia requirements in time for the 2014–15 school year.[50]

A CAUTIONARY NOTE: LET LEARNING COME FIRST

When contemplating the obstacles technology presents for Common Core
implementation, it is also important to reflect on how the Common Core
will impact the digital learning movement writ large.

On the surface, the Common Core can seem like a blessing to education technology enthusiasts. Forty-five states must now upgrade bandwidth,
acquire newer devices, and ensure their teachers can capably use technology
in the classroom. The Common Core will also create a new national marketplace for instructional materials and professional development, encouraging

the production of digital content. As chief information officer Valerie Truesdale of North Carolina's largest school district, Charlotte-Mecklenberg, has said, the Common Core is "an opportunity to upgrade every aspect of our schooling."[51]

But, while the Common Core may push schools to adopt new technologies, there are other valid reasons for those excited about the promise of technology to transform schooling to be skeptical of this movement. What often becomes lost in headlines about district iPad sales is that many who support the digital learning movement maintain that it's less about the technology than about changing and improving the environment in which students learn. As one of the editors of this volume, Frederick M. Hess, has written, "Technology can be a powerful lever for rethinking schools and systems. But it's the rethinking that matters, not the technology. . . . Unfortunately, too many educators, industry shills, and technology enthusiasts seem to imagine that the technology itself will be a difference maker."[52] When it comes to technology's contribution to education, the focus has to stay on the learning. As Kaplan's chief learning officer Bror Saxberg explains, "The problem with learning is not with technology, nor with the assessments—it's with the lack of focus on what works for learning. . . . The key is not to just add screens and silicon and hope for the best."[53]

Because it should be more strategic than random, integrating technological tools in the classroom should come with a great deal of patience and careful planning. If districts hastily procure new technologies solely to meet the Common Core specifications, they risk stifling the opportunity that technology presents to improve learning and fundamentally rethink schooling altogether. Michael Horn, executive director of education at the Clayton Christensen Institute and one of the authors of *Disrupting Class* (2008, McGraw-Hill), worries that some districts may "buy into technology for the wrong reason, rather than starting with the 'What are we trying to enable? What's the problem we're solving?' perspective and then attacking it from there."

For example, districts might choose devices in order to meet testing requirements, and not necessarily think about how they can be used for learning. Dennis Villano, director of technology integration at Burlington Public Schools, explains, "I think too many schools are making their decisions based on what the [assessment consortia] requirements are—not what's best for the students and teachers." He encourages districts that are serious about transitioning to digital learning to stick to their own plans first and think of Common Core second, "We will never allow the PARCC to make a decision or force our hand on what we think is best for the classroom. So if the iPad minis are best, that's what we'll go with. And if we have to find another solution for testing, we will."

Similarly, Riverside Unified School District in California has taken on a "Bring Your Own Device" program, in which students are allowed to bring any device they own to use for work during the school day. Riverside's chief technology officer Jay McPhail says that his district is holding firm and continuing the model despite Common Core testing requirements, but explains he sees other places making decisions based on consortia specifications, "Districts are saying, 'Well, I'm not going to buy anything other than a 10-inch screen,' hedging their bets in terms of what's going on." But this may be easier said than done, especially for districts with tight budgets.

If these attitudes endure, this wave of education technology will prove no more fruitful than past enthusiastic, yet unrealized, claims about the potential of the radio or filmstrips to transform education. Many may recall Stanford Emeritus Professor Larry Cuban's depressing account of education technology's failure to impress, *Oversold and Underused: Computers in the Classroom*. Cuban reminds us that we have so often swung from hype to disappointment when introducing new technologies and computers into schools.[54] This is because we have traditionally layered technology on to existing practices—replacing chalkboards with smartboards but using them for the same tasks—instead of using them to actually redesign teaching and learning. As Cuban writes, "Although promoters of new technologies often spout the rhetoric of fundamental change, few have pursued deep and comprehensive changes in the existing system of schooling."[55]

Michael Horn notes that online testing is promising, but because of what it allows teachers to do and students to learn, not because it's impressive looking. The underlying motivation is what's important; Horn says, "Technology should not be the end. If that's the case, we've really screwed up. It's a means to the end, and making that something that's reasonable can actually use technology that's full service. Otherwise it's just going to replace textbooks, which would be kind of lame." Lame, and a waste of technology's real potential to help craft new school designs, as has been done successfully in districts like North Carolina's Mooresville Graded School District and charter school networks like Rocketship Education and Summit Public Schools. Both Rocketship and Summit have embraced a model in which students spend part of their day learning at computer workstations, leaving behind the typical 30-students-per-class lecture model with the help of technology.

Yet, standards can play a vital role in the redesign process. Mooresville's chief technology officer Scott Smith explains:

> Common Core is a complement to what we've done. We've trained a lot of our teachers on different aspects of the digital environment. When you tie that with the Common Core standards, it creates an environment where every kid can have individualized instruction, remediation, and acceleration if they need it.

When approached with a "learning first" mindset, the Common Core can be a natural partner to those districts already using new technologies for instruction.

POLICY RECOMMENDATIONS

Technology will play a central role in the Common Core's triumph or failure. In order to maximize the chance of triumph and see the requisite changes in content, instructional strategies, and assessments, we suggest three areas for policy makers and educational leaders to consider.

Plan, Plan, and Plan Again

Policy makers and practitioners know that the Common Core assessments are coming, and they should plan accordingly. Scott Smith emphasizes the preparation aspect:

> Plan, plan, and plan again. I mean we joke about it, but before we were down this road, we talked through all the scenarios and we did extensive planning on what we thought was going to happen, and what it was going to look like, and, OK what are you going to do when this happens? And then, what's Plan B for this when this happens? And so, the preparation side of it is very important.

One strategy to help in the planning stages would be to pilot the tests within the district. Currently, 33 states offer some form of online testing.[56] Michigan recently piloted its online MEAP test for about 35,000 students in nearly 100 districts. The pilot served as a helpful rehearsal for the Common Core–aligned tests, allowing administrators and teachers to navigate questions such as how to troubleshoot technical problems with the hardware, collect student log-in information, and maintain test security.[57] However, like Scott Smith of Mooresville noted earlier, it is almost impossible to replicate what this will look like on testing day.

Consortia Should Keep in Mind District Capacity When Writing Requirements

To some districts knee-deep in digital learning programs, the requirements of the testing consortia may seem arbitrary. As Riverside's Jay McPhail explains, "People say, well, a kid can't take a test on a 4-inch screen. And so, we actually took them in to some third-grade classrooms where low and behold, the kid can actually can take the test on a 4-inch screen." The consortia and whatever governance structure emerges (see Chapter 8 for Patrick McGuinn's in-depth look at likely governance structures) should be wary that districts may be ahead of the movement. Based in part on districts' response the first time around, this governance structure may need to open up its requirements in order to prevent states and districts from opting out.

The consortia should acknowledge that some districts will be ill-prepared to take the online tests, and make the necessary modifications to ensure that they are able to take a nontech version. PARCC guidance assures that its assessments "will be available in paper-and-pencil format for students with disabilities whose Individualized Education Plans (IEPs) require it, and for schools that have gained approval for paper-and-pencil-based testing from their State Educational Agency (SEA)."[58] While waivers provide a safety valve for unprepared schools and districts, those that do not apply may decide to renege on the Common Core tests altogether, thus stifling the movement and impairing the reliability of the test results.

Leaders Should Get Creative

School, district, and state leaders should get creative with their existing resources in order to meet the testing requirements. For example, for Burlington Public Schools, a district in Massachusetts that is pursuing a one-to-one iPad program, tablet considerations are key. Specifically, the district has to figure out how to provide keyboards to meet PARCC requirements. Dennis Villano, the district's director of technology integration, describes Burlington's strategy, "We looked at some creative ways of using older keyboards—you actually can use a traditional old desktop keyboard with the camera adapter on an iPad—so instead of throwing away all those old keyboards, we can use them." This move has helped the district save substantial dollars that can be spent for other initiatives.

Districts can also get crafty in determining how to complete the tests within the allocated testing windows. Carissa Miller, deputy executive director of the Council of Chief State School Officers (CCSSO) and former deputy superintendent for the 21st Century Classroom at the Idaho Department of Education, describes how schools in Idaho's Meridian School District use a "hot seat" model to meet the allocated time frame. When one student finishes his or her test, he or she can leave the computer and allow another student to start. Therefore, students can take the test within a smaller window, avoiding interrupting teacher instructional time.[59]

Finally, districts can get creative to find the money to meet these requirements. Understanding the importance of technology and the Common Core, Charlotte-Mecklenburg school district worked with the local Parent Teacher Association (PTA) and local businesses to solicit device donations. The district also charted out its needs for funding per month for the next 24 months, so business partners could help assist in particular months with particular projects. They didn't need to ask for a big chunk of money up front, but the move helped to secure the local business community as a partner in the Common Core effort.[60] Such a strategy could serve useful in the long run, in order to keep the business community as an out-front supporter of the Common Core.[61]

CONCLUSION

It is unclear whether the Common Core will complement or conflict with the existing digital learning movement. At first glance, the Common Core has created a viable market for instructional materials, improved access to teacher professional development resources, and has prompted investors and education technology–driven entrepreneurs to invest in the market. Further, the tests that will accompany the standards are largely thought to be of higher quality than existing tests, in part because their digital nature allows for otherwise impossible new capabilities.

However, there are real reasons to be concerned about the relationship between technology and the Common Core. First, there does not appear to be any mechanism for vetting resources or providers in a growing market for instructional materials. Second, while new online tools are emerging to help teachers prepare to teach the standards, teachers aren't fully equipped to use technology in their classrooms. Lastly, the online testing challenges may be the most onerous of all. It is unclear whether states, districts, and schools have the capacity to make the necessary purchases and changes to meet the consortia specifications. The requirements may frustrate policy makers and practitioners, leading to backlash against the Common Core that may derail the effort altogether.

Ultimately, schools should ensure that learning comes first. They should shy away from making purchases solely because of the consortia requirements, but instead should consider how these purchases will enable them to provide a better learning environment for students. Only then will the Common Core effort be both sustainable and able to take advantage of the unique opportunities technology presents.

NOTES

1. Common Core State Standards Initiative. (2012). *English language arts standards, writing, kindergarten*. Retrieved from http://www.corestandards.org/ELA-Literacy/W/K; Common Core State Standards Initiative. (2012). *English language arts standards, writing, grade 11–12*. Retrieved from http://www.corestandards.org/ELA-Literacy/W/11-12

2. Roscorla, T. (2010). *Technology permeates common core standards*. Retrieved from Center for Digital Education website: http://www.centerdigitaled.com/policy/Technology-Permeates-Common-Core-Standards.html

3. Bailey, J., Schneider, C., & Vander Ark, T. (2012, December). *Getting ready for online assessments*. Retrieved from Digital Learning Now! website: http://www.digitallearningnow.com/wp-content/uploads/2013/01/Getting-Ready-for-Online-Asst.-Updated-Jan-2013.pdf

4.   Ravitch, D. (2004). *The language police: How pressure groups restrict what students learn.* New York: Vintage Books.

5.   Bimbaum, M. (2010, March 18). Historians speak out against proposed Texas textbook changes. *Washington Post.* Retrieved from http://www.washingtonpost.com/wp-dyn/content/article/2010/03/17/AR2010031700560.html

6.   Ash, K. (2011, January 7). Common Core conversation with Susan Patrick. *Education Week.* Retrieved from http://www.edweek.org/ew/articles/2011/01/12/15edtech_standardsqa.h30.html

7.   Vander Ark, T. (2012). *Getting smart: How digital learning is changing the world.* San Francisco, CA: Jossey Bass.

8.   Education Sector. (2012, June). *Getting to 2014 (and beyond): The choices and challenges ahead.* Washington, DC: Education Sector. Retrieved from http://www.educationsector.org/sites/default/files/publications/Gettingto2014_BEYOND_Release.pdf

9.   Vander Ark, *Getting smart,* p. 70.

10.   Henry, D. (2012, November 26). McGraw-Hill sells textbook unit to private equity. Retrieved from Reuters website: http://www.reuters.com/article/2012/11/26/us-mcgrawhill-apollo-idUSBRE8AP0N120121126

11.   Davis, M. R. (2013, February 6). "Big three" publishers rethink K–12 strategies. *Education Week.* Retrieved from http://www.edweek.org/dd/articles/2013/02/06/02textbooks.h06.html

12.   Alliance for Excellent Education. (n.d.). What are Common standards? Retrieved June 11, 2013, from http://www.all4ed.org/common-standards/what_are_common_standards

13.   Chingos, M., & Whitehurst, G. (2012). *Choosing blindly: Instructional materials, teacher effectiveness, and the Common Core.* Washington, DC: Brookings Institution, Brown Center on Education Policy. Retrieved from http://www.brookings.edu/~/media/research/files/reports/2012/4/10%20curriculum%20chingos%20whitehurst/0410_curriculum_chingos_whitehurst.pdf

14.   Unless otherwise specified, quotes were obtained during personal interviews with the authors between February 1 and March 30, 2013.

15.   Baker, A. (2013, February 28). "New state academic standards are said to require $56 million outlay for city's schools." *New York Times.* Retrieved from http://www.nytimes.com/2013/03/01/education/new-york-schools-detail-cost-of-meeting-new-standards.html?_r=2&

16.   Scholastic & the Bill & Melinda Gates Foundation. (2012). *Primary sources: 2012: America's teachers on the teaching profession.* Retrieved from http://www.scholastic.com/primarysources/pdfs/Gates2012_full.pdf

17.   National Council on Teacher Quality. (2012). *State of the states 2012: Teacher effectiveness policies.* Retrieved from http://www.nctq.org/p/publications/docs/Updated_NCTQ_State%20of%20the%20States%202012_Teacher%20Effectiveness%20Policies.pdf

18.   Scholastic & the Bill & Melinda Gates Foundation, *Primary sources: 2012.*

19.   Quilllen, I. (2012, August 7). Can technology replace teachers? *Education Week.* Retrieved from http://www.edweek.org/ew/articles/2012/08/08/37replace_ep.h31.html

20. Purcell, K., Heaps, A., Buchanan, J., & Friedrich, L. (2013, February 28). *How teachers are using technology at home and in their classrooms.* Washington, DC: Pew Research Center, National Writing Project, and The College Board. Retrieved from http://www.pewinternet.org/~/media//Files/Reports/2013/PIP_TeachersandTechnologywithmethodology_PDF.pdf

21. Rotherham, A. (2012, January 26). "Can computers replace teachers?" *Time Ideas.* Retrieved from http://ideas.time.com/2012/01/26/can-computers-replace-teachers/

22. Pierce, D. (2013, February 7). Aspiring teachers ill-prepared to use ed tech effectively. *ESchool News.* Retrieved from http://www.eschoolnews.com/2013/02/07/aspiring-teachers-ill-prepared-to-use-ed-tech-effectively/?ps=118746-0013000000j0TKX-0033000000q5ntC

23. Wilhoit, G. (2012) Make-or-break state action. *Phi Delta Kappan,* 94(2), 47–49. Retrieved from http://intl.kappanmagazine.org/content/94/2/47.full.pdf+html

24. Yoon, K. S., Duncan, T., Lee, S., Scarloss, B., & Shapley, K. (2007). *Reviewing the evidence on how teacher professional development affects student achievement* (Issues & Answers Report, REL 2007–No. 033). Washington, DC: U.S. Department of Education, Institute of Education Science, National Center for Education Evaluation and Regional Assistance, Regional Laboratory Southwest. Retrieved from http://ies.ed.gov/ncee/edlabs/regions/southwest/pdf/REL_2007033.pdf

25. Duncan, A. (2010, September 2). *Beyond the bubble tests: The next generation of assessments—Secretary Arne Duncan's remarks to state leaders at Achieve's American Diploma Project leadership team meeting.* Washington, DC: U.S. Department of Education. Retrieved from http://www.ed.gov/news/speeches/beyond-bubble-tests-next-generation-assessments-secretary-arne-duncans-remarks-state-l

26. Vander Ark, T. (2012, March 29). Getting ready for online assessment [Web log post]. *Getting smart.* Retrieved from http://gettingsmart.com/cms/blog/2012/03/getting-ready-for-online-assessment/

27. Bailey et al., *Getting ready for online assessments.*

28. Weiss, D., & Von Minden, S. (2011). Measuring individual growth with conventional and adaptive tests. *Journal of Methods and Measurement in the Social Sciences,* 2(2), 80–101.

29. Vander Ark, "Getting ready for online assessment."

30. Purcell et al., *How teachers are using technology.*

31. Gray, L., Thomas, N., & Lewis, L. (2010). *Educational technology in U.S. public schools: Fall 2008.* (NCES 2010-034). Washington, DC: U.S. Department of Education, National Center for Education Statistics, p. 8. Retrieved from http://nces.ed.gov/pubs2010/2010034.pdf

32. Kirk Glasgow, quoted in Lieszkovszky, I. (2013, March 21). *Rural schools struggle to prepare for Common Core's online tests.* Retrieved from StateImpact Ohio website: http://stateimpact.npr.org/ohio/2013/03/21/rural-schools-struggle-to-prepare-for-common-cores-online-tests/

33. Partnership for Assessment of Readiness for College and Careers (PARCC). (2013, March). *PARCC assessment administration guidance version 1.0.* Retrieved

from http://www.parcconline.org/sites/parcc/files/PARCC%20Assessment%20 Administration%20Guidance_FINAL_0.pdf

34. PARCC's *Common Core Implementation Workbook* can be downloaded from the PARCC website (http://www.parcconline.org/CommonCoreImplementation Workbook).

35. Associated Press. (2013, April 1). "Sioux Falls students can't use computers for tests." *Daily Republic*. Retrieved from http://www.mitchellrepublic.com/ event/article/id/78064/

36. Louisiana Department of Education. (2012, July). *Louisiana believes: Louisiana's technology footprint*. Retrieved from http://www.doe.state.la.us/data/ files/footprint/2012/Lafourche_Footprint_July_2012.pdf

37. Davis, M. (2012, October 15). Are you tech-ready for the Common Core? *Education Week*. Retrieved from http://www.edweek.org/dd/ articles/2012/10/17/01readiness.h06.html

38. American Institutes for Research. (2013, March 15). *Smarter Balanced Assessment System: Technical specifications manual for the pilot test*. Retrieved from http://sbac.portal.airast.org/Pilot_Test/resources/Smarter_TechSpecsManual_Pilot.pdf

39. Smarter Balanced Assessment Consortium. (2013, February 6). *Hardware & operating systems*. Retrieved from http://www.smarterbalanced.org/wordpress/ wp-content/uploads/2011/12/Hardware-Operating-Systems-Infographic_2-6-13.pdf

40. State Education Policy Center (SEPC). (2012). *State education policy center* [Database]. Retrieved from http://sepc.setda.org/

41. Cavanagh, S. (2013, March 1). New guide offered to help schools gauge Internet needs [Web log post]. *Education Week, Digital Education blog*. Retrieved from http://blogs.edweek.org/edweek/DigitalEducation/2013/03/new_guide_offered_to_test_scho.html

42. Education Superhighway. (n.d.). *Broadband information gap*. Retrieved June 12, 2013, from http://www.educationsuperhighway.org/broadband-information-gap.html

43. Cavanagh, S. (2013, January 15). Districts look to e-rate program to help with Common Core tech costs. *Education Week*. Retrieved from http://www.edweek.org/ew/articles/2013/01/16/17e-rate.h32.html

44. Schroeder, D. (2012, January 27). *E-rate demand: The true story*. [Web log Post]. Retrieved from Funds for Learning website: http://www.fundsforlearning. com/blog/2012/01/e-rate-demand-true-story

45. Wyatt, E. (2013, March 12). Fund that subsidizes Internet for schools should expand, a senator says. *New York Times*. Retrieved from http://www.nytimes.com/2013/03/13/technology/fund-that-subsidizes-internet-for-schools-should-expand-a-senator-says.html?_r=0; Funds for Learning. (2012). Funds for Learning survey reveals priorities of e-rate applicants. Retrieved from Funds for Learning website: http://www.fundsforlearning.com/release/2012/08/funds-learning-survey-reveals-priorities-e-rate-applicants

46. AccountabilityWorks. (2012). *National cost of aligning states and localities to the Common Core Standards*. (A Pioneer Institute and American Principles Project white paper). Retrieved from http://www.accountabilityworks.org/photos/ Cmmn_Cr_Cst_Stdy.Fin.2.22.12.pdf

47. Murphy, P., Regenstein, E., with McNamara K. (2012, May). *Putting a price tag on the Common Core: How much will smart implementation cost?* Washington, DC: Thomas B. Fordham Institute. P 42. Retrieved from http://edexcellencemedia.net/publications/2012/20120530-Putting-A-Price-Tag-on-the-Common-Core/20120530-Putting-a-Price-Tag-on-the-Common-Core-FINAL.pdf

48. Gray, L., & Lewis, L. (2009). *Educational technology in public school districts: Fall 2008* (NCES 2010-003). Washington, DC: National Center for Education Statistics, Institute of Education Sciences, U.S. Department of Education, p. 3. Retrieved from http://nces.ed.gov/pubs2010/2010003.pdf

49. Davis, Are you tech-ready?

50. Whiteboard Advisors. (2013, February). *Education insider: Digital learning and Common Core assessments.* Retrieved from http://www.whiteboardadvisors.com/files/Feb%202013%20-%20Education%20Insider%20(Digital%20Learning-Common%20Core)_2.pdf

51. Editorial Projects in Education, Inc. (Producer). (2013). *Getting tech-ready for Common Core testing* [Video webcast]. Retrieved from http://www.edweek.org/media/2013-3-7techreadycommoncore.pdf

52. Hess, F. (2012, November 28). Technology as "Hamburger Helper" [Web log post]. *Education Week, Rick Hess Straight Up.* Retrieved from http://blogs.edweek.org/edweek/rick_hess_straight_up/2012/11/technology_as_hamburger_helper.html

53. Saxberg, B. (2011, September 4). Technology driving learning, or learning driving technology: Which way 'round? [Web log post]. Retrieved from Bror's Blog website: http://brorsblog.typepad.com/brors-blog/2011/09/technology-driving-learning-or-learning-driving-technology-which-way-round.html

54. Cuban, L. (2003). *Oversold and underused: Computers in the classroom.* Cambridge, MA: Harvard University Press, p. 195.

55. Ibid., p. 195.

56. State Educational Technology Directors Association. (2011, June 22). *Technology requirements for large-scale computer-based and online assessment: Current status and issues,* p. 2. Retrieved from http://assess4ed.net/sites/default/files/techrequirements_june22_combined_0.pdf

57. Michigan Department of Education. (2012). Fall 2012 Social studies online pilot. Retrieved from http://www.michigan.gov/mde/0,4615,7-140-22709_31168-136745--,00.html

58. PARCC, *Assessment administration guidance,* p. 4.

59. Editorial Projects in Education. *Getting tech-ready for Common Core testing.*

60. Ibid.

61. Business Roundtable. (2010). Statement from Business Roundtable on the release of proposed K–12 Common Core Standards [Press release]. Retrieved from http://www.corestandards.org/assets/k12_statements/StatementK12Business Roundtable.pdf

CHAPTER 8

Visions and Challenges for Multistate Governance and Sustainability

Patrick McGuinn

MOST OF THE DEBATE surrounding the Common Core State Standards (CCSS) effort to date has focused on substantive issues related to what's in these standards and what will happen regarding their implementation and assessment. Less attention has been paid to crucial questions surrounding the governance of such an effort over the longer term, particularly if the federal government's role in it is limited (or nonexistent). How might decision making for a voluntary, state-based, but multistate set of common standards in education be institutionalized? How can the interests of diverse governmental and nongovernmental actors operating at the national, state, and local levels be accommodated? What kind(s) of institutional structure(s) can ensure that common standards and assessments remain rigorous and up-to-date, incentivize state participation, and create a stable governance and financing mechanism able to sustain the venture over time?

Although there were many participants in the development—and funding—of CCSS, at the end of the day the National Governors Association (NGA) and Council of Chief State School Officers (CCSSO) kept a tight rein on actual decisions. Today, the two groups literally hold the copyright on those standards on behalf of their respective memberships.[1] It appears that they are, in effect, "in control" of the Common Core until/unless an alternative structure is developed that meets with their assent. In some ways it resembles a privately held firm. Such firms have many advantages in the corporate world, but they also have disadvantages. A number of key players and stakeholders in the education space appear to believe that the Common Core—over the long haul, given its likely central role in American K–12 education—should be more akin to a publicly traded firm accountable to multiple shareholders, maybe even a public utility. This approach would, of course, bring its own complexities and disadvantages, as well as potential gains.

There is increasingly the sense that a more formal governance structure needs to be developed for managing the standards revision process and perhaps other ancillary tasks such as coordinating communications and tracking state implementation over the longer term.[2] The implementation of the CCSS poses many challenges for governance at the district, state, and national levels, as officials need to come to an agreement as to who "owns" what part of the standards, their assessment, and the systems of accountability and management built off of them.

Questions about governance are no longer esoteric, as debates are already raging about the content of the standards (such as the amount of fiction versus nonfiction reading) and assessments (such as where and how to set cut scores), and what the federal role will be in managing or funding them. It remains unclear who will make the decision about when and how the standards will be revised. This chapter is intended to facilitate and inform this conversation by laying out a variety of essential questions that are central to thinking about governance, irrespective of any particular structure, in this context. It will synthesize the results of interviews with 20 stakeholders representing a wide range of perspectives related to the Common Core.[3] The chapter will conclude by offering several possible governance models for further consideration, together with a preliminary appraisal of their strengths and weaknesses.

Most people seem to recognize that some kind of governance structure needs to eventually be put into place to make decisions about the Common Core Standards. That said, one of the most interesting findings to emerge from my interviews is how little most people outside of the NGA and CCSSO have thought about long-term governance issues. Among the few who have, much greater attention has been devoted to identifying the governance challenges that are likely to emerge than to how a particular structure or set of structures might be assembled to ameliorate them.

TIMING AND FORMALIZATION: WHEN DO THESE GOVERNANCE ISSUES NEED TO BE SETTLED?

The first question around governance centers on timing—*when* a new structure, whatever its form, should be announced. Or more specifically, at what point do different kinds of governance questions need to be answered? Opinions vary widely on this point, with some observers believing that long-term governance questions—and, in particular, the process by which the standards will ultimately be revised—need to be resolved now, while others believe that this is premature, that there is no rush, and that these questions are best left to a later date.

Several interviewees argued against creating *any* kind of new formal governance structure for the Common Core and advocated instead for a continuation of the loose coalition/network approach that has existed to date. Some fear that any national governing body—even if it keeps its distance from the federal government—could be depicted as a "national school board" and inflame the suspicions of Tea Party conservatives. Others felt that institutionalizing governance is unnecessary and may prove unworkable in practice.

So it appears that there is both a short-term and long-term dimension to thinking about Core governance. Why make an announcement about interim governance and the standards revision timetable now? There is tremendous concern in the field about the implementation of new standards and assessments and fear that the standards will be revised too early and/or too often, which would make implementation much harder both substantively and politically. There is also concern about the large turnover in governors (26 out of 45 adopting states so far) and state chiefs since the Core was adopted, as well as about future turnover that is likely to come in the 2014 elections. There is a sense that key organizations need to connect themselves more formally to the standards and for their members to publicly recommit themselves to them to provide some collective political cover.

Many interviewees also expressed concern about the political turbulence that will be created when the first test results are released in 2015, since they are expected to reveal worse student performance—and larger racial and socioeconomic achievement gaps—than previous state tests did. In addition, the major curricular and instructional changes—and sizable costs—necessary to implement the Common Core are becoming clearer as the process moves forward, which is making states skittish in the face of budgetary challenges.[4] There are fears that unless NGA and CCSSO and their members own the Common Core and are tightly connected to it, when the test results come in the Common Core could start to unwind and people will start to walk away from it. Additionally, the creation of a state-led governance structure—and the declaration that it will not accept any federal funding—is intended to combat the ongoing fear among some that the federal government will ultimately dictate decision making about the Core. It is also important to note that the timetable for governance decisions about the assessments is likely to be quite different from the timetable for the standards. New structures and resources may not be necessary for standards governance until the revision process begins, but the federal grants that fund the two assessment consortia will run out in 2014. As a result, the leaders of the assessment consortia will need to resolve questions about ownership, process, and funding sooner.

STRUCTURE AND REPRESENTATION: WHO GETS TO DECIDE? WHAT IS THE PROCESS? WHAT DO THEY DECIDE?

The most important governance questions center on who should have the power to make decisions about the future of the Common Core. Which individuals or groups should have a seat at the table? There are several tensions at work here—in particular, the need to balance inclusiveness with decisiveness in the decision-making process and the need to maintain states' commitment to the standards and assessments while keeping them rigorous and depoliticized. The question about power can be further subdivided into three subcomponents: representation, structure and process, and function. First, which individuals and groups should be involved in decision making? Second, what are the structures and processes that should guide their decision making? And third, which decisions/activities should they be responsible for?

Representation and Membership

The first question about representation centers on the appropriate size of the decision-making body. This is a particularly thorny issue because of the large and diverse array of organizations that have a stake in the implementation and revision of the standards and assessments. There is a fundamental tension here between the desire to be broadly inclusive—to include as many stakeholder groups as possible—and the desire to have an efficient decision-making process that can resolve policy questions in a timely and harmonious manner. One observer noted that even if the decision-making body is limited to governors and chiefs, there needs to be more than just a handful of them represented. "There needs to be a way to weave states into this institutionally more than they currently are, a tighter knitting together of states into this so there is a feeling that they are more invested in it." Others argued, however, that limiting the number of organizations and individual members on the executive committee would help to promote attendance, engagement, and ownership by those organizations and individuals because they will not just be "one of many." What is needed, one observer said, is "a 'Goldilocks' middle ground between coherence and inclusion, and between stability and adaptability—[the governance entity] should not be too easy to move or too quick to move. The whole point of the standards is that you don't want them to be static, but they also should not change every year. We have to think about what the right pace for changing them is and what the criteria should be."

A related question, but slightly different from that of the size of the governing entity, concerns membership: Which particular organizations or kinds of organizations are best suited to sit on such a governing body? Some interviewees expressed confidence that placing the governance of the Common Core in the hands of membership organizations like the NGA and CCSSO is a good idea because it is their members who play the critical role in adopting and implementing the standards. Other observers caution, however, that membership organizations are inevitably captive to the self-interest of their members and that this could threaten the objectivity of their decision-making process around the standards, ultimately undermining the rigor of the standards and assessments themselves. One interviewee remarked, "Having just NGA and CCSSO lead this is too slim—membership organizations are notoriously bad at doing anything that would be controversial for any of their members."

Another question related to representation is whether the standards decision-making entity should include only (or mostly) representatives from "supportive" organizations, or should it bring into the fold groups that have influence over the standards adoption and implementation process at the national or state level but who may be less "sold" on the ideas of common standards and assessments? Several interviewees, for example, highlighted the absence of state legislators from the long-term governance conversation as a major concern. It is widely acknowledged that legislators have not been consistent supporters of the Common Core and that they also may have a contentious relationship with governors and state chiefs. However, is it wise to exclude them from the standards decision-making body, given the central role that they will inevitably play at the state level in determining the future of the standards?

Another interviewee stated:

> To think that NGA and CCSSO would try to make decisions about the standards without having governing input—beyond just advisory—from the other two key state policy-making (state boards and legislatures) is a mistake. [We need] to have them at the table, even though I know full well that those relationships can be problematic and there is a lot of political tension among the four groups. But if you want people to stay on board you have to involve them in the process and give them ownership in the process—maybe it takes a little longer to make decisions but keeping people involved and informed is critical. And if the four organizations can demonstrate cooperation and the ability to interact with each other effectively at the national level than it could flow to the state level as a model and facilitate state level cooperation.

Several people argued for representation for the business and higher education communities on any CCSS governance entity given their crucial role in certifying the Common Core Standards as valid indicators of college and career readiness.[5]

Whatever specific *organizations* are given a seat on an executive committee, attention must also be paid to the kinds of *individuals* that should be chosen to represent the designated organizations. In particular, should the representatives be elected (or appointed) policy makers, their deputies, or the staff of national membership organizations? Do governors, state chiefs, and school-board presidents have the time and knowledge necessary to undertake engaged and informed leadership of the CCSS? Many of my interviewees believe that high-level public officials lack the necessary expertise to deal with the technical issues that will be at the heart of the standards implementation, validation, and revision process. Several wondered what a group of governors and chiefs would actually discuss at their meetings.

Several of the folks I spoke with also highlighted the political challenges that they believe would make it very difficult for sitting governors and chiefs to provide effective leadership for the CCSS. One questioned whether they would be able to decide when the standards are "good enough" during the revision process, since their governing responsibilities on the CCSS Executive Committee would inevitably conflict with their governing responsibilities in their home states. In addition, the hope is often expressed that state officials who serve on the Executive Committee will represent the interests not just of their particular state but of states in general, but several observers questioned whether it was realistic to expect members to subordinate their state's interests to the interests of the Common Core itself.

Decision-Making Structure and Process

What kind of governance structure is best suited to the CCSS? One way to think about the structural and procedural issues involved here is to identify the different types of decisions and decision makers that will be involved. There appear to be three quite distinct types of decisions that will need to be made in relation to the CCSS: *political* decisions, *operational* decisions, and *technical* decisions. Theoretically, all three kinds of decisions could be made by a single governing entity, but there may also be advantages to separating them out and housing them in different kinds of structures with different memberships and decision-making authorities and processes. On the one hand, elected political leaders will need to be involved in some capacity, given the fiscal and policy implications of CCSS governance decisions and the need to give them public legitimacy. But many of the people with whom I spoke expressed skepticism that elected leaders would be able or willing to make politically difficult or technically complicated decisions. For example, one interviewee remarked, "There is a struggle/trade-off between the desire to have broad buy-in and engagement at the highest policy-making level, and getting the work done and avoiding political posturing."

As a result, several of the people I interviewed suggested a governance structure that would include some combination of the following:

1. A small executive committee that would be in charge of the day-to-day operational decision making around the CCSS
2. A technical advisory board comprised of experts
3. A high-level political board that would meet quarterly or biannually to set broad policy

Others recommended that an advisory board—with a large and diverse membership—also be included to make recommendations to the executive committee and political board. The crucial question will be to determine which groups should have actual decision-making authority (on the executive committee) and which will be limited to making recommendations (on the advisory council). A related question centers on the independence of any new governance structure: Should it be housed inside of an existing organization, or should a new 501(c)(3) be created? One observer cautioned, however, "You could consider starting up a new place for it to live but watching the assessment consortia try to figure out their own sustainability shows how hard it is to create a new organization logistically and to build trust and reputation and brand and capacity—that takes a long time."

In addition to the size, composition, and structure of any decision-making body, careful thought needs to be given to *how* it will make decisions. What will the voting protocol be? Three possibilities come to mind—a majoritarian system (50% plus one), a supermajority system (perhaps a two-thirds or three-quarters threshold), or decision making by consensus/unanimity. Each model has advantages and disadvantages, and the approach chosen will have enormous consequences for governance, both in terms of how decisions are reached as well as how likely the body will be able to resolve contentious issues.

Function: What Tasks Should the Governance Entity Take on?

What kinds of functions need to be undertaken in support of the implementation of Common Core Standards and assessments? A 2010 Fordham report recommended that an interim monitoring and coordinating council be created to help guide the Common Core through the transition period until the standards need to be revised.[6] It called for this body to take on five tasks: (1) tracking and reporting on state implementation of standards and assessments; (2) promoting interstate collaboration around implementation; (3) initiating research programs to prepare for revision of standards; (4) undertaking public relations work to promote standards; and (5) recommending a long-term governance structure.

Many interviewees highlighted the importance of communications/public relations work related to the CCSS, particularly in the face of a growing political backlash. The Republican National Committee has taken a public stand against the Core and legislation calling for states to withdraw from the CCSS has advanced in several state legislatures (including Alabama, Indiana, Michigan, and Wyoming). One interviewee emphasized, "We have to have a real resetting of expectations in advance of release of new assessment results—going to be a lot fewer *proficient*, *advanced*, or *college-ready* students and big differences from what states have been reporting in the past." Another offered, "Communications help is a real need for states—states usually have one communications person and the districts none. They need elevator speeches—how to talk to principals, teachers, parents. Helping states to communicate with their legislators, working with NCSL [National Conference of State Legislatures]—need a neutral group to do this—NGA can't because they don't get along well with legislators."

Another possible function centers on research: Who should sponsor and conduct the validity studies and other "projects" that are vital to the long-term success of these standards and assessments—and that may lead to revisions of them over time? One observer believes, "You need a research and evaluation unit that collects and shares data and this should be part of this governance structure so that information can be brought into the standards revision process. There needs to be a mechanism for understanding how implementation is going and what adjustments need to be made. There needs to be a feedback loop—conduct surveys, focus groups with teachers and principals and superintendents and then bring that information back to policy makers." Other interviewees suggested additional tasks that a new governance entity might undertake. One emphasized the importance of creating an entity to certify Common Core–aligned instructional materials, and others called for working with professional development and teacher preparation programs to ensure that teachers are trained to understand the Common Core and how to align their teaching with it.

A majority of respondents agree that there was a tremendous need for technical assistance to the states, but opinions were divided about whether any single entity should provide it. A recent survey of state departments of education found that few have comprehensive implementation plans in place, despite a lot of planning work that is underway.[7] And early reports on implementation indicate that states are struggling to address some of the data collection and technological challenges around implementing the standards and assessments.[8] While some individual states have contracted with private companies to provide technical assistance around the Core, this fragmented state-by-state approach may not be conducive to the sharing of information and lessons across the country. One interviewee said, "There is a conundrum right now because the good news is that there is a lot of energy and resources going into developing supports. But the problem is that it is all over the place, not coherent and of very uneven quality, no synergy or bang for the buck. But the value of this work is the inventiveness and innovation that is happening, even though it will be messy for a while."

Several interviewees cautioned that "communications," "oversight," and "technical assistance" mean very different things to different people and that each function can be handled badly in such a way that it might damage the political support behind the Common Core. And any effort to try and assign supporting functions to a wide array of organizations may be stymied by the fact that many stakeholders are playing multiple roles/wearing multiple hats in and around Common Core and assessments. A good example of this phenomenon is Achieve, Inc., which, in addition to representing the interests of governors and the business community in education, contracts with states to provide technical assistance and is the project manager for PARCC.

ORGANIZATIONAL CAPACITY AND TECHNICAL VERSUS POLICY ISSUES

One issue related to the question about representation and function centers on what kind of decisions should be left to "political" leaders such as governors and state chiefs and which issues should be left to staff. A high-level governing board comprised of elected officials, for example, appears unlikely to be able by itself to devote much time toward direct work on the Common Core Standards, and its members are unlikely to possess the kind of technical expertise necessary to grapple with many of the important substantive issues that will inevitably arise. One interviewee noted, "I worry about a committee that has governors and chiefs on it because you won't be able to get them there and there will be a lot of turnover. I don't think it will be real, won't be able to get them together to talk about serious issues. They don't have the expertise to do the work either." In such a situation, by default if not by design, the real decision-making power of the executive committee is likely to devolve to the committee's staff. One observer noted, "The truth is that those folks will be figureheads and staff will do the real work and run the show. It will be like NAGB [National Assessment Governing Board] where the board provides general policy direction and then the staff fleshes it out; in these situations the quality of the staff and where they are housed becomes very important." Another interviewee warned, however, that it can be "problematic to hand technical work off to staff who are disconnected from the broader politics around the standards."

Whatever existing organizations are charged with leading CCSS—or whatever new organization is created to do it—it will be important that sufficient attention is paid to ensuring that adequate capacity exists to fulfill its mission over the longer term. If the work in support of the Common Core is going to be spread out among multiple organizations, it will be necessary to indicate precisely how staffing resources and responsibility will be shared operationally. In addition, many of the organizations often mentioned as potential leaders of the CCSS going forward—such as ECS (Education Commission of the States), NGA, and CCSSO—have recently undergone major leadership and/or staff turnover, which some interviewees cautioned may impede their ability to serve in this leadership role. Clearly, whatever kind of governance structure is ultimately set up, greater attention needs to be paid to the infrastructure that will be necessary to support all of this work.

IMPLEMENTATION AND MAINTENANCE OF STATE COMMITMENT

One of the crucial long-term governance issues revolves around how to sustain states' participation in a rigorous Common Core, particularly when—as is likely—state achievement results drop on the new assessments.[9] It is likely that there will be considerable pressure on states to either drop out of the CCSS and shift to a different set of standards or to relax the elements under their control (such as cut scores on the tests). Others fear that governors and state school chiefs in underperforming states will put pressure on the Common Core governing body to dumb down the standards and/or the assessments. There is a fundamental tension between the desire (for both political and substantive reasons) to gives states the maximum amount of flexibility in the implementation of standards and the desire to ensure that there is fidelity of implementation—that standards are implemented vigorously and effectively so that they can have a positive impact on teaching and learning. One observer noted, "That tension exists in just about everything that we do—it is the nature of the education business. You want to give states the flexibility to be able to deal with each state's politics and content and interest needs and priorities—that is really important. The key is how to find the right balance—total freedom can turn everything to mush and it has no meaning, but if you are too strict with it and there is rigidity then there you are not really responding to the different needs of each state. There is some kind of moderating place to be—have to create an organization or a process to find and sustain the happy balance between the two."

One of the questions that any CCSS governance entity must contemplate is how far they are willing to go to placate the concerns of individual states. There may be the danger of or need for "side deals" to gain and maintain individual states' support for standards. Leaders have to be careful, however, not to water down the standards so that the effort fails to accomplish what it set out to accomplish and the standards lose their credibility.

A related issue centers on who, if anyone, can and should play the role of "Common Core cop." Historically, as John Chubb has noted, states have often lacked the will to stay the course with difficult education reforms—and, in particular, higher academic standards—unless pressed by outsiders to do so.[10] The federal government has played this role in recent years, but few if any state leaders are desirous of it doing so in the case of common standards and assessments. There was a shared sense that there needs to be a watchdog to make sure that states don't set cut scores for their proficiency levels so low that proficiency becomes meaningless (like what happened with NCLB). While both consortia have agreed to set a common cut score for proficiency on their assessments across all of their member states, individual states retain the ability to establish their own cut scores for state accountability purposes (e.g., for graduation eligibility or for teacher evaluation).[11] Florida's decision to lower its cut score in 2012 in the face of low scores and public criticism is illustrative here.[12] While observers believe NGA and CCSSO can play a role, there is the sense that they don't have the will or authority to tell states they aren't implementing standards well. There is a sense that it has to be a third-party entity that doesn't really have any connection to either of the consortia, someone with gravitas and respect in the community. Some interviewees suggested that "you can and should rely on other organizations and researchers (such as the National Academy of Sciences, RAND, and the National Research Council for example) to play the watchdog role—they have the expertise and are universally respected." As the Gordon Commission has emphasized, the key point is that someone outside of the testing consortia needs to validate that any assessment (consortia or otherwise) that claims to be "aligned to the CCSS" is truly aligned.

FUNDING: WHO PAYS FOR ALL THIS?

It also remains unclear how any new Common Core governance entity and its related activities will be financed. As noted above, there are a variety of different tasks that this body might undertake, and the size of the budget necessary to fund its operation will of course depend on the scope of its mission. Perhaps the easiest and cheapest way to finance a new governance structure is to attach it to an existing organization in order to piggyback on its staff, facilities, and funding streams. As discussed below, however, while there are several plausible candidates that might be willing to take this on, there are some drawbacks to this approach. Many of the people I interviewed argued that creating an entirely new entity might be the best approach so that the independence and political neutrality of CCSS governance could be preserved. (Others, however, cautioned that a new entity would create a high-profile target for Common Core opponents.)

A new entity would likely take some time to get up and running and would be a more expensive undertaking, so who would fund it? Since there is considerable reluctance to accepting federal funds, there seem to be only two remaining options: member fees and foundation grants. Many of the people I interviewed suggested that foundations could fund a new governance entity for the CCSS; Gates, Hewlett, and Carnegie have been primary supporters of this work and are prime candidates to fund it in future.[13] However, even if these groups have no direct *financial* interest in education, they—like all foundations—certainly have their own particular *agendas* in education that will bias their judgment on the Common Core and assessments and perhaps threaten the objectivity of its governance. As a result, one observer suggested that if the effort is going to be primarily foundation-funded, there should not be just one or two but maybe four or five so no one group's agenda dominates.

Others have suggested that the governance entity's operating budget could be resourced through the creation of an endowment to provide long-term financial security and stability and to limit the influence of donors. "If there is some federal money great but the problem is that when there is money there are always strings attached. Philanthropic dollars might be easier to digest—but foundations have their own agendas too and it's not like there will be any money that will come without strings. Even if we rely on membership fees, still going to have strings because need to accommodate the interests of the members." The challenge, then, is to discover a funding source that is adequate and stable and which flows to the governance entity in a way that minimizes interference with its decision making for the CCSS. It is also important to note that standards governance and revision is likely to be much less expensive than the assessment work.

WHAT ROLE FOR THE FEDS?

There is virtually unanimous agreement that the federal government should *not* be directly involved in the governance of the Common Core Standards or assessments, for both substantive and political reasons. Substantively, observers believe that the crafting and implementation of the standards and assessments will be done better if led by the states themselves. Politically, there is tremendous concern that even the appearance of federal influence over the standards and assessments will jeopardize the entire endeavor. One observer noted, "Anything that even remotely smells like the federal government would make the conservatives go crazy." Another confirmed this point, stating, "Every time President Obama starts talking about the Common Core, the doomsday clock starts ticking." And another interviewee stated, "The feds should be standing on the sidelines cheering us on—that is their appropriate role." Even this cheering must be handled delicately, however, as one observer cautioned that "on many, many occasions we cringed when the feds tried to helpful. They have to be very, very careful and smart about how they talk about this."

At the same time, however, there is general agreement that federal dollars (through the American Recovery and Reinvestment Act [ARRA] and Race to the Top [RTTT]) and the No Child Left Behind (NCLB) waiver process provided crucial incentives for states to adopt the common standards and that federal funding—in some capacity—will be necessary to sustain the effort over the long haul. There is some support for having the federal government continue to fund assessments but disagreement about how this could best be done to minimize fears of federal control. There is also considerable support for having federal funds support research—either conducted directly by federal research institutions or through grants to individual researchers. A common sentiment was that there are not enough research dollars out there without the feds. One looming question is how to intersect the Common Core and its assessments with the next iteration of Elementary and Secondary Education Act (ESEA) when it eventually moves forward in Congress; there is a sense that someone needs to "represent" the Common Core in that negotiation.

POTENTIAL GOVERNANCE MODELS FOR CCSS

How might decision making for a voluntary, state-based, but multistate set of common standards in education be institutionalized? This section will highlight several governance models that might be employed for use with the Common Core Standards and/or assessments, along with a brief summary of some of the strengths and weaknesses of each approach.

The National Network Model

Some have called for governance through a loose, informal, and diffuse group of stakeholders with little defined structure or decision-making authority. Several interviewees saw this as more in line with the original approach to drafting standards and believe it worked well. Others noted that the informal network that has developed around the Hunt Institute offers a model (or an actual candidate) for future governance. Achieve, CCSSO, NGA, Hunt Institute, the Alliance for Excellent Education, National PTA, ASCD, and lots of others (36 organizations all together) currently hold a conference call every week to share information about what organizations are doing around implementation of the standards and assessments. Paul Manna has noted that networks can operate with varying degrees of formality and connectedness:

Depending on the configuration of nodes and links, a network's shape can suggest different degrees of connectedness among the organizations involved. At one extreme, networks with high centrality contain a single node linked to all others, with the remaining nodes primarily connected to the organization at the hub, but not each other. In contrast, networks with high density represent situations in which each node is directly connected to every other node. In the latter instance, no single node is the hub because all possible connections exist.[14]

This approach builds on established networks of policy professionals in the states: trusted, experienced administrators who have established relationships with one another and are seen as honest brokers rather than advancing a political agenda. It permits a broad and diverse array of groups and interests to participate and is less hierarchical and more fluid and nimble. The network approach, however, may preclude ownership and leadership, make it hard to agree on goals, and present challenge for accountability.

The NAGB Model

Another approach is to institutionalize governance but to do so in a structure that incorporates a large and diverse array of organizations and perspectives. This approach combines the broad representation of the Network model with a more formal decision-making structure. The best example of this approach inside of education is the National Assessment Governing Board (NAGB), which Congress established to oversee the National Assessment of Educational Progress (NAEP).[15] To make sure the governing board is widely representative, the law (Public Law 107-279) requires that the board be comprised of a representative group of stakeholders including governors, teachers, the business community, and the director of the Institute of Education Sciences. A big-tent approach for the Common Core would not necessarily include the same kinds of representatives as NAGB, and this larger board could be constructed to ensure that governors and chiefs constitute a majority (or even supermajority) of voting members. But it would have the advantage of including a broader array of interests—not merely in an advisory capacity but in a governing capacity. As with the network approach, however, the inclusiveness creates the potential for incoherent decision making. It is also unclear who would nominate individuals to sit on this board.

The Consolidation Model

Some have called for governance powers and functions to be consolidated under the leadership of one or two existing organizations, with many calling for the NGA and CCSSO to continue to serve in this capacity. Rather than the large membership and broad representation of groups outlined above, this approach would rely on a small executive committee of state policy makers selected with an eye toward political and geographic balance. A Memorandum of Understanding (MOU) could be created between the organizations, which would contribute staff time and raise the initial funding to support the operation of the committee and any ancillary structures formed. A larger advisory structure could include representatives from a broader array of stakeholders. The small executive committee may promote ownership, engagement, and decisiveness. The trade-off, however, is that only a few groups would have representation on the decision-making body for the CCSS. Whatever efforts are made to ensure a diverse mix of perspectives, this consolidated approach would ensure that a majority of states—as well as a majority of state policy makers—would not have a vote/voice in governance.

Create a Regional (or National) MOU

The Network, NAGB, and consolidation approaches to governance focus on representing particular groups and perspectives in a national decision-making body and, as a result, do not treat states as states in this process. But some multistate regional organizations have been created that focus on states as the crucial unit of analysis. Some have also done so without official interstate compacts (discussed below) by relying instead on Memoranda of Understanding (MOUs) or other more informal agreements. Rather than taking a national approach, states could group themselves together on the basis of geographical proximity or a shared approach to common standards and assessments and create regional entities, each with its own governing body.

One promising example here from outside of education is the Regional Greenhouse Gas Initiative (RGGI), the first multistate commitment to a market-based effort in the United States to reduce greenhouse gas emissions. The RGGI MOU, a blueprint of RGGI operations, was signed by seven states in December 2005, and three others have subsequently signed on. In July 2007, however, a regional organization (RO), RGGI Inc., was created as a potentially important regional advisory institution for multistate climate control, albeit within tightly circumscribed boundaries.[16] The RGGI has been called "federalism without the federal government,"[17] since the regional organization it created is given the power to track emissions and allowances from states in an effort to provide transparent data to document progress in meeting climate control standards. RGGI achieved considerable success over its first 3 years in operation, reducing annual emissions by 23% and raising almost $1 billion from allowance auctions to fund clean energy programs.[18]

The New England Common Assessment Program (NECAP) offers another interesting regional model. In response to NCLB's requirement that states expand annual testing in math and reading, three states (New Hampshire, Rhode Island, and Vermont) joined together to create a testing consortium in 2004. McDermott notes that the legal foundation of NECAP is weak: "Rather than formal written policies and memorandums of understanding, a great deal is done through 'gentlepersons' agreements.'"[19] Significantly, NECAP opted not to create a new organization with its own dedicated funding and staff. Instead, Pat DeVito writes,

> The consortium operates as an association of state departments of education, not a formal legal entity. The state assessment directors act as the management team for NECAP. While the goal is to arrive at consensus across states, if state staff members cannot agree on an important issue, the management team decides on the course of action. Each state carries equal weight in the decisions, regardless of the size of the student population or other factors.

This more informal approach to governance meant that approval of NECAP by governors and state legislatures was not necessary, only the approval of the standards and assessments by state boards of education.[20]

Since NECAP has no capacity of its own, it relies on the staff capacity and technical expertise that resides in its member states' departments of education and when necessary contracts with private consultants such as the National Center for the Improvement of Educational Assessment and testing companies such as Measured Progress. The NECAP states were able to reach agreement on common assessment materials, common achievement standards, common administration and allowable accommodations, a common administration period, and that a single set of reports would be generated. Crucially, however, the NECAP states decided to report test results in and for individual states rather than across states in a way that would facilitate interstate comparisons (which is, of course, one of the central goals of the Common Core). Each state retained its own separate accountability system based on the assessment results. Even with only a handful of small states involved, NECAP faced a number of governance challenges. McDermott concludes that "although the NECAP provides an encouraging example, the scale of the new assessment consortia dwarfs NECAP, and the states in the Partnership for Assessment Readiness for College and Career (PARCC) and the Smarter Balanced Assessment Consortium (SBAC) are more diverse in their approaches to accountability. [It] may be difficult for the consortiums to make the kind of generally acceptable decisions that have been so important to NECAP."[21]

The Interstate Compact Model

One of the most interesting developments in intergovernmental relations in the United States—and one with potential salience for the governance of CCSS—is the growing use of interstate compacts as mechanisms for collective action on common challenges that cross geographical boundaries.[22] These compacts create a much more centralized and powerful decision-making structure than any of the other potential models for Core governance discussed above, but retain a national rather than federal character. Compacts serve as formal agreements between states and resemble both statutory law and contracts. That means they cannot be unilaterally repealed or amended by a state, as is possible with administrative agreements.[23] Crucially, compacts then compel a commitment by states that they cannot unilaterally abandon absent an explicit exit option contained in the compact agreement.

While participation in compacts remains fundamentally voluntary—states choose to join them and can always withdraw—the purpose of the agreement is to create a public commitment and a high-enough exit cost to deter states from leaving once they have signed on. Of course, the more difficult that compacts make it for states to leave—or the more regulatory authority that is placed in a compact governing body—the less likely states may be to sign on in the first place. Interstate compacts must also address political, constitutional, and policy questions about the appropriate federal role in these ventures.[24]

Interstate compacts offer a middle ground of coordination between state autonomy and federalization and, as such, may represent an attractive option in areas like education, where there is a strong tradition of local control but growing pressure for common standards. States could create a new national interstate compact, which would enable a "fresh start" to deliberations about Common Core governance and would permit a new structure to be designed specifically to meet its needs. (Others caution that a debate over a new compact would offer an opening for detractors to derail the entire CCSS effort.) Another approach would be to utilize an existing interstate compact, and several interviewees suggested that the Education Commission of the States (ECS) might be a good home for it.

ALIGNING COMMON STANDARDS AND ASSESSMENTS

Much of the conversation above has focused on the governance issues surrounding the Common Core Standards. However, there is also tremendous concern around ensuring that the new tests being developed by the two assessment consortia are aligned with the common standards and that the two sets of tests are aligned (or comparable) with each other. There is widespread recognition that "bad" assessments could undermine the potential impact of the standards—and good assessments could enhance their impact. Should coordination be limited to alignment or should it extend to the kinds of auxiliary functions described above—research, advocacy, technical assistance, and public relations? There appears to be little appetite for a single, unified governance structure that would unite decision making for the two assessment consortia or formally connect the consortia with the standards. One observer indicated, "It is not clear how decisions are being made now between standards and assessments folks—but you can't divorce standards implementation from the assessments, there needs to be some coordinating role." How exactly to do this one observer calls "the great unknown." Another interviewee cautioned that any coordinating structure "needs to have firewalls to ensure that the standards need to define the assessments and not the other way around."

Some observers think that while coordination between the standards and the assessments is important, so too is maintaining operational independence as well as public distance so that the failure of one effort does not drag down the other. One interviewee argued,

> Standards need to continue and will continue even if assessment consortia fail and regardless of whether there are 45 states in the consortia or 25 states in the consortia. Key is whether states that are interested in doing this are able to find ways to work together collectively to reallocate resources and support implementation as a group. Assessment offers one critical way to show that this can be done. Others include multistate purchasing from vendors and the sharing of technology across states.

Unlike the Common Core Standards, the assessment consortia had a formal governance structure in place from the beginning. The original PARCC and SBAC governance structures were defined to a considerable extent in the requirements of the federal grants that provided their initial funding. They contained an explicit definition of what it means to be a governing (voting) state and an advisory/participatory state. PARCC and SBAC each have a governing board (which contains a subset of state members) and a steering/executive committee (with an even smaller group of states). SBAC, for example, has an executive committee of nine members—six from the 21 governing states, the Washington state rep (as fiscal agent), and two at-large seats elected by higher education leaders from states. The delegations from governing states (which contain a K–12 lead—usually the state assessment director—and a higher education lead) each get one vote.[25] The consortia are planning to put new governance structures in place when their federal grants run out; PARCC announced in March 2013, for example, that it will reorganize as a 501(c)(3) nonprofit.

There are several important distinctions between the standards and assessments that have important implications for governance. When states joined the assessment consortia, they made an explicit commitment to join an established organization with a set governance structure (and one determined in large part by terms of the federal grant). In the case of CCSS, states adopted the standards themselves but did not agree to join a particular organization/accept a particular governance structure because they did not exist yet. Another key distinction between the standards and assessments is that while the standards only need to be revised once every several years, an updated version of the assessments needs to be made available every year. So the assessment governance bodies need to make major decisions more frequently and more quickly than any standards entity. There would seem to be four models for coordinating policy making for the standards and assessments.

- *Coordinating Committee.* Staff from each of the assessment consortia and from the CCSS governance entity would meet regularly to consult and coordinate, but the committee would have no independent decision-making authority.
- *A Seat at the Table.* Another approach would be simply to place representatives from each of the two assessment consortia on the governing body for the CCSS and vice versa. These representatives could be given a vote or be limited to observer status.
- *Shared but Circumscribed Governance.* CCSS and the two assessment consortia would retain their independent governance bodies, but each would send representatives to a new governance council that possesses limited decision-making authority over specified issues related to the alignment of the standards and assessments.
- *Unified Governance.* A new governance council could be created that would unite decision making for both CCSS and both assessment consortia in a single entity.

CONCLUSION

The Common Core Standards and assessments movement in education is at a crucial juncture. Considerable support exists for having common performance targets and metrics to provide greater transparency about educational outcomes and to drive school improvement. As this analysis has demonstrated, however, how multistate efforts such as CCSS are institutionalized and governed is crucial to their ultimate sustainability and impact. In this respect, the intergovernmental challenge in education is similar to that in other policy areas: How do we simultaneously limit federal control and respect state rights, while also developing collective institutions that can advance national goals? Many multistate organizations in other spheres have found it difficult to create structures that facilitate joint action in pursuit of common goals while vouchsafing to individual member states the maximum in policy sovereignty and programmatic flexibility.[26]

Efforts to create governance structures for the Common Core State Standards must be cognizant of the "foxes-watching-the-henhouse" problem, as the very public officials and professionals that will be impacted the most by standards are likely to be the ones most involved in their revision and implementation. The governance of the CCSS initiative is thus likely to be buffeted by the political self-interest of governors and school chiefs and the professional self-interest of educators and school administrators, such as has influenced the evolution of standards in other sectors. Indeed, the CCSS will be pressed from many directions, including universities, employers, commercial interests, civil rights groups, and more. A backlash against rigorous standards or embarrassing results on common assessments must be anticipated, and the future Common Core governing body must be given sufficient institutional, procedural, and political insulation to protect its independence and integrity.

This returns us to the central questions of governance: What kind of institutional structure might best serve the Common Core initiative over the long haul? What powers, resources, and independence does it need? This chapter has sought to provide an overview of different visions and challenges for multistate governance of the Common Core Standards and assessments. It has highlighted fundamental questions that any governance structure must address and has outlined the inherent trade-offs between different governance approaches. The CCSS enterprise has generated momentum behind an ambitious reform agenda in education, but it remains to be seen whether states have the political will or institutional capacity to act collectively in multistate organizations to advance shared policy goals. And while the federal government used RTTT money to incentivize states to sign onto the Common Core, it is unclear whether states will maintain that commitment over time in the face of implementation challenges and costs, leadership turnover, or the end of federal funding.[27] As Conlan and Posner have noted, this is an inherent problem with "opt-out federalism": Voluntary state participation always leaves open the door to withdrawal.[28] In this sense, the outcome of the Common Core effort is an enormously important experiment, not just for education but also for American intergovernmental relations more generally. And the odds of the experiment succeeding will be greatly enhanced by close attention to questions of governance and institutional design.

NOTES

1.   For a comprehensive overview of the historical development of the Common Core, see Rothman, R. (2011). *Something in common: The Common Core Standards and the next chapter in American education.* Cambridge, MA: Harvard Education Press.

2.   As Katie McDermott has observed, "The CCSSI and the two assessment consortiums are all still in the institution-building stage. None of the three has independent organizational existence, such as 501(c)(3) status; they are simply projects being undertaken by their host institutions. Neither the CCSSI nor the consortiums necessarily needs to become an independent organization, but at some point they have to decide on their long-term structure." See Shattuck, P., & Sosland, D. (2013, January 24). Northeast faces stark choice on climate pollution. *New York Times.* Retrieved from http://www.nytimes.com/2013/01/25/opinion/northeast-faces-stark-choice-on-climate-pollution.html?_r=0

3.   Given the politically sensitive nature of the issues surrounding the Common Core, the people interviewed for this paper requested that their names—and the names of their organizations—remain anonymous.

4.   See, for example, Council of Great City Schools. (2012, Fall). *Implementing the Common Core State Standards in urban public schools.* Retrieved from http://www.cgcs.org/cms/lib/DC00001581/Centricity/Domain/4/Implementing%20the%20Common%20Core%20State%20Standards%20FINAL.pdf.   See also Murphy, P., & Regenstein, E. (with McNamara, K.). (2012, May). *Putting a price tag on the Common Core: How much will smart implementation cost?* Washington, DC: Thomas B, Fordham Institute. Retrieved from http://www.edexcellencemedia.net/publications/2012/20120530-Putting-A-Price-Tag-on-the-Common-Core/20120530-Putting-a-Price-Tag-on-the-Common-Core-FINAL.pdf

5.   It is also unclear what role the influential College Board will play in all of this going forward, particularly in light of the fact that its new president, David Coleman, led the writing of the Common Core language arts standards and that its new chief of policy, advocacy, and government relations, Stefanie Sanford, funded the development of standards from her perch at the Bill & Melinda Gates Foundation.

6.   Finn, C. E., & Petrilli, M. J. (2010, October 19). *Now what? Imperatives and options for Common Core implementation and governance.* Washington, DC: Thomas B. Fordham Institute. Retrieved from http://www.edexcellence.net/publications/now-what-imperatives-and.html

7.   Education First and the Editorial Projects in Education Research Center. (2012). *Preparing for change: A national perspective on Common Core State Standards implementation planning.* Washington, DC: Education First and the Editorial Projects in Education Research Center.

8. Kober, N., & Rentner, D. S. (2012, January). *Year two of implementing the Common Core State Standards: States' progress and challenges.* Washington, DC: Center on Education Policy.

9. An NGA analysis of data from the Institute for Education Sciences and state departments of education has demonstrated that a large gap exists between current state proficiency levels and the NAEP, for example.

10. Chubb, J. (2012, December). *Let history not repeat itself: Overcoming obstacles to the Common Core's success.* Washington, DC: Education Sector. Retrieved from http://www.educationsector.org/publications/let-history-not-repeat-itself-over-coming-obstacles-common-core%E2%80%99s-success

11. In PARCC, for example, there will be five performance levels, one of which will be called *proficient* (or something similar; the labels have not been decided yet). These would not be modifiable. A state may use a different performance level (say, Level 2 rather than Level 4) to determine eligibility for a high school diploma. Alternatively, a state could set its own performance level (in effect, add a 6th) for high school graduation. Ideally, PARCC states that need a graduation test would work together to agree on a common standard for high school graduation—so that the cut score is the same in GA and TN, for example—but there is no guarantee that this will happen.

12. Ujifusa, A. (2013, January 24). With eye on Common Core, Illinois raises state test cut scores. *Education Week.*

13. See Robelen, E. (2013, January 17). Common-Core work gets aid from many philanthropies [Web log post]. *Education Week, Curriculum Matters Blog.* Retrieved from http://blogs.edweek.org/edweek/curriculum/2013/01/common_core_work_gets_aid_from_many_philanthropies%20%20%20.html?print=1

14. Manna, P. (2010). *Networked governance in three policy areas with implications for the Common Core State Standards initiative.* Washington, DC: Thomas B. Fordham Institute. Retrieved from http://pmanna.people.wm.edu/research/Manna2010_FordhamCommonCoreGovernanceProject.pdf

15. For a detailed analysis of NAGB's relevance to the Common Core, see Musick, M. (2010). *What can the Common Core State Standards Initiative learn from the National Assessment Governing Board?* Washington, DC: Thomas B. Fordham Institute. Retrieved from http://www.edexcellencemedia.net/publications/2010/201006_CommonEdStandards/201006_EducationGovernance_Musick.pdf

16. The MOU carefully notes that "The RO is a technical assistance organization only. The RO shall have no regulatory or enforcement authority with respect to the Program, and such authority is reserved to each Signatory State for the implementation of its rule." The text of the RGGI MOU is available at: http://www.rggi.org/design/history/mou

17. Rabe, B. (2008, October 9). *The complexities of carbon cap-and-trade policies: Early lessons from the states.* Washington, DC: Brookings Institute.

18. Shattuck, P., & Sosland, D. (2013, January 24). Northeast faces stark choice on climate pollution. *New York Times.* Retrieved from http://www.nytimes.com/2013/01/25/opinion/northeast-faces-stark-choice-on-climate-pollution.html?_r=0

19. McDermott, p. 143. See McDermott, K. A. (2013). Interstate governance of standards and testing. In P. Manna & P. McGuinn (Eds.), *Education governance*

for the twenty-first century: Overcoming the Structural Barriers to School Reform (pp. 130–155). Washington, DC: Brookings Institute.

20. "As such," McDermott notes, "the commissioners were able to develop the consortium under the radar politically" and there was little public dissent. Ibid., p. 147.

21. McDermott, Interstate governance, p. 149.

22. For a more detailed discussion of interstate compacts and their potential in education, see McGuinn, P. (2010, June). *E Pluribus Unum in education? Governance models for national standards and assessments from outside the world of K–12 schooling*. Washington, DC: Thomas B. Fordham Institute. Retrieved from http://www.edexcellencemedia.net/publications/2010/201006_CommonEdStandards/201006_EducationGovernance_McGuinn.pdf

23. As Bowman and Woods observe, "Once a state ratifies a compact, its provisions have legal superiority, taking precedence over conflicting state laws. The compact itself establishes the rules for state *compliance with, and withdrawal from, the compact, and its* amendment and termination" (p. 349). See Bowman, A. & Woods, N. (2007). Strength in numbers: Why states join interstate compacts. *State Politics and Policy Quarterly, 7*(4), 347–368.

24. Article I of the U.S. Constitution proclaims that "No state shall, without the consent of Congress . . . enter into any Agreement or Compact with another State." Read literally, that clause would seem to require that all interstate compacts be subjected to congressional approval. However, as Matthew Pincus has noted, in practice many compacts have not been submitted to Congress and yet their validity has been respected by public officials and the courts. In a series of cases beginning with *Virginia v. Tennessee* (1893), and upheld most recently in *U.S. Steel v. Multistate Tax Commission* (1978), the U.S. Supreme Court has ruled that only a small subset of compacts—those that "enhance state power quoad the national government" and thereby threaten federal supremacy—need explicit congressional consent. See Pincus, M. (2009). When should interstate compacts require congressional consent? *Columbia Journal of Law and Social Problems, 42*, 511–544.

25. SBAC uses a consensus approach—on the first ballot 100% of states must approve to pass policy; otherwise dissenting states get to express reservations and changes can be contemplated before a second ballot is cast in which a two-thirds majority is needed to secure passage. (To this point, SBAC has gone to a second ballot twice but then measures passed.) The challenge is that SBAC is a fast-moving process but the consensus process can be slow. As a result they are judicious about what gets put to a vote—reserve for "significant" policy issues.

26. Usdan, M. (2010, October 25). Political peril for the Common Core? *Education Week*.

27. Klein, A. (2010, August 20). ECS education forum spotlights policy fault lines. *Education Week*.

28. Conlan, T. J., & Posner, P. L. (2011). Inflection point? Federalism and the Obama administration. *Publius: The Journal of Federalism, 41*(3), 444.

CHAPTER 9

A Reform at Risk?
The Political Realities

Ashley Jochim

THE COMMON CORE STATE STANDARDS initiative not only represents an unprecedented collaboration between the National Governors Association (NGA), the Council of Chief State School Officers (CCSSO), and 45 states to create common standards in English and mathematics; it also represents an intriguing experiment in federalism. With virtually every state in the union an adopter and strong supporters on both sides of the aisle, the Common Core has an air of inevitability that few reforms can tout, especially in the contemporary political environment.

Yet, the initiative also faces significant challenges as it moves beyond adoption. The commitment of fractured state legislatures, interest groups, and other stakeholders will be tested as the rhetoric of high standards meets the realities of implementation. Implementation will demand new investments in curriculum, tests, technology, professional development, and other instructional supports at a time of profound fiscal constraint. It will require potentially messy reforms to accountability systems that may anger students, parents, and other stakeholders, as schools that thought they were performing well fare poorly on new tests, and new cut points exacerbate the appearance of already wide achievement gaps among student subgroups. And this will all unfold at a time when issues of federalism and the relative roles of the state and federal government have reemerged as central debates in education reform conversations. Navigating this terrain is possible, but it won't be easy.

POLITICAL WILL AND IMPLEMENTATION

Observers of politics often forget that fights don't simply end once agreements are forged and written into law. Implementation involves more than vague proclamations of support; it involves highly specific decisions about who to target, how much money to invest, and which stakeholders to engage. These choices profoundly shape the winners and losers of political debates, as some individuals face greater oversight, some programs win a greater share of available dollars, and new oversight authorities are established and threaten existing power bases. Political scientist Aaron Wildavsky termed this cycle "policy as its own cause" and suggested that policies take new forms during implementation.[1] Viewed in political terms, implementation is successful to the extent that it reinforces existing political commitments or creates new ones. This is different from securing a policy's substantive objectives. Crime rates go down, more children graduate from high school, fewer senior citizens enter poverty, and air quality improves— these are all indicators that a given policy has achieved its substantive goals.

But policies can be politically robust without being good. That is, they can achieve political aims without actually solving any problems and often by creating new ones. Much has been written about the policy failures associated with the "War on Drugs," for example, including the lack of attention toward treating addiction, sentencing disparities, and overcrowded and financially strapped jails, but these have failed to substantially weaken policy makers' support for a "tough-on-crime" approach to America's drug problem.[2] Similarly, policies can be successful in ameliorating a public problem but draw little in the way of political support. Most economists agree that preserving Social Security and Medicare for future generations will require substantial changes to program eligibility, funding, and structure, but thus far, policy makers have not found it in their political interests to advance entitlement reform.[3]

However, political success and substantive success are inherently connected because public policies in democratic societies are sustained through politics, not around them. Policies are crafted, implemented, and sometimes repealed through politics. While public policies can serve political purposes without addressing public problems, the reverse is not true—no policy can achieve its substantive objectives without securing political support.

Public policies become sustainable when they create or mobilize groups with a stake in the reform's continuation.[4] But mobilization is not automatic. Those interests with the most at stake tend to be mobilized most readily. For example, the business community tends to win a seat at the negotiating table because it is frequently a target of particularistic benefits and/or regulatory programs; these increase their incentives to mobilize.[5] But the mobilizing effect of public policy is not limited to narrowly targeted programs. In separate considerations, Andrea Campbell and Suzanne Mettler identify powerful mobilization effects for the Social Security program and GI Bill, respectively, with participation resulting in higher rates of political activism among the elderly and veterans.[6]

Policies that fail to achieve their public purpose or that have negative, unintended side effects can result in a strategic retreat, as potential constituencies of the reform fail to see their benefit or become meaningfully harmed. The No Child Left Behind Act of 2001 (NCLB) transformed the education system by instituting performance-based accountability. However, rather than empower reform-minded education advocates, the policy's political implications tended to be negative, as states rejected the prescriptive federal approach[7] and parents and teachers disliked the emphasis on test-based accountability.[8] As a result, despite the fanfare that accompanied its passage, a retreat from many of the law's key provisions seems not just possible, but likely.[9]

THE POLITICS OF THE COMMON CORE

Stemming from its legislative history (or in most cases, lack thereof), the political challenges of Common Core implementation loom particularly large. Most public policies emerge through the labyrinth of legislative politics fully vetted by those with the most at stake, giving them at least an initial veneer of political legitimacy. But the Common Core followed an unconventional path, passing instead through state boards of education, whose members are often appointed by the governor and are thus largely immune from the political pressures that shape reelection-sensitive policy makers. Indeed, the use of such politically insulated bodies, which often lack strong executive or legislative oversight, is often grounded in the assumption that policy making is best when it is conducted as a technocratic enterprise.[10] If policy change is supposed to be hard—stemming from the separation of powers between the legislative and executive branches—then the Common Core bypassed those institutional arrangements, making change considerably easier, but emerging also on less politically stable ground.

The air of inevitability around the Common Core is further tainted by incentives created by the Obama administration's signature education initiatives, Race to the Top (RTTT) and the Elementary and Secondary Education Act Flexibility (ESEA Flexibility) program. Both all but required states to adopt the Common Core to secure additional federal funds, in the case of RTTT, or regulatory relief, in the case of ESEA Flexibility. Of the 46 states that have adopted all or part of the standards, 29 had done so by August 2, 2010, the administration's deadline for states applying for round one of RTTT (including at least one state, California, which approved the standards on the day of the deadline).[11]

The lack of legislative limelight and incentives provided by the Department of Education likely enabled the reform to spread further and faster than it would have if it had been drawn into the far messier policy process. Consider, for example, that the promise of federal funds through

RTTT was *not* enough to win over Kentucky legislators' support for charter schools. (The state's application was all but doomed in the first round as a result.)[12]

But opting out of the legislative process is not possible in the long run because Common Core implementation hinges on a variety of changes to state accountability systems, adequate funding, and other reforms that will require legislative action. These decisions will be harder than the vague, more symbolic commitments expressed during the Common Core's adoption. And they will involve a set of political actors who had less at stake during the adoption stage, including teachers, administrators, curriculum developers, professional development providers, parents, students, and as a result, policy makers themselves.

Early efforts at legislative oversight suggest the fight is far from over. In 2012, as implementation was just beginning, Utah's Senate education committee sought to force the state school board to rescind its adoption of the standards. Ultimately, the committee approved a milder resolution encouraging the board to "continually monitor" policy implementation—but the threat of a renege nonetheless remains very real.[13] In South Carolina a bill barring Common Core implementation was met with a full hearing by the senate education committee, though the subcommittee ultimately rejected its adoption.[14] Early in 2013 Indiana Republican state senator Scott Schneider introduced legislation that would require the state to abandon the standards, though the legislation was ultimately weakened, essentially leaving the standards intact as well as reaffirming the state board's authority over repeal.[15] Such efforts are likely to continue. The question is: How successful will they be in derailing implementation or forcing legislative repeal?

ASSESSING THE POLITICAL LANDSCAPE AND THE THREATS

Just as policy makers do not enact policies without carefully assessing their political implications, maintaining support for policies hinges on forging agreements in implementation that satisfy key stakeholders. These stakeholders include: ideological activists and party leaders who come to define the partisan issues of the day; interest groups, many of which will have a hand in implementation and whose members fund and support political campaigns; and the broader public whose electoral support policy makers ultimately depend. Because of the varied nature of the threat, based on both states' individual political contexts and how implementation decisions affect specific constituencies, political challenges are far from uniform across states.

Threat #1: What Happens When Great Minds *Don't* Think Alike

We call it Obama Core. It's been co-opted by the Obama administration. They've done everything they can to tie us into these standards. We're Republicans and we're letting Obama take over our education system.
—Gayle Ruzeicka, president of the Utah Eagle Forum and a delegate to the Republican National Convention[16]

Prototypical depictions of legislative repeal suggest such processes often rest in changes in the majority party and/or legislators' ideological preferences.[17] That is, reforms that are purely partisan in nature tend to hinge on retaining party control in the legislative and executive branches. Ideological disagreements are "hard" because they aren't generally amenable to debate or compromise.

Of course, not all issues draw the ideological or partisan rancor that dominates news headlines. For much of its existence, the Common Core was one of these issues. The initiative drew bipartisan support, including backing from prominent members from both sides of the aisle, such as former Florida governor Jeb Bush, New Jersey governor Chris Christie, and Kentucky governor Paul Patton.

However, just because an initiative fails to activate the ideological divide at one time doesn't mean that it won't ever do so. Indeed, history is replete with examples of partisan instability, including on diverse issues such as Medicare, immigration, energy, criminal justice, and indeed, education itself, as so clearly revealed by the stalled reauthorization process for the No Child Left Behind Act. Because the strength of the ideological divide stems both from elections as well as other political pressures, issues can evolve in terms of how they engage partisan coalitions.[18]

At least two forces have worked against the Common Core in this regard: mobilization and competition. With regard to mobilization, ideological activists in the Republican Party have rallied since Obama's election in 2008 and especially during and after the debates around health care and financial services reform. The 2010 congressional elections brought many of these activists' most impassioned members into the House of Representatives as well as state houses across the country. This shift has important implications for Common Core implementation because it reinvigorated the divide in the Republican Party over the appropriate role for the federal government in education reform, essentially ending the compromise politics that had emerged during the passage of the No Child Left Behind Act.

The ideological divide was on display in Utah, where administrators were caught off guard by conservatives' increasingly vocal opposition to the

Common Core long after the standards were adopted.[19] Republican senator Howard Stephenson, cochair of the Education Interim Committee in the Utah State Legislature, emphasized the ideological nature of the disagreement in observing, "The federal government may be trying to do good in education, but many of us believe that they have no business doing anything."[20] Reflecting the seriousness of the threat, the state superintendent, Larry Shumway, wrote a letter to secretary of education Arne Duncan asserting Utah's right "to complete control of . . . learning standards in all areas of our public education curriculum."[21]

Obama and the Democratic Party have exacerbated this ideological tension. Partisan conflicts in American political institutions are often driven by the parties' competition for political power—a competition that is a zero-sum game; you either have a majority or you don't. As a result, parties become more likely to diverge by virtue of the fact that one of them takes a position. Such dynamics are especially likely as elections near.[22]

The Obama administration fueled the association by requiring states to adopt the Common Core through RTTT and ESEA Flexibility, endorsing the standards in the Democratic Party's 2012 platform, and promoting them on the presidential campaign trail. Secretary Arne Duncan exacerbated this suspicion by publicly denouncing state legislators in South Carolina and Utah after those legislatures made movement on bills rescinding Common Core adoption (both bills failed).[23] At least in part as a reaction to these events, in April 2013 the Republican National Committee supported a resolution attacking the standards as misguided and affirming their support for states' rights in the realm of standards and curriculum.[24]

While these events have brought the ideological and partisan dimensions of the Common Core debate to the fore, their impact on implementation has been limited by the fact that intraparty tensions are stronger than interparty ones. Establishment Republicans—including the vast majority of governors and others holding statewide office—are overwhelmingly supportive of the standards. This is evident by the support voiced by many prominent and well-known Republican Party members, as well as the solid backing of Republican-dominated state legislatures in states like Louisiana, Tennessee, and West Virginia. Opposition, in contrast, has been driven by smaller, less-well-known state-based activist networks (though a handful of D.C.-based think tanks, including the Cato Institute and the Heritage Foundation, have also thrown their hats into the ring).

Reflecting the tensions among conservatives, the American Legislative Exchange Council (ALEC), a group with considerable influence amongst conservative state legislators, considered two resolutions in 2011 related to the Common Core—one calling on states to back out of the initiative and a second instructing the Obama administration to stay away from the state-led standards. The second easily became ALEC's policy, but the organization's board failed to approve the first after a delayed vote. Instead, the board issued a statement suggesting they would remain neutral.

While it is unclear what stymied the first proposal's passage, it is likely that the organization's board was under substantial pressure from Republican supporters of the Core to stay the course. The American Principles in Action, one of the sponsors of the proposal, attributed the delay to former Indiana superintendent Tony Bennett and Republican Jeb Bush's Foundation for Excellence in Education's opposition.[25] The very fact that such divisions are present is more a testament to the resiliency of the Common Core than its fragility. It's hard to focus on fighting your political opponents when some of those opponents are on your team.

Without these internal divisions, Common Core implementation would likely come to be defined by its partisan dimensions, and implementation success would depend on the stability of legislative coalitions in the state house—a dangerous proposition considering that parallel debates have unfolded over health care reform. But intraparty disagreement—especially when driven by prominent party leaders—dilutes the potency of debate and conflict.

Because the ideological debates have failed to sway the vast majority of Republican lawmakers, success likely hinges on activists' ability to broaden the appeal of their argument beyond their own ranks. They could partner with other interest groups like business associations, who are concerned about the relationship between economic development and the quality of education. This would require that they more prominently highlight debates over the quality of the standards and their potential impact on individualized instruction and blended learning. Such issues are more likely to resonate with business groups than the more principled concerns over the relative role of the federal government in education.[26]

Or they might pursue their cause popularly by taking the debate to the electorate. Political scientist Mark Smith shows that activists are usually most effective when they act indirectly via public opinion.[27] Of course, such efforts would have to tie the standards to broader themes around loss of local control in education and centralization of curriculum, as few in the general public preoccupy themselves with arcane debates around federalism.[28]

All this suggests that in the short run, regardless of how or whether ideological activists continue to oppose the standards, partisan politics may not be the biggest threat to Common Core implementation. Indeed, in many states, it is probably not an issue at all.

Threat #2: Program Politics and the Hidden Army of Interest Groups

> For states to perform, they will have to change things and changing things will require help.
> —Jonathan Grayer, chief executive officer of Weld North, an investment company with interests in education[29]

One of the reasons the politics of implementation can be so different from that of enactment is because implementation can create new winners and losers. Consider, for example, the evolution of debates over the Social Security program, which was first dominated by ideological activists concerned about the size of the social safety net, but is now dominated by senior citizen groups interested in maintaining eligibility standards. While interest group politics can and do change over time, the Common Core has transformed from being what Peter May calls a "policy without a public"—technocratic and largely apolitical in nature—to one characterized by a highly diversified set of interest group stakeholders, including curriculum and instructional support providers and teachers unions.[30]

Interest groups often have strong and direct interests in programmatic decisions because such decisions can enrich them (via contracts or other resources), empower them (via decision-making authority), or control them (via regulation). Other interests are engaged from the perspective of issue advocacy and are less personally affected by gains or losses in implementation, but also less easily "bought off."

It is clear that interest groups seek to influence policy makers to shape such decisions. What is perhaps less known is that implementation often provides a more important (and effective) venue for interests to express their preferences and lobby policy makers. As Susan Webb Yackee notes, observers of politics often portray interest groups as actors who influence implementation by working *through* or *with* legislative actors.[31] But interest groups often effectively lobby bureaucrats independently through the formal rulemaking process, where they voice their preferences during the notice and comment period, and by influencing the selection of provider groups in grant making and contracting. Indeed, interest groups often have more at stake during implementation and can be more effective, given the limited visibility of bureaucratic politics.

Navigating these realities is not always easy. For instance, legislative initiatives can sometimes sail through the policy process only to encounter significant opposition as interest groups become aware of how the program changes will affect their bottom lines. In the case of the expansion of Medicare to cover catastrophic care, for example, elderly Americans who already had access to such coverage were reluctant to accept a tax to expand coverage to others.[32] Such "delayed-onset" political opposition often stems from a lack of awareness of how a new law will be implemented.

While many interest groups have remained officially neutral on whether states should adopt the Common Core, they are less likely to do so once implementation decisions begin imposing concentrated costs (or benefits) on their membership.[33] Indeed, such threats are the primary motivator for interest group formation in the first place.[34] Thus the challenge is to use the implementation process to bolster the position of potential supporters while weakening or neutralizing potential opponents. The support of any one group is less important than the contours of coalitions that emerge for or against.

Who are the key players and how might their interests be impacted? There is little doubt that the two major teachers unions—the National Education Association (NEA) and the American Federation of Teachers (AFT)—are the two most politically powerful interests in education. While teachers unions are generally not thought to be strong advocates for standards (national or otherwise) and indeed, remain highly critical of test-based accountability, they have been supportive of the Common Core. The NGA and CCSSO invited the NEA to be a partner in the development of the standards[35] and the AFT publicly voiced their support for national standards as early as 1992.[36] Indeed, many credit the late AFT president, Albert Shanker, with sparking the movement toward national standards.[37] Their early support has been rewarded—in December of 2012, the Leona M. and Harry B. Helmsley Charitable Trust announced the two teachers unions, along with Student Achievement Partners, had won $11 million to build an online warehouse of instructional tools to support standards implementation.[38]

While such support seems to bode well for the Common Core, the connection between the standards and teacher evaluation systems could lead to backpedaling or an outright reversal, especially if professional development is perceived as inadequate. As Morgan Polikoff discussed in Chapter 3, value-added assessments, which rely on student growth, are likely to be affected by the change in content standards, as teachers adapt to new expectations and teaching strategies.

Early signs from the states suggest that few are attending to the potential political complications.[39] As reported by Education First and the EPE Research Center in 2013, most teacher evaluation plans submitted by states to demonstrate alignment with Common Core do not even mention the standards and instead focus on student academic growth.[40] On the one hand, this makes sense—why would states want to connect a controversial reform (like teacher evaluation) with a less controversial one (standards) when doing so could taint both initiatives? But in ignoring how these reforms relate to each other, states give up an opportunity to align teacher evaluation policies with those targeted toward improving teachers' instructional practice. In the process, they introduce more political risk into implementation.[41]

The program politics don't stop there. Private instructional support providers, including publishers and related companies, are particularly poised to win (or lose) in Common Core implementation as districts move toward online testing and require new textbooks, curriculum, and formative assessments that align with the standards. Just as new opportunities for contracts tend to exacerbate tensions between Boeing and Airbus, decisions about who will provide instructional supports related to implementation are likely to shake up the marketplace for education providers. This will occur even if states largely rely on repurposing existing resources, as appears to be happening in many states.[42] The competitive pressures will be exacerbated by the fact that common standards open up opportunities for new providers to enter, as well as create the potential for securing near monopoly status on service provision.[43]

Groups representing state and local education authorities and their staff have long been active and influential in state and federal education reform debates.[44] The Council of Great City Schools (CGCS) and the American Association of School Administrators (AASA) are key players in national education debates and have largely remained neutral or cautiously supportive of the Common Core.[45] Partnerships with these groups could diffuse any lingering opposition, both within and outside the organizations. CGCS, for example, has received funding from the Gates Foundation to aid members' implementation efforts, giving them a tangible stake in the reform's durability. Both New Jersey and Arkansas have partnered with professional associations to deliver professional development to teachers and principals.[46]

Of course, those with something directly at stake in the reform are not the only ones who will shape implementation politics. Advocacy groups like the Chamber of Commerce and higher education allies could provide a potent reform buffer if tapped early and often for assistance. These groups have been overwhelmingly supportive of the Core and are at least partly responsible for the strong Republican support for the standards.[47] Their engagement is even more important for implementation, however, especially as difficulties emerge and commitment wanes. It will be at those critical moments when reform supporters can tap advocates to remind policy makers why they committed to the enterprise in the first place.

Threat #3: Public Relations and the Politics of Unintended Consequences

If they need to see 500 angry moms, we can make that happen.
—Dineen Majcher, an Austin lawyer who helped launch the parent group
Texans for Meaningful Student Assessment[48]

While it can be difficult to see at times, public opinion is a potent source of change in American politics. Policy makers' electoral considerations can trump ideology and interest group pressures. Political scientist Douglas Arnold noted more than 2 decades ago that policy makers become highly sensitive to public opinion when issues are salient (or have the potential to become so).[49]

As a result of this electoral connection, policy makers often pursue ambitious reforms to education policy. As Frederick Hess and Patrick McGuinn argue, Republican president George W. Bush successfully used an accountability platform to neutralize the Democratic advantage on education and secure his electoral fate among moderate swing voters weary of debates over school choice and the existence of the federal Department of Education. When public opinion is on the side of reform, its impact can be powerful—delivering political benefits to those whose support is critical not just for whether a reform passes, but also for whether it endures.

But, of course, public opinion can also deliver political costs when voters turn against a reform. The tide may turn because a disengaged public becomes newly aware of a law's intended or unintended impacts, stemming from poor policy design or ineffective implementation efforts. Either way, when citizens move against a reform initiative, policy makers become more likely to rescind their support.[50]

While the principles of testing, accountability, and achievement gap reduction in the No Child Left Behind Act were initially well received, implementation turned many supporters into opponents. As Frederick Hess discusses, many parents do not think schools are broken. As a result, when they came to experience some of the law's consequences, including an increased focus on testing and tough accountability measures, they were less than satisfied with the results.[51]

Standards-based reforms like the Common Core are particularly susceptible to these political dynamics because people *directly* experience the impact of school accountability policies. When schools are labeled as failing, accountability becomes real for wide swaths of the public in a way that many laws never will.

How these opinion dynamics come to shape policy makers' commitment to the Common Core depends on several factors, including rigor of current state standards and the consequences for poor performance. For instance, states vary widely in the rigor of their existing standards.[52] If we assume that the common assessments being developed will raise standards to the average National Assessment of Educational Progress (NAEP) scale equivalent—a measure of highly rigorous state standards—roughly 15 states would raise their standards by one standard deviation and ten states by two standard deviations. Schools that are currently rated highly based on state accountability systems will be downgraded with the change.

State accountability systems will also influence public opinion about the Common Core. The higher standards (and resulting lower performance levels) will probably generate less concern in states with few serious consequences for poor performance, compared to those with tough consequences like school closure or charter conversion. The stakes are particularly high for the 25 states with high school exit exams. Many states plan to use Common Core–aligned exams, which will be significantly more rigorous than existing tests. Therefore, fewer at-risk students will graduate, though alternative graduation procedures and other transition plans may soften the blow.

These factors will likely put pressure on states to change the cut points for proficiency levels, leaving the standards officially intact but weakening their impact on schools. Or, states may repeal and return to (in many cases) less rigorous state standards, in which poor outcomes can be better disguised and less easily compared to other states.

The Wild Card: "A Day Late and a Dollar Short"

In flush fiscal times, policy makers may seek to buy off individual stakeholders using favorable legislative, programmatic, or regulatory treatment as the currency of exchange.[53] It is a highly effective method of building political support.[54] Deficits reduce implementers' ability to sweeten these deals, which often rely on the investment of new dollars, rather than the reallocation of old ones. The latter process is inevitably fraught with greater conflict given the potential for offending constituents of existing programs and yields more trade-offs between competing providers, programs, and services.

Unfortunately for supporters, the Common Core is being implemented in one of the toughest fiscal environments since the Great Depression. States have been trimming their obligations to schools and K–12 education since 2008. Even among states where the fiscal reality is improving, it's hard to imagine how new resources for implementation will be identified.

Early movement by instructional support providers reveals the political logic. As the Parthenon Group's Education Center of Excellence found, the strongest business opportunities rest in the states with big performance challenges and budget growth.[55] It is likely that for-profit instructional support providers will be attracted to such states, yielding potentially powerful political consequences by creating constituencies with a direct stake in continuing the standards. States seeking to do implementation "on the cheap" because of deficits are unlikely to as readily gain such supporters.[56]

The lack of resources also gives potential opponents ammunition to charge that the program isn't worth the cost. This has certainly helped to add "fuel to the fire" for the Pioneer Institute and the Eagle Forum, right-leaning think tanks opposed to the standards.[57] Publishers, who not surprisingly have a stake in finding the money for implementation, are clearly concerned about the fiscal situation. As Jay Diskey, the executive director of the school division of the Association of American Publishers, said, "The three traditional drivers of this market are changes in standards, enrollment increases, and availability of funding. If one of those things isn't there, such as funding, well, what do you have?"[58] According to the Center for Education Policy, of the three states that indicated they might rescind their decision to adopt the Common Core Standards, all suggested insufficient funds as a key factor that would prompt the change.[59]

Skimping on implementation supports like professional development because of financial pressures not only shapes whether the reform is implemented with fidelity, but also whether parents and teachers remain supportive of the initiative. Lack of professional development in places like Idaho, for example, may lead to lower than expected student achievement, which in turn could embolden opponents and shift the tides of public opinion. Even absent such political feedback effects, charges that the Common Core is an unfunded mandate can erode state and district support.

SUSTAINING THE COMMON CORE: RECOMMENDATIONS FOR MOVING FORWARD

Good politics is good government.
—Lyndon B. Johnson, October 12, 1964

These considerations suggest that a well-designed and implemented public policy—that is, a policy that achieves its substantive objectives—rarely depends on its technical design attributes alone. Indeed, democratic politics is premised on the notion that public policies are adequately endorsed prior to securing legal status. In the American system, the number of actors who must endorse a policy prior to adoption is large, and these actors don't simply disappear once change is secured. Lyndon B. Johnson recognized this political logic and was masterful at transforming the politics to support his policy objectives, as illustrated by his strategic mobilization of powerful Southern Democrats to pass his War on Poverty initiative.[60] Good politics is what sustains government, and in turn, the policies it produces.

The threats to Common Core that will emerge during implementation are serious but not insurmountable. Building a cadre of strong supporters who are willing to protect it from current and future opponents will be key to sustaining the reform. Supporters of the standards in advocacy groups, state departments of education, state legislatures, and governors' offices can shape this dynamic by using the following strategies:

- Mobilize their existing allies.
- Build new constituencies and limiting opposition by making smart implementation choices.
- Above all, remember that fights don't end once agreements are forged.

Mobilize Existing Allies

Perhaps the best way to deal with the political implementation challenges is to confront them head on. No strategy is better in this regard than directly engaging allies and mobilizing them on behalf of the reform enterprise. In some states, reform advocates are already engaging in these types of activities. But in many others, the political threats seem too distant to motivate strong action, and most advocacy groups focus their attention on the process of policy adoption, not implementation. When allies do not directly mobilize, it is up to the leaders of state education agencies and their supporters in state legislatures and governors' offices to press advocates into action.

In Tennessee, the State Collaborative on Reforming Education (SCORE), a reform advocacy organization founded by former Senate majority leader Bill Frist, helped to improve receptivity to a change in standards. SCORE began to help in 2007 when Tennessee's state standards received an F from the Chamber of Commerce.[61] Analyses revealed that while 95% of students achieved proficiency according to state tests, only 25% did on the NAEP. This generated new urgency for business organizations, local philanthropists, and others concerned about educational quality.

SCORE engaged a variety of stakeholders, including parent groups, teachers, and administrators, around standards reform prior to Common Core adoption. This helped to foster consensus across the major political actors in the state. But they didn't stop there. SCORE continued to mobilize stakeholders after the Common Core Standards were adopted, spending 3 years between 2009 and 2012 messaging the reform to the public, policy makers, and other members of the education community. They've poll-tested communication strategies for the move toward electronic assessments (the answer: technology doesn't sell itself, it must have a distinctive purpose) and launched a "listening" campaign to assess promises and challenges for teacher evaluation reform.

At least in part as a result of these efforts, standards reform in the state survived a leadership transition to a Republican governor and encountered little, if any, serious opposition from stakeholders. This occurred despite the fact that Tennessee remains a deeply red state with citizens equally as skeptical of federal intervention as their counterparts in Utah or South Carolina. Indeed, according to reform advocates, the Common Core isn't viewed in partisan terms at all.[62]

Similar efforts have unfolded in other states as they adopted the reform, though few have been as successful at sustained mobilization. Massachusetts secretary of education Paul Reville engaged the business community to support the Common Core, leading the Massachusetts Business Association for Education and the Progressive Business Leaders Network to endorse the reform.[63] These efforts have helped marginalize opponents, who in the Massachusetts case, credibly suggested that their own standards were more rigorous than the Common Core. Similarly, the Vermont Department of Education solicited feedback from curriculum coordinators, superintendents, business interests, and unions, helping to develop stakeholder buy-in prior to implementation.[64] While these efforts are noteworthy, they have not been as effective at building a durable and engaged reform coalition as Tennessee's, in part because they largely ended once the standards were adopted.

Build New Constituencies and Minimize Opposition Using Smart Implementation Choices

While mobilizing allies can get you through tough times, ultimately states need a constituency deeply committed to the reform over the long haul. While reform advocates, like Democrats for Education Reform (DFER) or the Chamber of Commerce, are important for a reform's sustainability, they also have less directly at stake in the enterprise. As a result, they may not always be as effective compared to more materially oriented interests like teachers unions.

Policy design and implementation choices can profoundly affect this process by creating winners and losers. When resources are concentrated on a particular interest, stakeholders have powerful incentives to mobilize on behalf of reform. Consider, for example, senior citizens' efforts to protect Social Security and Medicare from retrenchment. But, sometimes, implementers spread resources too thin—what Eric Patashnik and Julian Zelizer call a "diffuse policy design"—resulting in too few incentives to sufficiently mobilize a constituency.[65] As a result, potential beneficiaries fail to protect the reform from opponents' efforts at repeal (or retrenchment).

Reform advocates should carefully assess their implementation plans to consider where the risks and opportunities are in terms of professional development programs, curriculum service providers, and other types of instructional supports. For example, engaging professional associations and unions as implementation partners can provide them a stake in the process, making them less likely to rescind their support over time.

Absent new implementation resources, states should repurpose existing resources carefully, making choices that make sense not just from a technical perspective, but also from a political one. For example, states might expand a popular professional development program in a fashion that builds on what already works and has political support. States might also seek partnerships with districts or regional educational services to help deliver professional development more economically, thus freeing up additional dollars to support implementation. Such choices would help them avoid appearing to skimp on what is sure to be a massive change in state educational systems.[66]

Marginalizing potential opponents is just as important as building new constituencies. As a result, a key task of smart implementation is to reduce the opportunities for this pressure to expand and grow. For Common Core implementers, this means two things.

First, states must carefully think through *how* the change in standards will be experienced by teachers and parents and act early to reduce the potential for fallout. Tennessee's "Expect More, Achieve More" campaign is a model for other states in this regard. While many states have large quantities of information about the Common Core available on their websites, such messages are too complex and convoluted to be effective for those who matter the most. The best messages are simple, personal, and delivered by someone whom the recipient already respects. In Tennessee, former senator Bill Frist helped to inform stakeholders about the reform and its implications. Recognizing the importance of messaging, Arizona unveiled a set of tools for educators and business leaders to explain and promote the standards to parents and others. The Arizona Public Engagement Task Force, along with governor Jan Brewer and state superintendent John Huppenthal, crafted a "toolkit" including an "elevator speech," talking points, and an informative letter for educators to share with parents.[67]

Second, states should not rush through the implementation process. Unlike a Band-Aid, which you try to remove quickly, speed is not the best way to avoid political pitfalls or reduce political conflicts, especially when they involve complex and impactful policy changes. Stakeholders will feel the consequences regardless of how quickly policy makers act. Indeed, policy implications are usually more noticeable the more quickly changes are made. Consider, for example, that the architects of health reform carefully timed implementation, with the more controversial individual mandate unveiled much later than the more popular provisions around expanding coverage.

States might consider a moratorium on implementing changes to teacher evaluation systems, as Morgan Polikoff suggests in this volume (see Chapter 3), to reduce political fallout. A slower implementation pace also gives implementers time to continue to assess their messaging strategy and cultivate support from potential skeptics, as has been important in places like Utah, where misinformation has cultivated more opponents than expected.[68]

One way to help mitigate the fallout around higher standards is to sell them more as an effort around continuous improvement and professional development than as high-stakes accountability. This has been the approach in Utah and Massachusetts. Controlling the message and how it is framed— what one staffer in a state department of education called "linguistic somersaults"—is an important skill, usually not developed in state agencies. In the absence of such internal capacity, states can and should invest in skilled public relations support that can carefully craft messages. Letting opponents define the reform is a mistake and can embolden them.

Above All, Don't Forget That the Fights Don't End with Enactment

Just because you have buy-in today doesn't mean you'll have it tomorrow. Political winds change all the time. In Utah, opposition to the Core first emerged late in 2011.[69] Party control of state legislatures and governor's offices change with elections, new groups and activists mobilize, and new issues explode on the agenda without any notice. All of these changes can alter political dynamics. Reform advocates and implementers need to stay attentive if implementation is to be successful.

One way to stay on top of the threats is to engage state legislatures and governors early and often in the implementation process. Not only does keeping their pulse give clues about how the winds are shifting, but legislatures and governors will be involved in implementation as changes to state accountability systems require statutory approval. Such engagement can help to build greater support for reform, while also making it more sustainable, given that legislatively initiated reforms are less dependent on the good will of individual leaders.[70]

While anticipating and attempting to mitigate these challenge may seem to taint the Progressive era ideal of technocratic experts implementing policies free from political concerns, all it really does is make explicit what are already implicitly political choices. The most effective and durable public programs become so because of good politics, not in spite of them.

NOTES

1.   Wildavsky, A. (1979). *Speaking truth to power.* Boston: Little, Brown.

2.   See, for example, Becker, G. S., & Murphy, K. M. (2013, January 4). Have we lost the war on drugs? *Wall Street Journal.*

3.   Brown, C. B. (2013, January 22). President Obama dodges 'hard choices' on entitlements. *Politico.*

4.   Patashnik, E. (2003). After the public interest prevails: The political sustainability of policy reform. *Governance, 16*(2), 203–234.

5.   Wilson, J. Q. (1980). *The politics of regulation.* New York: Basic Books.

6.   Campbell, A. (2003). *How policies make citizens: Senior citizen activism and the American welfare state.* Princeton, NJ: Princeton University Press; Mettler, S. (2005). *Soldiers to citizens: The G.I. bill and the making of the greatest generation.* New York: Oxford University Press.

7.   Sunderman, G., & Kim, J. (2007). The expansion of federal power and the politics of implementing the No Child Left Behind Act. *Teachers College Record, 109*(5), 1057–1085.

8.   Howell, W., West, M., & Peterson, P. E. (2008). The 2008 Education Next–PEPG survey of public opinion. *Education Next, 8*(4).

9.   See Alexander, L. (2012, January 5). NCLB lessons: It is time for Washington to get out of the way. *Education Week.*

10.   Though it also often has its roots in executive efforts to limit legislative control over the bureaucracy. See Lewis, D. E. (2003). *Presidents and the politics of agency design: Political insulation in the United States government bureaucracy 1946–1997.* Stanford, CA: Stanford University Press. The Federal Reserve, as an example, is powerfully insulated from politics because the terms of its members span presidential and congressional terms and it receives no funds from Congress.

11.   Lewin, T. (2010, July 21). Many states adopt national standards for their schools. The *New York Times.*

12.   Brammer, J., & Truman, C. (2010, August 25). Kentucky loses again in "Race to the Top": Lack of charter schools again costs points toward federal education funds. *Kentucky.com.* Retrieved from http://www.kentucky.com/2010/08/25/1405003/kentucky-misses-out-on-federal.html

13.   Gewertz, C. (2012, March 12). Common standards rumblings in Utah and South Carolina. *Education Week.*

14.   Ibid.

15.   Elliott, S. (2013, February 13). Vote means state likely to retain Common Core education standards. *Indystar.*

16.   Klein, A. (2012, August 30). Common Core State Standards dividing GOP. *Education Week.*

17.   Berry, C. R., Burden, B. C., & Howell, W. G. (2009). After enactment: The lives and deaths of federal programs. *American Journal of Political Science, 54*(1), 1–17.

18.   Jochim, A. E. (2012). *The making of partisan issues: Groups, mass publics and the dynamics of politics.* Seattle: University of Washington.

19.   Brenda Hales, Utah State Office of Education, personal communication, October 24, 2012.

20. Barker, G. (2012, August 21). Common Core debate reaches lawmakers: Utah legislators hear from education office, opposition on issue. *Park Record*.

21. Schencker, L. (2012, March 5). Utah to U.S. Education Secretary: State controls standards. *The Salt Lake Tribune*.

22. Lee, F. E. (2009). *Beyond ideology: Politics, principles and partisanship in the U.S. Senate*. Chicago, IL: University of Chicago Press.

23. "The idea that the Common Core standards are nationally imposed is a conspiracy theory in search of a conspiracy. The Common Core academic standards were both developed and adopted by states and they have widespread bipartisan support. GOP leaders like Jeb Bush and governors Mitch Daniels, Chris Christie, and Bill Haslam have supported the Common Core standards because they realize states must stop dummying down academic standards and lying about the performance of children and schools. In fact, South Carolina lowered the bar for proficiency in English and mathematics faster than any state in the country from 2005 to 2009, according to research done by the National Center for Education Statistics." Duncan, A. (2012, February 23). Statement by U.S. Secretary of Education Arne Duncan: On a legislative proposal in South Carolina to block implementation of the Common Core Academic Standards [Press release]. Washington, DC: Department of Education. Retrieved from http://www.ed.gov/news/press-releases/statement-us-secretary-education-arne-duncan-1

24. Strauss, V. (2013, April 19). Common Core Standards attacked by Republicans. *Washington Post*.

25. American Principles in Action. (2012, May 11). ALEC delays decision on Common Core standards. Retrieved from http://www.americanprinciplesinaction.org/blog/preserving-innocence/education/alec-delays-decision-on-common-core-standards/

26. This is reinforced by the strong business support for previous federal efforts around standards-based education reform.

27. Smith, M. (2000). *American business and political power: Public opinion, elections and democracy*. Chicago, IL: Chicago University Press.

28. It is noteworthy, for example, that former Indiana school superintendent Tony Bennett was defeated by union supporters who successfully argued that reforms like vouchers, school takeovers, and tough accountability were destroying public education. While some commentators suggest that the Core factored into the defeat, this argument does not hold up to exit polling data which show that "very conservative" voters were 15% *more* likely to support Bennett than "somewhat conservative" voters, who broke at the rate of 52% toward the Republican incumbent. See Hayden, M. (2012, November 6). Ritz shocks incumbent Bennett for education post: Grassroots campaign, teachers helped her to take seat. *News and Tribune*. Local journalist Scott Elliot suggests that the Common Core was not a major campaign issue, reinforcing the notion that it was too much "tough love" that as was Bennett's downfall. See Elliot, S. (2012, November 11). Many seek to understand how Tony Bennett's heavily funded campaign failed. *Indy Star*.

29. Tomassini, J. (2012, September 25). Preparing for Common Core, firm acquires school improvement companies. *Education Week*.

30. May, P. J. (1991). Reconsidering policy design: Policies and publics. *Journal of Public Policy, 11*(2), 187–206.

31. Yackee, S. W. (2006). Sweet-talking the fourth branch: The influence of

interest group comments on federal agency rulemaking. *Journal of Public Administration Research and Theory, 16*(1), 103–124.

32. Rice, T., Desmond, K., & Gabel, J. (1990). The Medicare Catastrophic Coverage Act: A post-mortem. *Health Affairs, 9*(3), 75-87.

33. Wilson, *Politics of regulation.*

34. Olson, M. (1965). *The logic of collective action: Public goods and the theory of groups.* Cambridge, MA: Harvard University Press.

35. National Education Association. (2013). Common core state standards. Retrieved from www.nea.org/commoncore

36. American Federation of Teachers. (2013). Common core state standards. Retrieved from http://www.aft.org/issues/standards/nationalstandards/

37. Kahlenberg, R. D. (2007). *Tough liberal: Albert Shanker and the battles over school, unions, race and democracy.* New York: Columbia University Press.

38. Gewertz, C. (2012, December 17). NEA, AFT partner to build Common Core tools. *Education Week.*

39. Statement based on personal interviews October 1–November 30, 2012, in Utah, Idaho, and North Carolina.

40. Chalk, S. M., Hightower, A. M., Lloyd, S. C., Matthews, C. A., Porter, W., Riley, R., Swason, C. B., & Towne, L. (2013). *Moving forward: A national perspective on states' progress in Common Core State Standards implementation planning.* Washington, DC: Education First and EPE Research Center.

41. Youngs, P. (2013). *Using teacher evaluation reform and professional development to support Common Core assessments.* Washington, DC: Center for American Progress.

42. Statements based on personal interviews with the Council of Chief State School Officers and state departments of education in Idaho, North Carolina, Tennessee, Utah, Connecticut, California, and Vermont, October 1–November 30, 2012.

43. Early signs indicate the latter. The Gates Foundation invested $3 million into Pearson to fund free courses related to the Common Core. While the investment was intended to increase access to high-quality curricular materials related to the standards, it also had the effect of giving Pearson a considerable advantage.

44. DeBray-Pelot, E., & McGuinn, P. (2008) The new politics of education: Analyzing the federal education policy landscape in the post-NCLB era. *Educational Policy, 23*(1), 15–42.

45. The AASA supports "state-developed standards, which may include Common Core." But they also support "less intrusive and costly testing for accountability" (common tests will, at least initially, be costly given the transition to online testing) as well as "opposition to federally established national standards." See American Association of School Administrators (AASA). (2012, January). *2012 AASA Legislative Agenda.* Retrieved from the AASA website: http://www.aasa.org/uploadedFiles/Policy_and_Advocacy/files/2012AASALegAgenda.pdf

46. Council of Chief State School Officers, personal communication, October 31, 2012.

47. TN SCORE (Tennessee State Collaborative on Reforming Education), personal communication, November 30, 2012.

48. Dineen Majcher, quoted in Alexander, K. (2012, November 3). Political winds shifting over testing, accountability. *Statesman.*

49. Arnold, R. D. (1990). *The logic of congressional action.* New Haven, CT: Yale University Press.

50. Ibid.

51. Hess, R. (2006, Winter). Accountability without angst? Public opinion and No Child Left Behind. *Harvard Educational Review, 76*(4), 587–610.

52. National Center for Education Statistics. (2011). *Mapping state proficiency standards onto the NAEP scales: Variation and change in state standards for reading and mathematics, 2005–2009.* Washington, DC: Institute for Education Sciences.

53. Buchannan, J. M., & Tullock, G. (1962). *The calculus of consent: Logical foundations of constitutional democracy.* Ann Arbor: University of Michigan Press.

54. Evans, D. (1994). Policy and pork: The use of pork barrel projects to build policy coalitions in the House of Representatives. *American Journal of Political Science, 4*(38), 894–897.

55. Tomassini, J. (2012, August 7). Business opportunities seen in new tests, low scores. *Education Week.*

56. Of course, proponents in high-funding states would be careful not to spend too much at risk of making the Core look too expensive.

57. Accountability Works. (2012). *National cost of aligning states and localities to the Common Core standards* (A Pioneer Institute and American Principles Project white paper). Washington, DC: The Pioneer Institute; Common standards aren't cheap. (2012, January). *Education Reporter: The Newspaper of Education Rights,* no. 312. Retrieved from http://www.eagleforum.org/educate/2012/jan12/common-core-standards.html

58. Gewertz, C. (2012, March 13). Districts gear up for shift to informational texts. *Education Week.*

59. Kober, N., & Retner, D. S. (2011). *Common Core State Standards: Progress and challenges in school districts' implementation.* Washington, DC: Center on Education Policy.

60. Dellek, R. (1993). *Flawed giant: Lyndon Johnson and his times, 1961–1973.* New York: Oxford University Press.

61. TN SCORE, personal communication, November 30, 2012.

62. Ibid.

63. Council of Chief State School Officers, personal communication, October 31, 2012.

64. Vermont Department of Education, October 31, 2012, personal communication.

65. Patashnik, E. M., & Zelizer, J. E. (2009, September). *When policy does not remake politics: The limits of policy feedback.* Paper presented at the annual meeting of the American Political Science Association, Toronto, Canada.

66. Council of Chief State School Officers, October 29, 2012 personal communication.

67. Robelen, E. (2012, September 11). New Tennessee coalition aims to promote, support Common Core. *Education Week.*

68. Utah State Office of Education, personal communication, October 24, 2012.

69. Ibid.

70. Council of Chief State School Officers, personal communication, October 31, 2012.

The Common Core and the "Reform" Agenda

Frederick M. Hess
Michael Q. McShane

IN A SPELL of sudden and unexpected success, 45 states and the District of Columbia adopted the Common Core State Standards between summer 2010 and the start of 2013. The push for the standards enjoyed the support of an impressive lineup, including the National Governors Association (NGA), the Council of Chief State School Officers (CCSSO), the Gates Foundation, the American Federation of Teachers (AFT) Albert Shanker Institute, and prominent educational and political figures like former New York City schools chancellor Joel Klein, former Florida governor Jeb Bush, and U.S. secretary of education Arne Duncan.

This early success fueled high hopes. Mike Cohen, president of Achieve Inc., an organization of business and education leaders that has played a prominent role in promoting the Common Core, argued, "If American students nationwide are to benefit from rigorous, focused and internationally competitive expectations, the Common Core Standards Initiative is the best opportunity in a generation to finally realize this goal."[1] Arthur Rothkopf, former senior vice president at the U.S. Chamber of Commerce, said, "Common Core academic standards . . . are essential to helping the United States remain competitive and enabling students to succeed in a global economy."[2] Secretary Duncan promised that the Common Core, "Will enable states, school districts and teachers to more effectively collaborate to accelerate learning and close achievement gaps nationwide."[3]

When it came to assessments aligned to the Common Core, advocates were equally upbeat. In a 2010 speech Secretary Duncan referred to the Common Core–aligned exams as "an absolute game-changer in public education." He said that the Smarter Balanced Assessment Consortium (SBAC) and the Partnership for Assessment of Readiness for College and Careers

(PARCC) tests would "better measure the higher order thinking skills so vital to success in the global economy of the 21st century." He said that the tests would "help drive the development of a rich curriculum, instruction that is tailored to student needs, and multiple opportunities throughout the school year to assess student learning."[4]

In light of the preceding chapters, a fair-minded observer might question whether the Common Core effort will live up to this billing. Now, as we noted in the introduction, our aim in this volume has been neither to advocate for nor to critique the Common Core. Rather, it's been to help minimize the Monday-morning quarterbacking that often occurs when well-intended policies encounter the messy realities of implementation. The contributors to this volume have illuminated a number of challenges that educators, policy makers, advocates, and funders would do well to keep in mind as the Common Core moves from rhetoric to reality.

In perusing the chapters of this book, two things emerge. First is the ironic caution that even if the standards are educationally sound, the Common Core's net impact may be negative if implementation is fumbled or undermines other improvement efforts. After all, the Common Core is not just about standards and assessments. It requires schools to upgrade technology, changes the political calculus of test results, and risks infusing school improvement with a tinge of nationalization that may alienate many parents and educators. Mishandled, the Common Core will not simply disappoint; it will serve to complicate or even upend other ongoing improvement efforts.

Second, considerations of the Common Core Standards can't meaningfully be separated from the assessments, instructional materials, teacher preparation and development, and technology that complement them. Much commentary concerning the Common Core has addressed the standards in isolation. Common Core proponent Michael Petrilli, vice president of the Thomas B. Fordham Institute, has written, "We've said it before and we'll say it again: The Common Core Standards are worth supporting because they're educationally solid."[5] Even if one stipulates that to be true, the technical quality of the standards is just one (important) factor when determining how the endeavor will affect school improvement efforts more broadly.

Take the issue of assessments. In Chapter 4, Robin Lake and Tricia Maas quote one principal telling them, "The standards may be voluntary, but the assessments are mandatory." Josh Starr, superintendent in Montgomery County, Maryland, has expressed concern that the push to launch new Common Core–aligned assessments will lead to incoherent instruction as schools hurriedly switch from old standards and assessments to new. Starr took to the pages of the *Washington Post* in early 2013 to call for a 3-year moratorium on high-stakes testing so that schools have time to align their instruction appropriately.[6] AFT president Randi Weingarten seconded his call in April 2013, calling for an open-ended moratorium.[7] Weingarten went on to take a firm shot at Common Core advocates, saying, "These standards, which hold such potential to create deeper learning, are instead creating a serious backlash as officials seek to make them count before they make them work. They will either lead to a revolution in teaching and learning, or they will end up in the overflowing dustbin of abandoned reforms."[8]

Weingarten's stance occasioned much notice. After all, her hesitation represented a dramatic shift from 2010, when she said that the Common Core State Standards "are essential building blocks for a better education system—not a new educational fad—and they can help prepare all children, regardless of where they live, for success in college, careers and life."[9] Less than 1 month after Weingarten made her speech, the Department of Education granted states flexibility to states' No Child Left Behind (NCLB) waiver applications to allow more time to implement their new tests before attaching stakes to them. Upon careful reflection, Weingarten's seeming change of heart was less surprising than it might appear. Her stance on the standards themselves had not changed, and she continued to champion them as instructionally sound. Rather, she was reacting to the way those standards will be used when it comes to teacher evaluation and to school accountability. As a matter of course, as the once-fuzzy outline of the Common Core's practical impact comes into sharper focus, these kinds of practical disputes will proliferate.

In the introduction we noted that the Common Core raises three kinds of "implementation" challenges: those dealing with *policy*, *politics*, and *instruction*. In this volume, while contributors have necessarily touched upon the third, the predominant focus has been on policy and, to a lesser extent, on the related political challenges. This is the place where Common Core implementation may complement or clash with ongoing reform efforts, as possible pain points arise when it comes to teacher evaluation, school accountability, charter schooling, governance, technology, and the rest. Let's take a moment to distill some of the chapter takeaways that most struck us regarding the underappreciated challenges ahead.

POLICY CHALLENGES

Common Core implementation risks encouraging schools and districts to make decisions about technology procurement based on the requirements specified by the Common Core assessments, rather than on the basis of instructional need. As Taryn Hochleitner and Allison Kimmel explain in Chapter 7, the two testing consortia have released the technical specifications regarding which computers or devices students will be able to use when taking their assessments. For example, both SBAC and PARCC require that students take tests on devices with screens that measure at least 9.5 inches across. Practically speaking, most districts cannot afford to procure one set of devices for instruction and another for assessment (plus, it makes little sense to offer advanced assessments which cannot be readily linked into smart devices to help inform daily instruction). Thus Dennis Villano, director of Technology Integration at Burlington High School in Burlington, Massachusetts, fears that "Too many schools are making their decisions based on what the requirements are—not what's best for the students and teachers." Jay McPhail, chief technology officer in Riverside, California, says, "Districts are saying, 'Well, I'm not going to buy anything other than a 10-inch screen.'" As Hochleitner and Kimmel note, this risks handcuffing districts that choose to employ more affordable and ubiquitous smaller-screened devices, like smartphones or iPad minis.

There's also a question about whether SBAC and PARCC are well-positioned to deliver the assessments that have been promised. As Deven Carlson argues in Chapter 5, high-quality test items take time to develop and are typically expensive. However, SBAC and PARCC, the two organizations tasked with developing the Common Core assessments, were launched with 4-year Race to the Top grants in the conviction that states would eventually sustain them by purchasing their tests. The need to rapidly launch these entities, and for them to deliver assessments on a tight time frame, has posed significant challenges. Moreover, their multistate governing boards and complicated relationships with the states mean that SBAC and PARCC have simultaneously had to play the role of psychometrician, test developer, and navigator of complicated interstate politics.

The Common Core Standards and assessments represent a dramatic expansion in the grade levels included in the reading and math accountability regimes. Currently, under NCLB, the federal government requires states to administer reading and math tests to children in Grades 3–8 and then again once in high school. This means that the value-added assessments that undergird teacher evaluation systems typically encompass only Grades 4 through 8. By establishing a framework for reading and math assessments that could ultimately span K–12, the Common Core makes it possible to include a vastly larger number of students, classrooms, and teachers under the value-added umbrella. Most Common Core proponents see this as a terrific thing, allowing more robust and systematic assessment of student growth and teacher performance. Of course, this also means a sea change for schools that have existed outside of the tested grades, primarily high schools—and especially magnets, STEM or arts-focused schools, or career academies where educators may question whether value-added metrics are attuned to their mission and population. Building out the framework of value-added will inevitably mean a more standardized set of expectations and performance measures to more grades and schools, for good and ill.

In Chapter 3 Morgan Polikoff notes that educators are positioned for success when it's clear what students are expected to know, are prepared to teach it, and can count on assessments that measure whether students have mastered the content and concepts. That requires teachers to have access to instructional materials that contain the information that students need to know and that will show up on their assessments. However, a particular challenge on that score is that the market has been flooded with resources claiming to be "aligned to the Common Core," but neither districts, states, nor any third parties have a reliable way to ensure that these resources are actually aligned. Some state education leaders, like John White in Louisiana, have made it a personal commitment to vet materials, but the scale of the challenge—a simple search of Amazon.com yields tens of thousands of results—makes that a particularly daunting prospect.[10]

One way to address "alignment" would be to create a new national body able to vet materials and serve as a clearinghouse for those that met with approval. Such an effort, of course, would make the Common Core increasingly into an engine of nationalization and standardization. After all, such an entity would inevitably exert substantial power over instructional resources and curriculum, playing a key role in determining whether materials would or would not have to emphasize the classic literature alluded to in the standards. One way to minimize such standardization would be the creation of multiple vetting agents, as in the case of the federal Reading First program a decade ago. But that, naturally, yields concerns about inconsistency, fragmentation, and quality control. The upshot: Efforts to police the quality of instructional materials will inevitably cause concern among parents, educators, and local officials skeptical of standardization, while the absence of such a mechanism will ensure that school and system officials have a tough time sorting through vendor offerings to tell which resources really are Common Core–aligned. In technical jargon, this presents quite the pickle.

Preparing teachers to succeed under the Common Core relies on a lever that many policy makers and educators view with skepticism: colleges of education. As Morgan Polikoff highlights, state and system leaders have remarkably little control over what education professors actually teach. Academic freedom in higher education means that faculty training preservice teachers are free to pay lip service to the Common Core, assert that they're training teachers for it (whether they are or aren't), or outright oppose it. Given the skepticism toward testing in many colleges of education and the inertia characteristic of most any preparation program in any walk of life, finding ways to leverage deep-seated change in preparation and professional development will pose an ongoing challenge for state and system leaders.

POLITICAL CHALLENGES

There are also a host of political challenges. For one, the interest groups that will shape implementation have only begun to show up to the fight. In Chapter 9, Ashley Jochim refers to these groups as a "hidden army" that will emerge only as implementation decisions start to create winners and losers. Teachers unions are a leading indicator of this trend. While vocally supporting the standards at first, they have now begun to sour on the enterprise as the assessments are linked to evaluation, compensation, and tenure. Textbook companies whose materials are not deemed "Common Core–aligned" will have reason to disparage the standards. Parents, educators, state leaders, and school system officials may have reason to start bad-mouthing the standards if the performance of their school, system, or state declines precipitously under the new assessments and proficiency thresholds. In short, the broad coalition that supported the Common Core when it was an exciting initiative with vague practical consequences may start to fray as the initial enthusiasm dissipates and the frustrating trade-offs of implementation become clear.

Federal support is sure to fuel further concerns and pushback among conservatives. The Obama administration's efforts to help the Common Core along—via such measures as the Race to the Top program and its NCLB waivers—lent the enterprise a partisan coloring. In early 2013, amid Republican grumbling about "Obamacore" (a play on the "Obamacare" moniker hung on the president's signature health care reform act), the Republican National Committee formally announced its opposition to the Common Core. Such a development makes it much more difficult for the effort to maintain the broad support that will be needed in many state legislatures to push forward with meaningful implementation and to allocate the requisite funds.

While early success of the Common Core may have created the impression that much of the heavy political lifting had been readily accomplished, it turns out that the work for governors and other state leaders is not over—in truth, it has barely begun. In Chapter 2, Dane Linn, who played a key role in helping to shepherd the Common Core from his perch at the National Governors Association, offers words of caution for governors and other state leaders. He warns them: Adoption was the easy part. Due partly to the emerging interest groups that Ashley Jochim enumerates and partly to the partisan conflict that has emerged, the Common Core may become politically perilous, especially for Republicans.

On a related note, many, if not most, governors tasked with implementing the Common Core will not be the governors who got the laurels for adopting it. During adoption, governors could sign up for an amorphous, exciting initiative, one that promised to perhaps bring federal Race to the Top dollars (in the midst of the Great Recession) and that enjoyed the backing of the National Governors Association, prominent education reformers, foundations, and the U.S. secretary of education. While those leaders got to go to the champagne ball, it will be the governors in office in 2014, 2015, and beyond who will be expected to clean up after, return the tux, and pay the bills. Governors in states that have trimmed spending for a number of years face eager claimants in K–12 and elsewhere. Directing funds to Common Core assessment, materials, and training, rather than to class-size reduction or teacher pay, for instance, may be an unpopular call in many states. In more than a few states, organized opposition from teachers unions on the left and Tea Party conservatives on the right will make it harder still.

One of the hopes for many who have embraced the Common Core is that coupling rigorous assessments with high bars for proficiency will jolt suburbanites and bolster the constituency for dramatic change. Of course, a pronounced decline in school and student performance may cut many ways. In middle- and upper-class communities that are currently content with their schools, there are two possible reactions. One is that parents, teachers, and community members will be shocked into declaring, "We need to work a lot harder to reform our schools." The other is that they will decide the tests are problematic, as are any accountability policies linked to those tests. If it's the second, which we think somewhat more likely (especially in light of the history of NCLB), it would have far-reaching significance. As AFT president Randi Weingarten said in early 2013, "When scores drop as sharply as they're expected to, it will send an inexcusable message to parents: Your child is far from meeting the standards."[11] Many suburban parents and educators may reject the judgment that their children are indeed failing. It may turn out that Common Core advocates find themselves essentially asking these parents, "Who are you going to believe, our assessments or your own lying eyes?" If that happens, Common Core supporters may find themselves quietly yearning for the halcyon days of 2010.

Importantly, it may prove remarkably easy for opponents in a given state to hold up the Common Core—it's really as easy as opponents convincing legislators to spend limited dollars on other things. While the path to adoption was marked by soaring rhetoric, implementation will be about assessments, instructional materials, training, retooling teacher preparation, technology, and so on. These things all have price tags, and any state legislator or governor skeptical of the Common Core need simply elect to put resources elsewhere. That will leave the standards in place but, as Common Core advocates have frankly acknowledged, the standards themselves don't change anything. It's what happens next that matters. In practice, it will be more difficult for state leaders to marshal the political will *to* fund Common Core necessitated costs than to *not* do so. Whether Common Core advocates will be able to surmount that hurdle in many states, or in a few, remains to be seen.

THE COMMON CORE AND THE "REFORM" AGENDA

Beyond the complex policy and political challenges that the contributors have surfaced, there are also more fundamental tensions that will loom increasingly large as the Common Core moves forward—and whose resolution will only be clear in the fullness of time. How these play out will help determine just what really does happen when the Common Core meets the "reform" agenda.

The first tension relates to *technology*. As Hochleitner and Kimmel note, the Common Core may prove either a booster or a bottleneck when it comes to education technology. On the one hand, the technology requirements for the Common Core assessments could compel states and school systems to upgrade their technology infrastructure, permitting schools to more fully embrace tech-infused instructional opportunities. Similarly, a national marketplace for instructional materials and professional development could spur the creation of new and different low-cost resources. On the other hand, it is a real possibility that the particular requirements attached to the Common Core assessments will impede schools or systems from utilizing the most effective new technologies. Something very much like this has long plagued the U.S. space program. In order to ensure that hardware and software are reliable and trustworthy, and given its need to design spacecraft that may take years to complete and then launch, NASA has long operated spacecraft with computers far less capable than those commercially available at a given point in time. Such a development would do more to hamstring the movement to digital instruction than enhance it.

A second tension concerns *governance*. As Patrick McGuinn explains in Chapter 8, there's a need for *some* kind of governing entity to oversee the Common Core Standards and assessments. Exactly what that means, though, is an open question. For instance, McGuinn points out that the cognoscenti agree that such a governing body needs to provide "technical support" and "oversight," but don't especially agree on what those terms mean or what the body would actually do. Providing technical support could simply entail convening meetings of state officials to troubleshoot problems with bandwidth or test administration, meaning it could be done by a loose organization of state chiefs. It could also mean a much more formal body with its own staff, one that works directly with states, districts, and schools to perform these functions. A critical challenge, however, is that settling upon any given structure poses problems. If leaders institute a robust governance model that features a legally binding multistate organization like the National Assessment Governing Board (which oversees the federal NAEP assessments), those protective of state autonomy will argue that the step is a bridge too far. If a less robust model is adopted, the effort will lack any mechanism for ensuring that participating states faithfully embrace high standards and rigorous implementation of the Common Core and the new assessments. There is no golden mean here, only compromises that balance the two sets of concerns.

A third tension relates to the complicated relationship needed to make teacher evaluation work. If teachers embrace the Common Core standards, and deem the PARCC and SBAC assessments to be fair and accurate measures of student learning, the Common Core could offer a substantial boost to the legitimacy of test-based accountability. (After all, a common concern among teachers has been that today's assessments generally provide a shallow or highly incomplete view of student learning.) However, if unions generally oppose the standards, the tests, or how the tests are used for accountability purposes, the Common Core is in for a tough slog. Indeed, because the Common Core will ultimately be so intertwined with assessment, accountability, and teacher evaluation, fierce resistance could provide occasion to relitigate these policies.

One pressing question is what it will take for teachers and unions to stand firmly behind the Common Core. Asked directly: What exactly *is* the price of teacher buy-in? At the research conference where these chapters were first presented in March 2013, National Education Association vice president Lily Eskelsen said, "We should never use these tests for high-stakes decisions for principals, for teachers, for schools, or for students unless and until we have validated these as indicators of a teacher's performance or a school's performance." Suggesting that such a day was a long way off, she said, "We have to insist before we go forward that these assessments are going to measure what we say they measure."[12] Eskelsen said what she had embraced in the standards was the promise of deep and rich learning—seeing a respite from the emphasis on test-based accountability.

Meanwhile, many other Common Core advocates have embraced the effort in large part because they see it as a tool to rationalize and improve test-based accountability. The lesson here is that it is easy for unions to support standards solely in terms of improved pedagogy, partnerships fracture over evaluation. Tim Daly, president of TNTP, argued, "Students don't have the liberty of treating the initial years of Common Core as a grace period" and "teacher evaluation work has already proceeded slowly."[13] Given that a careful process of validation and confidence-building in the assessments could take multiple test administrations over several years, the price of union support could mean suspending consequential teacher evaluation systems until 2017 or beyond. Especially with dozens of states due to start implementing new, post–Race to the Top teacher evaluation systems over the next few years, the stakes are high.

A fourth tension concerns *innovation*. Key proponents of the Common Core have seen it as an example of healthy innovation and a mechanism for spurring more of the same. In 2011 former Florida governor Jeb Bush and former New York City schools chancellor Joel Klein wrote, "The beauty of our federal system [is that] it provides 50 testing sites for reform and innovation. The Common Core State Standards are an example of states . . . working together, sharing what works and what doesn't."[14] Advocates see the Common Core as providing a common set of metrics by which to judge reforms, interventions, training, and materials, enabling better solutions to crowd out worse. They hope that a more common national set of standards will enable publishers and technology providers to focus on quality and less on customizing their wares for state after state. This offers much to recommend. At the same time, there are very reasonable concerns that the Common Core will promote a heightened degree of uniformity and standardization, hampering alternative approaches to instruction, narrowing curriculum, and ultimately stifling healthy innovation. A related challenge is that creating state-of-the-art assessments in 2012–13, with a burst of spending fueled by onetime federal funds, risks leaving the two testing consortia with assessments that are difficult to change in future years. As Robin Lake and Tricia Maas explain in Chapter 4, there is a wealth of task- and game-based assessments that will become available in the years ahead. But, if the SBAC or PARCC assessments are the official scorecard, the ability of schools or systems to take full advantage may turn on the degree to which those consortia are willing and able to update their handiwork.

A final tension concerns *school choice*. It's unclear how charter schools and private schools participating in voucher programs will be affected by the Common Core. The new assessments promise to create metrics by which schools in various states and sectors can be more readily compared. The result will mean that measures of growth and outcomes in reading and math will become ever more ubiquitous when gauging school performance. Increased standardization of training and instructional materials will make it easier for national charter networks or Catholic dioceses to cooperate across state lines when purchasing resources or delivering professional development. At the same time, more than a few charter leaders express concerns that the prescriptiveness of the standards and assessments may unduly constrict curriculum and instruction.

If, for example, math assessments incorporate "through-course" components that test for certain content at regular intervals throughout the academic year, it will restrict the freedom of schools to decide when and how to teach certain concepts and skills. Such developments could prove to be especially problematic for new school models, like Carpe Diem, the Summit Academies, or the Rocketship Academies, which allow students to move at their own speed and even do away with traditional notions of curricular scope and sequence. An interesting attendant concern, as Lake and Maas note, is whether charter schools (or private schools subject to state assessment due to voucher programs) will have the resources to install the technology needed to administer the assessments.

PEERING AROUND THE CORNER

Political scientists have long recognized that it's easiest to forge broad coalitions when the idea is alluring, practical implications are fuzzy, and you've got a little money to help ease things along. The practical stuff of implementation was always going to ruffle feathers and spur the emergence of opposition. New standards and tests would pose concerns for teachers and unions when tied to new evaluation and tenure systems. Legislators and governors (many of whom weren't in office when the Common Core was adopted) would have to come up with hundreds of millions of dollars for implementation. Proficiency rates would either remain high (angering advocates) or would be slashed (angering parents). The national machinery of implementing the Common Core would become more disconcerting to the right as it became more concrete and visible.

In short, the very things that helped the Common Core rush to its surprising success in 2010 and 2011 carried a price tag. The decisions that will determine the success of the Common Core enterprise will each bear their own trade-offs, many of them impacting other key pieces of the school improvement agenda.

Building assessments that push the envelope of what's possible with today's technology would require school systems to make enormous investments in hardware and software. So, to keep costs manageable, the ambition of the assessments had to be scaled down.

Maintaining teacher support will require sensitivity to the fact that standards in states which adopted the Common Core won't be aligned with their assessment until the SBAC and PARCC assessments are rolled out. And once they are, teachers will have justifiable reservations about the reliability and validity of the initial results, and how those will be used for teacher evaluation. Addressing those concerns requires compromises that could upend hard-fought victories.

Such disputes speak not only to the fidelity of Common Core implementation or impact. They remind us that efforts to alter standards and assessments affect so many other improvement efforts that rest on that edifice. The plight of the Common Core will matter not just for that effort, but will play an outsized role in determining the fate of so many other developments that have defined 21st-century school reform. Whether educators, policy makers, advocates, and funders recognize that, and what they do about it, will in many ways be *the* educational story of the second decade of this young century.

NOTES

1. Achieve. (2009, September 21). Achieve supports nation's governors and chief school officers in mission to prepare all high school graduates for college and careers [Press release]. Retrieved from http://www.achieve.org/achieve-supports-nations-governors-and-chief-school-officers-mission-prepare-all-high-school

2. U.S. Chamber of Commerce. (2010, March 10). U.S. Chamber applauds the issuance of Common Academic Standards [Press release]. Retrieved from http://www.uschamber.com/node/6015/%252Fmay

3. Duncan, A. (2010, June 2). Statement on National Governors Association and State Education Chiefs Common Core Standards [Press release]. Retrieved from http://www.ed.gov/news/press-releases/statement-national-governors-association-and-state-education-chiefs-common-core-

4. Duncan, A. (2010, September 2). Beyond the bubble tests: The next generation of assessments. Secretary Arne Duncan's remarks to state leaders at Achieve's American Diploma Project leadership team meeting. Retrieved from http://www.ed.gov/news/speeches/beyond-bubble-tests-next-generation-assessments-secretary-arne-duncans-remarks-state-l

5. Petrilli, M. J. (2013, April 18). The RNC on the CCSSI, OMG! [Web log post]. Flypaper (Thomas B. Fordham Institute). Retrieved from http://www.edexcellence.net/commentary/education-gadfly-daily/flypaper/2013/the-rnc-on-the-ccssi-omg.html

6. Starr, J. P. (2013, February 7). Schools need a timeout on standardized tests. *Washington Post.*

7. Weingarten, R. (2013, April 30). Making Common Core Standards work before making them count: Remarks for [sic] AFT president Randi Weingarten, Association for a Better New York [Speech transcript]. Retrieved from the AFT website: http://www.aft.org/newspubs/press/weingarten043013.cfm

8. Ibid.

9. Weingarten, R. (2010, June 3). Statement by Randi Weingarten, president, American Federation of Teachers, On Common Core Standards [Press release]. Retrieved from the AFT website: http://www.aft.org/newspubs/press/2010/060310.cfm

10. Almy, S. (2012, March). *Instructional supports: The missing piece in state education standards.* Washington, DC: The Education Trust.

11. Weingarten, Making Common Core Standards work.

12. Eskelsen, L. (2013, March 25). Public remarks on panel: Teacher quality and accountability. at *Common Core Meets the Reform Agenda*, research conference held by the American Enterprise Institute, Washington, DC. Retrieved from http://www.aei.org/events/2013/03/25/common-core-meets-the-reform-agenda/

13. Daly, T. (2013, April 29). Don't put the brakes on teacher evaluation [Web log post]. *TNTP Blog*. Washington, DC: The New Teacher Project. Retrieved from http://tntp.org/blog/post/dont-put-the-brakes-on-teacher-evaluation

14. Bush, J. & Klein, J. (2011, June 23). The case for common educational standards. *Wall Street Journal*. Retrieved from http://www.wsj.com

About the Editors and Contributors

Frederick M. Hess is resident scholar and director of education policy studies at AEI (American Enterprise Institute for Public Policy Research). An educator, political scientist, and author, he studies a range of K–12 and higher education issues. He pens the *Education Week* blog "Rick Hess Straight Up" and has authored influential books on education including *The Same Thing Over and Over*, *Education Unbound*, *Common Sense School Reform*, *Revolution at the Margins*, and *Spinning Wheels*. He has edited widely cited volumes on education philanthropy, urban school reform, how to stretch the school dollar, education entrepreneurship, what we have learned about the federal role in education reform, and No Child Left Behind. He also serves as executive editor of *Education Next*; as lead faculty member for the Rice Education Entrepreneurship Program; on the Review Board for the Broad Prize in Urban Education; and on the boards of directors of the National Association of Charter School Authorizers, and 4.0 Schools. A former high school social studies teacher, he has taught at the University of Virginia, the University of Pennsylvania, Georgetown University, Rice University, and Harvard University.

Michael Q. McShane is a research fellow in education policy studies at AEI. He is coauthor of *President Obama and Education Reform: The Personal and the Political*, published by Palgrave MacMillan in 2012. His scholarship has been published by *Education Finance and Policy* and in various technical reports. He has contributed to more popular publications such as *Education Next*, *Huffington Post*, *National Review*, *Chronicle of Higher Education Review*, and the *St. Louis Post-Dispatch*. He began his career as an inner-city high school teacher in Montgomery, Alabama. He holds an MEd from the University of Notre Dame and a PhD in education policy from the University of Arkansas.

Deven Carlson is assistant professor of political science at the University of Oklahoma. Deven earned his PhD in the Department of Political Science at the University of Wisconsin–Madison in 2012, where he was a graduate research fellow at the Wisconsin Center for Education Research and a graduate affiliate of the Institute for Research on Poverty. His research interests include the relationship between individuals' educational experiences and their later life participation in the political process, the operations and effects of education policies—particularly school choice policies, public policy, and research design and causal inference. His work has been published in journals such as *Educational Evaluation and Policy Analysis*, the *Journal of Policy Analysis and Management*, the *Journal of Urban Economics*, the *Economics of Education Review*, and *Educational Policy*.

Taryn Hochleitner is a research associate at the American Enterprise Institute. She has contributed to work on digital learning, parent empowerment, college ranking, and teacher quality. She earned her BA in sociology from American University.

Ashley Jochim is a research analyst at the Center on Reinventing Public Education. Her research expertise includes performance management, state education policy, district governance, and the politics of education. Her work can be found in the *Policy Studies Journal* and *Political Research Quarterly*, as well as numerous edited volumes including the *Handbook of Research on School Choice* and the *Oxford Handbook of American Bureaucracy*. Jochim holds a BA in political science and psychology and a PhD in political science, all from the University of Washington.

Allison Kimmel is a legislative assistant to Rep. Jared Polis (D-Co). Prior to that, she worked as a research assistant at the American Enterprise Institute, where she contributed to work on school and system leadership, parent empowerment, and teacher voice. She earned her BA in politics from Harvard University.

Robin Lake is the director of the Center on Reinventing Public Education (CRPE) at the University of Washington. She is the editor of *Unique Schools Serving Unique Students: Charter Schools and Children with Special Needs* (CRPE, 2010) and editor of the annual report, *Hopes, Fears, & Reality: A Balanced Look at American Charter Schools*. She coauthored, with Paul Hill, *Charter Schools and Accountability in Public Education* (Brookings, 2002).

Dane Linn is a vice president for the Business Roundtable (BRT). Prior to his work at BRT, he served as director of the educational policy division of the National Governors Association (NGA) Center for Best Practices. At the NGA he coled the development of the Common Core State Standards. He began his career as a teacher and later the assistant principal at Matheny Grade School in West Virginia. Linn is a PhD candidate at Virginia Polytechnic Institute and State University.

Tricia Maas is a PhD student in education policy at the University of Washington (UW) and a research assistant at the Center on Reinventing Public Education (CRPE). Her primary research interests relate to charter school policy and outcomes, blended learning systems, and human capital pipelines in education. Prior to coming to CRPE and UW, Tricia taught high school math at a KIPP school in California and at a traditional public school in North Carolina. Tricia holds bachelor's degrees in economics and French from the University of Richmond and a master's degree in education policy from Stanford University.

Patrick McGuinn is associate professor of political science and education and chair of the political science department at Drew University. He holds a PhD in government and an MEd in education policy from the University of Virginia. Patrick's first book, *No Child Left Behind and the Transformation of Federal Education Policy, 1965–2005* (Kansas, 2006), was honored as a Choice outstanding academic title. He is the editor (with Paul Manna) of *Education Governance for the 21st Century: Overcoming the Structural Barriers to School Reform* (Brookings Institution Press, 2013). Patrick has produced a number of policy reports for the American Enterprise Institute, the Center for American Progress, and the Thomas B. Fordham Institute, and is a regular commentator on education in media outlets such as *Education Week*, the *New York Times*, the *Wall Street Journal*, and the *NJ Star Ledger*. He is a former high school social studies teacher and the father of four girls.

Peter Meyer is a former news editor for *Life* magazine, author of numerous nonfiction books, and contributor to such national magazines as *Harper's, Time, Life, National Geographic, Vanity Fair,* and *New York*. Since 2004 Meyer has been an editor at *Education Next*, since 2010 a senior fellow at the Thomas B. Fordham Institute, and since 2012 the program manager at the CUNY Institute for Education Policy.

Morgan Polikoff is assistant professor of education at the University of Southern California's Rossier School of Education. His primary line of work is on the design, implementation, and effects of standards, assessment, and accountability policy. He has written extensively about teachers' implementation of state standards under No Child Left Behind (NCLB). His current work includes the evaluation of states' NCLB waiver policies, the alignment of textbooks with the Common Core Standards, and the design and effects of hybrid learning at USC's Hybrid High School. He earned his PhD in education policy from the University of Pennsylvania.

Index

Accountability. *See* State accountability systems
Accountability Works, 152n.46, 196n.57
Achieve Inc., 35–36n.1, 38, 39, 43, 47, 50, 61n.28, 127, 129, 170, 174, 206n.1
Achievement gaps, 92, 112, 164, 185, 195, 206
Achieving By Changing (ABC), 89
ACT, 26–27n.22, 39
Adams, J., 122n.14
Adequate Yearly Progress (AYP), 7, 25, 101
Adkins, D. G., 25n.19
Adler, S. A., 122n.14
Advanced Placement, 146, 148
Airbus, 193–194
Alabama, 3, 20, 45, 107, 114, 169
Alaska, 40
Albert Shanker Institute, 206
Alexander, K., 194n.48
Alexander, Lamar, 124–125, 187n.9
Alliance for Excellent Education, 10, 47, 129, 144n.12, 174
Almy, S., 210n.10
Amazon.com, 210
America Achieves, 145
American Association of School Administrators (AASA), 194n.45
American Association of State Colleges and Universities, 42
American Council on Education, 42
American Enterprise Institute (AEI), 9, 124
American Federation of Teachers (AFT), 3, 41–42, 129, 193n.36, 206, 208, 212
American Historical Foundation, 122
American Institutes for Research, 150n.38
American Legislative Exchange Council (ALEC), 70, 190–191n.25
American Philosophical Society, 121
American Principles in Action, 191n.25
American Recovery and Investment Act (ARRA), 174
American Society of News Editors, 4n.5
Anand, A., 129n.50
APEX Learning, 52
Apollo Global Management, 143
Apple, 149

Apple, M. W., 62n.31
Arizona, 37–38, 200
Arkansas, 20, 88, 89, 194
Arnold, Douglas, 194
Arnold, R. D., 194–195nn.49–50
ARRA (American Recovery and Investment Act), 174
ASCD (Association for Supervision and Curriculum Development), 9, 174
Ash, K., 143n.6
Assessment
   alignment with standards, 21–23, 55, 59–60, 64, 67–69, 71–72, 97–99, 178–180, 210
   charter schools and, 81, 83, 85–86, 92–93
   college placement and, 44
   computer adaptive testing (CAT), 7, 19, 60, 99–100, 147
   computer-based/online, 19, 81, 83, 141, 143, 147–151, 152, 154, 155–156
   defining proficiency levels, 100–102, 120–121, 172
   establishing common assessments, 43–45
   evolution of proficiency thresholds, 107–108, 114–115
   expected dips in proficiency, 23–24, 32, 44, 164, 169, 195–196, 212
   graduation requirements and, 43, 195–196
   implementation timeline, 7, 14, 17, 44, 49–50, 56, 67–68, 99–100, 108, 140, 144, 148, 152
   importance of, 47–48
   international assessments, 26, 37, 38n.4, 41, 48, 101
   transition from old to new system, 49–50
Associated Press (AP), 150n.35
Association for Supervision and Curriculum Development (ASCD), 9, 174
Association of American Publishers, 196

Bailey, John, 141n.3, 144, 145–146, 147n.27
Baker, A., 144n.15
Baker, B. D., 67n.46
Banchero, S., 76n.2

Bandeira de Mello, V., 7n.10, 104–107
Barghaus, K. M., 60n.20
Barker, G., 190n.20
Barnes, Ray, 44
Barney, H., 25n.18
Barrett, Craig, 36, 38
Beach, R. W., 58n.9
Becker, G. S., 186n.2
Benchmarking for Success, 35n.1, 38, 50
Bennett, Tony, 152, 191
Beran, Michael K., 123n.19
Berry, C. R., 189n.17
Berry, F. S., 110n.13
Berry, W. D., 110n.13
Berson, M. J., 122n.14
BetterLesson, 19, 63, 145
Bevilacqua, Linda, 134n.62
Bhatt, R., 62n.32
Bill & Melinda Gates Foundation, 3, 10, 26,
    54, 63, 68n.49, 89, 145n.16, 146n.18,
    166n.5, 194n.43, 206
Bird, T., 61n.22
Birnbaum, M., 142–143n.5
Blackboard Inc., 146
Blended learning, 77, 79–83, 89, 93, 141–142,
    143
Bloom, Allan, 123
Bloom, H. S., 100n.7
Boeing, 193–194
Bowman, A., 178n.23
Brammer, J., 188n.12
Brewer, Jan, 200
"Bridge" textbooks, 15, 20
Brown, C. B., 186n.3
Brown, C. G., 46n.8
Buchanan, J. M., 146n.20, 196n.53
Burden, B. C., 189n.17
Burns, J. M., 58n.8
Burns, Leslie D., 62n.30
Burris, Carol, 8n.16
Bush, George H. W., 6n.6, 124n.24, 126, 129
Bush, George W., 6, 195
Bush, Jeb, 3, 9n.17, 47, 189, 190n.23, 191,
    206, 215n.14
Bushaw, W. J., 23n.13, 61n.27
Business community, 51–52
Business Roundtable, 157n.61

California, 20, 41, 46, 86–87, 142–143, 154,
    187, 209
Calkins, Lucy, 9
Camoy, M., 96n.2
Campbell, Andrea, 186n.6
Campbell, Joseph, 120n.8
Carcieri, Don, 43, 44
Cardinal Principles of Secondary Education, 122

Carlson, Deven, 6, 11, 25, 96–117, 209
Carmichael, S. B., 58n.9, 110n.15
Carpe Diem, 215–216
Carr, David, 120n.7
Cato Institute, 8, 190
Cavanagh, Sean, 127n.40, 150n.41, 151n.43
CCSS. *See* Common Core State Standards
    (CCSS)
Center for Education Policy, 127, 196–197
Cermak, Kate, 22n.12
Chalk, S. M., 193n.40
Charter schools, 11, 76–94, 187–188
    assessment concerns, 81, 83, 85–86, 92–93
    autonomy concerns, 76–77, 80, 82–84, 92
    blended learning and, 77, 79–83, 89, 93
    examples of leaders and laggards, 88–91
    financial issues for, 86–88
    implementation of CCSS, 77–82, 84–88,
        91–94
    professional development and, 88–89,
        215–216
    in "reform" agenda, 215–216
    rigor and scalability, 80–82
Cheney, Dick, 124
Cheney, Lynne, 6n.7, 124, 125–126n.31, 129,
    132
Chingos, M., 144n.13
Chou, Luyen, 144
Christensen, Clayton N., 19n.7, 153
Christie, Chris, 3, 47, 189, 190n.23
Christie, K., 57n.6
Chubb, John E., 19n.7, 172n.10
Clinton, Bill, 126, 129
Closing of the American Mind, The (Bloom),
    123
Cobb, P., 58n.9
Cochran-Smith, Marilyn, 61nn.23–24
Cody, A., 69n.52
Cogan, L. S., 59nn.13–14, 62n.33, 64n.39
Cohen, D. K., 61n.21
Cohen, Michael, 127, 129–133, 206
Coleman, David, 126, 127, 166n.5
College and Career Readiness standards, 40,
    107–108, 140
College Board, 39, 126, 166n.5
Colorado, 41, 44, 88, 90–91n.7
Commission on the Reorganization of
    Secondary Education, 122
Committee of Seven, 122n.13
Committee of Ten on Secondary School Studies
    (1892), 5–6, 122n.13
Common Core State Standards (CCSS)
    in charter schools, 77–82, 84–88, 91–94
    College and Career Readiness standards,
        40, 107–108, 140
    critique/opposition to, 4–5, 7–8, 61–62, 76,

Common Core State Standards (CCSS), *continued*
129, 169, 189–191, 199–200
development (*See* Standards development process)
English Language Arts and Math standards, 5, 7, 11, 41, 61, 63, 129–133, 185
as experiment in federalism, 185, 215
future predictions, 50–52, 66
governance (*See* Standards governance)
history of, 37–43
implementation (*See* Implementation of CCSS)
importance of, 35, 47–48
nature of, 1–2, 5–8
potential risks/threats, 2, 5, 70–72, 188–197, 206–217
"reform" agenda, 4–5, 213–217
revisions and, 47, 65–66, 181
role in school improvement, 5
as Rorschach test, 8, 79–80
Social Studies standards, 11, 118–134
state adoption, 1, 2, 3, 14–21, 30, 42–43, 55, 65, 113, 118, 129, 140, 179, 187–188, 206, 212, 216
Common Core State Standards Initiative (CCSSI), 39, 97n.3, 140n.1
Communications/public relations, 169, 170, 194–196
Computer adaptive testing (CAT), 7, 19, 60, 99–100, 147
Conlan, T. J., 181n.28
Connecticut, 89
Consolidation model of standards governance, 175–176
Coody, Kaylin, 150
Core Knowledge Foundation, 134
Council for Basic Education, 131
Council of Chief State School Officers (CCSSO), 3, 14, 24n.17, 26, 35–36n.1, 38, 40–44, 47, 52, 140n.2, 147n.23, 156, 162–169, 171–176, 185, 193–194n.42, 194n.46, 198n.63, 199n.66, 201n.70, 206
Council of Great City Schools (CGCS), 41–42, 164n.4, 194
Crabtree, Charlotte, 119n.2, 125, 126n.32
Cronin, J., 25n.19
Cross, Christopher, 129n.53, 130, 131
Cruz, B. C., 122n.14
Cuban, Larry, 66n.44, 96n.2, 154nn.54–55
Cultural Literacy (Hirsch), 123–124n.22
Curriculum
alignment with standards, 21–23, 55, 59–60, 64, 67–69, 71–72, 97–99, 178–180, 210
charter schools and, 87
online providers, 81

professional development and, 62–64
questions of curricular validity, 67
Social Studies standards and, 121–128, 130–131
technology and, 142–144
Cyr, Penni, 146

Dahlin, M., 25n.19
Daly, Tim, 214n.13
Daniels, Mitch, 190n.23
Darling, Hammond, L., 76n.1
Data Quality Campaign, 51
Davis, M. R., 144n.11, 150n.37
D.C. Association of Chartered Public Schools, 90
Debra P v. Turlington, 67
DeBray-Pelot, E., 194n.44
Declaration of Independence, 123n.18
Dee, T. S., 96nn.1–2
Delaware, 44
Dellek, R., 197n.60
Democratic Party, 35, 43, 190, 195
politics of CCSS implementation, 3, 14, 32, 197, 199
War on Poverty, 197
Democrats for Education Reform (DFER), 3, 199
Desimone, L. M., 63n.38
Desmond, K., 192n.32
DeVito, Pat, 177
Diegmueller, Karen, 125n.27, 125n.30, 126n.33
Digital Learning Now, 144
Diskey, Jay, 196
Disrupting Class (Christensen et al.), 153
District of Columbia, 90
Doyle, Jim, 45–46n.7
DreamBox Learning, 143
Duncan, Arne, 3, 4n.5, 43, 102, 147n.25, 190n.23, 191, 206–207nn.3–4
Duncan, T., 18n.4, 147n.24
Dunn, Ross E., 119n.2, 126n.32
Duplass, J. A., 122n.14

Eagle Forum, 196
Economic Development Administration, 100n.7
ECS (Education Commission of the States), 171, 178
The Editorial Board, 10n.18
Editorial Projects in Education, Inc., 63n.37, 153n.51, 156nn.59–60, 169n.7
Edmodo, 89
eDoctrina, 89
Education Commission of the States (ECS), 171, 178
Education First, 63n.37, 169n.7, 193
Education Next, 6–7n.9
Education Sector, 143n.8

EducationSuperHighway, 150n.42
Ehrenworth, Mary, 9
Elementary and Secondary Education Act
  (ESEA), 111–113, 174
  ESEA Flexibility, 187, 190
  ESEA waivers, 14, 49, 54–57, 63, 65,
    67–70, 156
Elliott, S., 188n.15, 191n.28
English Language Arts and Math standards, 5,
  7, 11, 41, 61, 63, 129–133, 185
EPE Research Center, 193
E-Rate program, 151
ERIC, 60
ESEA. *See* Elementary and Secondary Education
  Act (ESEA)
Eskelson, Lily, 214n.12
Evans, D., 196n.54
Evans, Ronald W., 122n.12, 122n.14, 122n.16,
  127–128n.43, 134n.60
Evers, W., 8n.15

Financial issues. *See also* Race to the Top
  (RTTP) Program
  CCSS funding levels, 27–28
  for charter schools, 86–88
  costs of instructional materials, 196–197
  pressures on state budgets, 28–29, 45–46,
    50–51, 164, 196, 212
  school improvement, 5, 45
  for standards governance, 172–173, 174
  for state accountability systems, 14–15,
    27–29
  technology and, 147–152, 154
Finkelman, P., 119n.3
Finn, Chester E., Jr. (Checker), 1n.1, 7–8n.11,
  126, 127n.36, 128n.46, 129, 130–132,
  133n.59, 134n.61, 168n.6
Finney, Ross, 122n.16, 123n.19
Finnish Lessons (Sahlberg & Hargreaves),
  25–26n.21
Floden, R. E., 58n.10
Florida, 3, 20, 23–24n.15, 41, 46, 47–48, 52,
  67, 152, 172, 189, 206, 215
Ford, Gerald, 124
Fordham Institute, 1, 7–8n.11, 20n.10, 27–28,
  27n.23, 32, 110, 126, 128, 129, 152n.47,
  164n.4, 168, 207n.5
Forster, G., 8n.15
Foundation for Excellence in Education, 191
Freeman, D. J., 58n.10
Friedrich, L., 146n.20
Frist, Bill, 198, 200
Fuhrman, S. H., 59n.18

Gabel, J., 192n.32
Gallup/Phi Delta Kappan, 23n.13
Ganske, K. A., 58n.8

Gates Foundation, 3, 10, 26, 54, 63, 68n.49,
  89, 145n.16, 146n.18, 166n.5, 194n.43,
  206
GE Foundation, 3n.4
Georgia, 6–7, 20, 38, 39, 41, 44
Gewertz, C., 1n.1, 98n.5, 188nn.13–14,
  193n.38, 196n.58
GI Bill, 186n.6
Ginsberg, R., 122n.14
Glasgow, Kirk, 149n.32
Goals 2000 initiative, 126
Goldstein, D., 126n.34, 127n.42
Google Chrome, 150
Gordon Commission, 172
Governance. *See* Standards governance
Governors. *See also* National Governors
    Association (NGA) *and names of
    individual states*
  budgetary concerns, 28–29, 45–46, 50–51,
    164, 196, 212
  challenges of CCSS implementation, 45–50,
    211–212
  common assessments and, 43–45
  role in standards development/
    implementation process, 11, 35–37,
    43–52
  turnover in, 164, 170–171, 181
Grading systems, 86–87, 112–113
Graduation requirements, 43, 195–196
Granholm, Jennifer, 43, 44
Gray, L., 148n.31, 152n.48
Grayer, Jonathan, 191
Great Depression, 196
Great Recession, 211–212
Green, P. C., 67n.46
Greenberg, J., 18n.3
Greene, J. P., 8n.15, 127n.36

Haertel, E. H., 25n.20
Hales, Brenda, 189–190n.19
Hamilton, L. S., 25n.18
Hansen, Matthew, 120n.7
Hanushek, E. A., 96n.2
Hargreaves, A., 25–26n.21
Haslam, Bill, 190n.23
Hayden, M., 191n.28
Heaps, A., 146n.20
Heartland Institute, 8n.13
Henry, D., 143n.10
Heritage Foundation, 190
Hernandez, J. C., 129n.50
Hess, Frederick M., 1–13, 6–7n.9, 46n.8,
  101n.8, 110n.14, 112n.17, 153n.52,
  194–195n.51, 206–218
Hess, R., 153n.52, 194–195n.51
Higgins, L., 22n.12
Higher Education Act (HEA), 57–58

Hightower, A. M., 193n.40
Hill, C. J., 100n.7
Hill, H. C., 63n.36
Hill, P. T., 76n.3
Hirsch, E. D., 121–122nn.9–11, 123–124n.22, 129, 130, 132
Hispanic Chamber of Commerce, 8n.12
History on Trial (Nash et al.), 119n.2, 124n.23
Ho, A. D., 25n.20
Hochleitner, Taryn, 11–12, 140–161, 208–209, 213
Horn, Michael B., 19n.7, 153, 154
Houang, R. T., 58n.11, 59n.13, 61n.25, 62n.33
Howell, W. G., 187n.8, 189n.17
Hunt, James B., 127n.38
Hunt Institute, 47, 174
Huppenthal, John, 200
Hutt, E., 67n.46
Hwang, J., 55n.2

Idaho, 20, 146, 156, 197
Illinois, 28
Implementation of CCSS, 1–4
    adoption and development, 1–3, 14–21, 30, 42–43, 55, 65, 113, 118, 129, 140, 179, 187–188, 206, 212, 216
    challenges of, 45–50, 66–70, 208–217
    charter schools and, 77–82, 84–88, 91–94
    comparability, 25–26
    flow chart of decisions, 16
    funding issues, 14–15, 27–29, 196–197
    governance in (*See* Standards governance)
    governors' role in, 11, 35–37, 43–52
    history of, 37–43
    instructional implementation, 2–3
    integration, 16, 17, 24–27
    pilot testing and alignment, 16, 17, 21–24, 55, 59–60, 64, 67–69, 71–72, 97–99, 178–180, 210
    policy (*See* Policy implementation)
    politics of (*See* Politics of implementation)
    potential risks/threats, 2, 5, 70–72, 188–197, 206–217
    preparing for dips in proficiency, 23–24, 32, 44, 164, 169, 195–196, 212
    professional development, 14–15, 18, 21, 30, 32, 49, 62–64, 194, 197, 199, 210, 215–216
    public perceptions, 26–27
    recommendations, 31–33, 155–157, 197–201
    teacher preparation, 14–15, 17–18, 21, 48–49, 54, 60–62, 72, 210
    teacher quality in, 58–63, 66–70
    technology in (*See* Technology)
    textbooks in, 15, 19–21, 62–63, 68–69, 211
    timeline, 7, 14, 17, 44, 49–50, 56, 67–68,
        99–100, 108, 140, 144, 148, 152
    timing of, 14
Implementation (Pressman & Wildavsky), 10, 29–31n.26, 100n.7
Indiana, 3, 20, 114, 169, 188, 191n.28
Individualized Education Plans (IEPs), 156
Individuals with Disabilities Act, 46
Ingersoll, R., 65n.42
"Innovation America" (National Governors Association), 36n.2
Institute of Education Sciences, 7n.10, 18n.4, 175
Instructional strategies, 2–3
    blended learning, 77, 79–83, 89, 93, 141–142, 143
    teachers and, 146–147, 153
    technology in, 141–147, 152–155
Intel, 36, 38
Interest groups, 191–194, 211
International assessments, 26, 37, 38n.4, 41, 48, 101
International Association for K-12 Online Learning (iNACOL), 143n.6
International Association for the Evaluation of Educational Achievement, 38
International Reading Association (IRA), 42
Interstate compact model of standards governance, 177–178
iPad, 149, 153, 154, 156, 209

Jackson, K., 58n.9
Jacob, B., 96nn.1–2
Jennings, Jack, 127n.41, 128n.45, 128n.47, 129n.51, 133
Jochim, Ashley E., 7, 12, 185–205, 189n.18, 211
Johnson, F., 76n.1
Johnson, Lyndon B., 197
Johnston, J. H., 122n.14
Jones, J. O., 123n.20
Jones, L. R., 101n.9

Kahlenberg, R. D., 193n.37
Kaplan, 153
Keeling, D., 56n.3
Kelly, A. P., 112n.17
Kendell, John, 9
Kennedy, Edward, 6n.8
Kennedy, M., 61n.22
Kentucky, 20, 24, 28, 32, 49–50, 67, 187–188, 189
Khan Academy, 19, 20, 72, 143
Kim, J., 187n.7
Kimmel, Allison, 11–12, 140–161, 208–209, 213
Kingsbury, G., 25n.19
KIPP, 85

Kitchens, Joe, 151
Klein, A., 181n.27, 189n.16
Klein, Joel, 9n.17, 206, 215n.14
Kober, N., 169n.8, 196–197n.59
Koedel, C., 62n.32

Lake, Robin J., 11, 76–95, 76n.3, 207, 215, 216
Language Police, The (Ravitch), 142n.4
Laptops, 151
Lautzenheiser, D. K., 46n.8
Layton, L., 129n.48
LearnZillion, 19, 145
Lee, F. E., 190n.22
Lee, H., 2n.3
Lee, S., 18n.4, 147n.24
Lehman, Christopher, 9
Leno, Jay, 120
Leona M. and Harry B. Helmsley Charitable Trust, 193
Lesson plans, online lesson-sharing sites, 63, 141, 145, 193
Levin, Doug, 150
Lewin, T., 187n.11
Lewis, D. E., 187n.10
Lewis, L., 148n.31, 152n.48
Lieszkovszky, I., 149n.32
Limbaugh, Rush, 126
Linn, Diane, 11, 35–53, 129n.51, 129n.54, 132n.56, 211
Lloyd, S. C., 193n.40
Lockwood, J. R., 68n.49
Loeb, S., 96n.2
Lopez, S. J., 23n.13, 61n.27
Louisiana, 20, 28, 58, 150n.36, 152, 190, 210
Loveless, T., 94n.8

Ma, L., 61n.26
Maas, Tricia, 11, 76–95, 207, 215, 216
Macia, L., 2n.3
Madaus, G. F., 67n.45
Majcher, Dineen, 194n.48
Making of Americans, The (Hirsch), 121–122nn.9–11
Malen, B., 59n.18
Manna, Paul, 174–175n.14, 177n.19
Markell, Jack, 44
Markow, D., 2n.3
Marsh, J. A., 25n.18
Martino, G., 58n.9, 110n.15
Maryland, 129, 207–208n.6
Massachusetts, 6, 41, 49, 101, 103, 110, 149, 151, 153–154, 156, 198–199, 200, 209
MasteryConnect, 19, 20, 145
Matthews, C. A., 193n.40
May, Peter J., 192n.30
McCaffrey, D., 68n.49

McCallum, William, 1n.2, 41
McCluskey, Neal, 8nn.13–14
McCombs, J. S., 25n.18
McDermott, Katie A., 163n.2, 177nn.19–21
McGraw-Hill, 143
McGuinn, Patrick, 12, 155–156, 162–184, 177n.19, 177n.22, 194–195n.51, 194n.44, 213
McKee, A., 18n.3
McKnight, C. C., 59n.13, 62n.33
McMaken, J., 55n.2
McNamara, K., 152n.47, 164n.4
McPhail, Jay, 154, 155, 209
McREL, 9
McShane, Michael Q., 1–13, 14–34, 206–218
Measured Progress, 177
Medicare, 186, 189, 192, 199
Mehta, J., 112n.17
Memorandum of Understanding (MOU)
   in consolidation model of governance, 175–176n.16
   regional or national, 176–177
Merrill, L., 65n.42
Metlife Survey of the American Teacher, 2n.3
Mettler, Suzanne, 186n.6
Meyer, Peter, 5–6, 11, 118–139, 123n.20
Michigan, 3, 22–23, 43, 44, 155n.57, 169
Microsoft, 148–149
Mihaly, K., 68n.49
Miller, Carissa, 156
Minnesota, 41, 45–46
Minnich, Chris, 140n.2
Mississippi, 6–7, 8, 20, 102
Mitchel, K. J., 101n.9
Moe, T. M., 19n.7
Moffitt, S. L., 61n.21
Moyers, Bill, 120n.8
Mulhern, J., 56n.3
Multiculturalism, 123
Multistate governance. *See* Standards governance
Murphy, K. M., 186n.2
Murphy, P., 27n.23, 152n.47, 164n.4
Musick, M., 175n.15

Naftel, S., 25n.18
NAGB (National Assessment Governing Board), 170, 175n.15, 176, 213–214
Napolitanom, Janet, 36–38
Nash, Gary B., 119n.2, 124n.23, 125, 126n.32
National Academy of Sciences (NAS), 101, 172
National Alliance for Public Charter Schools, 82, 88, 93
National Assessment Governing Board (NAGB), 170, 175n.15, 176, 213–214
National Assessment of Educational Progress (NAEP), 6, 23, 25, 37, 85, 101–102,

National Assessment of Educational Progress (NAEP), *continued*
103–110, 109n.12, 112, 120, 126, 128, 175n.15, 195, 198, 213–214
National Association of Charter School Authorizers, 88
National Association of State Boards of Education, 39
National Center for Education Statistics (NCES), 7n.10, 103, 120n.6, 128n.44, 148, 190n.23, 195n.52
National Center for History in Schools, 125
National Center for the Improvement of Educational Assessment, 177
National Center on Education and the Economy, 43
National Conference of State Legislatures (NCSL), 169
National Council for the Social Studies, 119n.4, 122n.15
National Council of Teachers of Mathematics (NCTM), 42, 65
National Council on Education Standards and Testing (NCEST), 6, 124n.25, 125, 126, 128n.47
National Council on Teacher Quality (NCTQ), 18n.3, 54n.1, 56n.54, 57, 129, 145n.17
National Education Association (NEA), 3, 5–6, 41–42, 122, 193, 193n.35, 214
National Education Goals initiative, 124n.24
National Endowment for the Humanities (NEH), 6, 124–125
National Forum for History Standards, 125n.29
National Governors Association (NGA), 3, 5, 10, 11, 14, 26, 35–36nn.1–2, 37–38, 40–44, 47, 52, 126, 129, 162–166, 171n.9, 172, 174–176, 185, 193, 206, 211–212
National History Standards, 132
National model of standards governance, 176–177
National network model of standards governance, 174–175, 176
National PTA, 174
National Research Council, 172
National Review, 7–8n.11
National Review of Teacher Preparation Programs, 57
National Writing Center, 148
National Writing Project Teachers, 146
NCSL (National Conference of State Legislatures), 169
Nebraska, 40
Nevada, 20
Nevins, Allan, 123n.17
New England Common Assessment Program (NECAP), 176–177
New Hampshire, 176–177

New Jersey, 3, 47, 189, 194
New Mexico, 20
New York Charter Schools Association (NYCSA), 81–82, 89–90
New York City, 8, 88, 89, 93, 144, 206, 215
New York state, 8
Next Generation Science Standards, 50
No Child Left Behind Act (NCLB; 2001), 6–8, 11, 14, 59–60, 68, 133, 148, 172, 176–177, 212
Adequate Yearly Progress (AYP), 7, 25, 101
learning from experiences with, 8, 62–66, 70–72, 111–113, 187, 189, 195, 209–210
NCLB waivers, 3, 25, 49, 51, 56–57, 97, 111–113, 174, 208, 211
passage, 6, 96
state accountability systems and, 96–97, 101, 103, 108, 111–113
state response and "gaming," 6–7
Noell, G., 58n.8
North Carolina, 6–7, 20, 48, 49, 127, 151–157

Obama, Barack, 3, 8n.12, 14, 17, 54, 69–70, 111, 127, 134, 145, 151, 173, 187, 189–191, 211
O'Day, J. A., 59n.18
Ohio, 88–89, 149
Oklahoma, 3, 6–7, 20, 102, 150, 151
Olson, M., 192n.34
Oluwole, J. O., 67n.46
Opening the Common Core (Burris), 8n.16
Oregon, 20, 43
Organisation for Economic Co-operation and Development (OECD), 38n.4
Oversold and Underused (Cuban), 154nn.54–55
Owen, I., 46n.8

Pandolfo, N., 19n.6
Parthenon Group, 196
Partnership for Assessment of Readiness for College and Careers (PARCC), 7, 15–20, 47, 51, 85, 88–90, 98n.4, 99n.6, 107–108, 110–111, 147–149, 149nn.33–34, 153–154, 156, 170, 172n.11, 177, 179, 206–209, 214–215
Patashnik, Eric M., 186n.4, 199n.65
Pathways to the Common Core (Calkins et al.), 9
Patrick, Susan, 143
Patton, Paul, 189
Pawlenty, Tim, 45–46n.7
Pearson Education, 63, 143–144
Pedagogy. *See also* Instructional strategies
learning about effective, 64
standards *versus*, 60–61
Pellegrino, J. W., 101n.9

Pennsylvania, 3
Perdue, Sonny, 38, 39
Perry, R., 40n.5
Peterson, Paul E., 6–7n.9, 101n.8, 110n.14, 187n.8
Petrilli, Michael J., 7–8n.11, 168n.6, 207n.5
Pew Center on the States, 27n.24, 28
Pierce, D., 146n.22
Pilot testing, in implementation of CCSS, 21–23
Pimental, Susan, 41
Pincus, Matthew, 178n.24
Pioneer Institute and American Principles Project, 45n.6, 151–152, 196n.57
PISA (Programme for International Student Assessment), 26, 38n.4
Policy implementation, 4, 10. *See also* Politics of implementation; Standards governance
    challenges of, 208–210
    maintenance of state commitment, 171–172
    recommendations for, 199–200
    technical *versus* policy issues in, 170–171
    technology and, 155–157
Polikoff, Morgan S., 11, 21–22, 54–75, 58–59nn.11–13, 59nn.15–17, 60nn.19–20, 62–63nn.34–35, 64n.41, 65n.43, 193, 200, 210
Politics of implementation, 5–6, 10, 12, 26–27, 32, 185–201, 211–213
    as challenge to CCSS influence on teacher policies, 69–70
    financial issues, 196–197
    ideological divide in, 3, 14, 169, 189–191
    interest groups in, 191–194, 211
    minimizing opposition, 199–200
    mobilizing existing allies, 198–199
    ongoing nature of, 201
    political will, 30, 48, 185–187
    politics of CCSS and, 187–188, 211
    public relations in, 169, 170, 194–196
    recommendations for moving forward, 197–201
    Social Studies standards, 125–126, 130–131
    threat assessment, 2, 5, 70–72, 188–197, 206–217
Porter, Andrew C., 55n.2, 58n.10, 59n.17, 60n.20, 62n.34, 68n.51
Porter, W., 193n.40
Porter-Magee, K., 58n.9, 110n.15
Posner, P. I., 181n.28
Postal, L., 23–24n.15
Powers, E., 17n.2
Prentice Hall, 20
Preservice teacher education. *See* Teacher preparation
Pressman, Jeffery L., 10, 29–31n.26, 100n.7
Professional development
    charter schools and, 88–89, 215–216
    curriculum materials and, 62–64
    in implementation of CCSS, 14–15, 18, 21, 30, 32, 49, 62–64, 194, 197, 199, 210, 215–216
    technology and, 146–147, 153
Progressive Business Leaders Network, 198
Progressive era, 201
Project Tomorrow, 146
Purcell, K., 146n.20, 148n.30
Putting a Price Tag on the Common Core (Thomas B. Fordham Institute), 27–28, 27n.23

Quillen, I., 146n.19

Rabe, B., 176n.17
Race to the Top (RTTP) Program, 3, 5, 7, 14, 17n.1, 40, 45, 54–55, 69–70, 98, 127, 133, 145, 147, 174, 181, 187–188, 190, 209, 211–212, 214–215
RAND, 172
Ravitch, Diane, 126, 142n.4
Ravitch, Richard, 28n.25
Raymond, M. E., 96n.2
Reading First, 210
Reagan, Ronald, 128, 129
Regenstein, E., 27n.23, 152n.47, 164n.4
Regional Greenhouse Gas Initiative (RGGI), 176
Regional model of standards governance, 176–177
Regional Service Agencies (RESA), 46
Rentner, D. S., 169n.8
Republican Party, 35, 43, 211
    battles with teachers unions, 54
    politics of CCSS implementation, 3, 14, 169, 189–191, 194–195, 198, 211
Rescorla, T., 140n.2
Retner, D. S., 196–197n.59
Reville, Paul, 198
RGGI Inc., 176
Rhee, Michelle, 54
Rhode Island, 43, 44, 176–177
Riccio, J. A., 100n.7
Rice, T., 192n.32
Rich, Motoko, 123n.21
Richards, E., 3n.4
Riley, Richard, 38, 193n.40
Ritter, Bill, 44
Robelen, E., 127n.39, 173n.13, 200n.67
Robyn, A., 25n.18
Rocketship Academies, 81, 154, 215–216
Rotherham, A., 146n.21
Rothkopf, Arthur, 206n.2
Rothman, Robert, 10, 118n.1, 124n.25, 126–127n.35, 127n.37, 129–132, 129n.52, 162n.1

Rud, A. G., 85n.6
Rudalevige, A., 6n.8
Rush, Benjamin, 121
Russell, J. L., 25n.18
Ruzeicka, Gayle, 189

Sahlberg, P., 25–26n.21
Sanderman, G., 187n.7
Sanford, Stefanie, 166n.5
Santayana, George, 119
Save Our Schools, 69
Sawchuk, S., 20n.9, 20n.11, 57n.5, 102n.10
Saxberg, Bror, 153n.53
Scarloss, B., 18n.4, 147n.24
Schenker, L., 190n.21
Schlesinger, Arthur, Jr., 126
Schmidt, W. H., 58nn.10–11, 59n.13, 59n.14,
    61n.25, 62n.33, 64nn.39–40
Schneider, Carrie, 141n.3, 147n.27
Schneider, Scott, 188
Scholastic, 145n.16, 146n.18
School improvement, 5, 45
School Review, The, 122
Schroeder, D., 151n.44
Schwille, J. R., 58n.10
Sexton, S., 56n.3
Shanker, Albert, 193
Shapley, K., 18n.4, 147n.24
Share My Lesson, 145
Shattuck, P., 163n.2, 176n.18
Shumway, Larry, 190
Smarter Balanced Assessment Consortium
    (SBAC), 7, 15–19, 22, 40, 43, 47, 51, 60,
    85, 98n.4, 99n.6, 100, 107–108, 110–
    111, 147–148, 177, 179n.25, 206–209,
    214–216
Smartphones, 148, 209
Smith, M. S., 59n.18
Smith, Mark, 191n.27
Smith, Scott, 151, 154–155
Smithson, J., 59n.17, 62n.34
Social Security, 186, 192, 199
Social Studies standards, 11, 118–134
    common curriculum and, 121–128
    moving forward with, 132–134
    National History Standards of the 1990s,
        119–120, 123–128, 131, 133
    national self-identity and, 118–120
    need for, 128
    proficiency levels, 120–121
    questions concerning, 129–132
Social Studies Wars, The (Evans), 122n.12,
    127–128n.43
Something in Common (Rothman), 10
Sosland, D., 163n.2, 176n.18
South Carolina, 20, 102, 188, 190n.23, 198
South Dakota, 150

Sparks, S., 67n.47
Staiger, D. O., 68n.49
Standards development process
    aligned assessments in, 21–23, 55, 59–60,
        64, 67–69, 71–72, 97–99, 178–180, 210
    College and Career Readiness standards,
        40, 107–108, 140
    decision to create standards, 39–40
    decreasing standards churn, 65–66
    English Language Arts and Math standards,
        5, 7, 11, 41, 61, 63, 129–133, 185
    governors in, 11, 35–37, 43–52
    interest groups in, 193
    learning from past experiences, 126–128,
        132–133
    Social Studies standards, 11, 118–134
    writing the standards, 41–42
Standards governance, 12, 50, 162–181.
    See also Council of Chief State School
        Officers (CCSSO); National Governors
        Association (NGA); Partnership for
        Assessment of Readiness for College and
        Careers (PARCC); Smarter Balanced
        Assessment Consortium (SBAC)
    advisory board, 168
    aligning common standards and
        assessments, 21–23, 55, 59–60, 64, 67–
        69, 71–72, 97–99, 178–180, 210
    Common Core cop/watchdog role, 172,
        180–181
    communications/public relations in, 169,
        170, 194–196
    decision-making structure and process,
        167–168
    federal government role in, 173–174
    formalization of, 163–164
    funding considerations, 172–173, 174
    maintenance of state commitment, 171–172
    membership, 165–167
    Memorandum of Understanding (MOU) in,
        175–177
    models for coordinating standards and
        assessments, 180
    organizational capacity in, 170–171
    potential governance models, 174–178
    in "reform" agenda, 213–214
    representation, 165–167
    research in, 169
    tasks in, 168–170
    technical assistance to states in, 169–170
    technical *versus* policy issues in, 170–171
    timing of implementation, 163–164
Starr, Josh, 207–208n.6
Start-up Bloomboard, 145
State accountability systems, 6–7, 11, 96–115.
    See also Governors; Standards governance
    adoption of CCSS, 1–3, 14–21, 30, 42–43,

55, 65, 113, 118, 129, 140, 179, 187–188, 206, 212, 216
alignment of standards with tests, 21–23, 55, 59–60, 64, 67–69, 71–72, 97–99, 178–180, 210
CCSS integration and, 25, 30, 96
defining proficiency levels, 100–102, 120–121, 172, 195–196
funding issues, 14–15, 27–29
implementation timeline, 44, 49–50, 67–68, 99–100
learning from past experiences, 8, 62–66, 70–72, 103–108, 111–113, 126–128
No Child Left Behind and, 96–97, 101, 103, 108, 111–113
variations across states, 103–111
State Budget Crisis Task Force, 28
State Collaborative on Reforming Education (TN SCORE), 194n.47, 198nn.61–62
State Educational Agencies (SEA), 41, 46, 156n.58
State Educational Technology Directors Association (SETDA), 150n.40, 155n.56
State Education Policy Center (SEPC), 150n.40
State governance. *See* Standards governance
State Higher Education Executive Officers, 39
State of State Standards, The (Thomas B. Fordham Institute), 110
Stecher, B. M., 25n.18
Steiner, David, 120n.5, 134n.63
Stephenson, Howard, 190
Stotsky, S., 8n.15
Strauss, V., 8n.16, 190n.24
STRIVE Preparatory Schools, 85
Student Achievement Partners (SAP), 3, 5, 10, 41, 145, 193
StudentsFirst, 54
Summit Academies, 154, 215–216
Surpassing Shanghai (Tucker), 25–26n.21
Sustainability Task Force, 100
Swason, C. B., 193n.40
Sykes, G., 61n.22
Symcox, Linda, 125n.28, 133n.58

Tablets, 148, 149
Tang, A., 67n.46
Teacher evaluation reforms, 48–49, 54, 56–58, 68, 71, 193, 214–215
Teacher preparation
comparison of teacher education programs, 64–65
evaluation and reform, 57–58
in implementation of CCSS, 14–15, 17–18, 21, 48–49, 54, 60–62, 72, 210
pedagogy in, 60–61
standards in, 60–62
technology and, 147

Teacher quality, 11, 54–72. *See also* Professional development; Teacher preparation
alignment of standards and assessment, 21–23, 55, 59–60, 64, 67–69, 71–72, 97–99, 178–180, 210
in implementation of CCSS, 58–63, 66–70
teacher evaluation reforms, 48–49, 54, 56–58, 68, 71, 193, 214–215
teacher tenure and, 57
Tea Party, 164, 212
Technical assistance to states, 169–170
Technology, 140–157
blended learning models and, 77, 79–83, 89, 93, 141–142, 143
charter schools and, 81, 83, 85–86, 89, 92–93
collaboration across state lines, 45–46
computer adaptive testing (CAT), 7, 19, 60, 99–100, 147
computer-based assessment, 19, 81, 83, 141, 143, 147–151, 152, 154, 155–156
district capacity, 155–156
financial issues, 147–152, 154
future of, 151–152
in implementation of CCSS, 11–12, 18–19, 30, 49, 52, 213
increasing use of, 141–142
innovation and, 156–157
instructional strategies based on, 141–147, 152–155
learning with, 141–144, 152–155
new content and instructional materials, 140–141, 142–144
online lesson-sharing sites, 63, 141, 145, 193
policy recommendations for, 155–157
professional development and, 146–147, 153
in "reform" agenda, 213
Teles, S., 112n.17
Tennessee, 6–7, 20, 103, 144, 190, 194n.47, 198nn.61–62, 200
Tenure of teachers, 57
Texas, 20, 40, 46, 142–143
Textbooks
cross-state collaboration in purchasing, 46
impact of new standards on, 196–197, 211
in implementation of CCSS, 15, 19–21, 62–63, 68–69, 211
pilot new texts, 20
technology and, 142–144
Thomas, N., 148n.31
Thomas, P. L., 61–62n.29
Thomas B. Fordham Institute, 1, 7–8n.11, 20n.10, 27–28, 27n.23, 32, 110, 126, 128, 129, 152n.47, 164n.4, 168, 207n.5

TIMSS (Trends in International Mathematics and Science Study), 26, 101
TNTP, 214n.13
Tomassini, J., 191n.29, 196n.55
Tonight Show, 120
Towne, L., 193n.40
Trachtenberg, J. A., 19n.8
Truesdale, Valerie, 153n.51
Truman, C., 188n.12
Tucker, M. S., 25–26n.21
Tullock, G., 196n.53
21st Century Classroom, 156
Tyack, D., 66n.44, 96n.2

Ujifusa, Andrew, 23n.14, 24n.16, 67n.48, 129n.49, 172n.12
Uncommon Schools, 85
Understanding Common Core State Standards (ASCD), 9
U.S. Chamber of Commerce, 194, 198, 199, 206n.2
U.S. Constitution, 36, 37, 127
U.S. Department of Education (DOED), 3, 17n.1, 37n.3, 40, 49, 51, 57n.7, 68, 97, 111–112n.16, 124–125, 127, 195, 208
University of California Press, 10
U.S. Steel v. Multistate Tax Commission, 178n.24
Usdan, M., 180n.26
Utah, 20, 107, 114, 188, 189–190, 198, 200nn.68–69, 201

Value-added model (VAM) scores, 64
Vander Ark, Tom, 81, 141n.3, 143n.7, 143n.9, 147nn.26–27, 148n.29
Vermont, 176–177, 199n.64
Viadero, Debra, 125n.27, 125n.30, 126n.33
Villano, Dennis, 151, 153–154, 156, 209
Virginia, 20, 43
Virginia v. Tennessee, 178n.24
Volcker, Paul, 28n.25
Von Minden, S., 19n.5, 148n.28
Voucher programs, 215–216

Walsh, Kate, 18n.3, 129, 130, 134n.64
Walton Family Foundation, 89
Wang, H., 62n.33
War on Drugs, 186
War on Poverty, 197
Washington, D.C., 90
Washington state, 179
Watchdog role, 172, 180–181
Webb, N. L., 68n.50
Weingarten, Randi, 1n.2, 129, 208nn.7–9, 212n.11
Weisberg, D., 56n.3
Weiss, D. J., 19n.5, 148n.28
Weiss, Joanne, 102n.10
West, M., 187n.8
West Virginia, 6–7, 20, 190
White, John, 20n.11, 210
Whiteboard Advisors, 152n.50
Whitehurst, G., 144n.13
Wildavsky, Aaron, 10, 29–31n.26, 100n.7, 186n.1
Wilentz, S., 126n.32
Wiley, D., 62n.33
Wilhoit, Gene, 24n.17, 40, 147n.23
Will, George, 129n.53
Wilson, J. Q., 186n.5, 192n.33
Wilson, W. S., 58n.9, 110n.15
Wisconsin, 45–46, 102
Wolfe, R. G., 62n.33
Woods, N., 178n.23
Wurman, Z., 8n.15
Wyatt, Edward, 151n.45
Wyoming, 8, 124, 169

Yackee, Susan Webb, 192n.31
Yang, R., 55n.2
Yoon, K. S., 18n.4, 147n.24
Youngs, P., 193n.41

Zeichner, Kenneth M., 61nn.23–24, 85n.6
Zelizer, Julian E., 199n.65
Zimmerman, Jonathan, 133n.57
Zinth, J. D., 57n.6